T0292109

Managing knowledge reserves the status quo argument that organizational change is driven by the specific demands of large companies. Instead of viewing firms as the catalysts for gradual change, Albert and Bradley argue that expert professionals have fuelled a break away from the traditional organizational structure to an organizational structure at the heart of which is an agent and/or an agency system.

The authors draw our attention to the growing phenomenon of atypical work manifested in workforce flexibility, mobility, the feminization of professional employment, and technological changes. They focus upon a group of knowledge-based employees – experts – who increasingly have influence over work and wealth creation. They show the way in which experts are ushering in changes in the work environment and consider their impact on our understanding of labour markets and organizational behaviour.

Case studies are developed from companies including AT&T, the Hollywood film industry, London accounting firms, and specialized agencies such as Labforce and Knowledge Net. In addition, cases of specific experts are described, as is the way in which the Internet is assisting them by acting as an agent.

Managing knowledge

Managing knowledge

Experts, agencies and organizations

Steven Albert and Keith Bradley

The Open University Business School, Milton Keynes

CAMBRIDGE
UNIVERSITY PRESS

PUBLISHED BY THE PRESS SYNDICATE OF THE UNIVERSITY OF CAMBRIDGE
The Pitt Building, Trumpington Street, Cambridge CB2 1RP, United Kingdom

CAMBRIDGE UNIVERSITY PRESS
The Edinburgh Building, Cambridge CB2 2RU, United Kingdom
40 West 20th Street, New York, NY 10011–4211, USA
10 Stamford Road, Oakleigh, Melbourne 3166, Australia

First published 1997

Typeset in 11/13pt Garamond

A catalogue record for this book is available from the British Library

Library of Congress cataloguing in publication data

Albert, Steven.
Managing knowledge: experts, agencies, and organizations / Steven Albert and Keith Bradley.
p. cm.
Includes bibliographical references and index.
ISBN 0 521 56150 7 (hbk). – ISBN 0 521 59887 7 (pbk.)
1. Information technology – Management.
2. Knowledge acquisition (Expert systems) – Management.
3. Commercial agents. 4. Expertise. 5. Specialists.
6. Professional employees. 7. Women in the professions.
I. Bradley, Keith. II. Title.
HD30.2.A38 1997
658.4′038–dc21 96–48935 CIP

ISBN 0 521 56150 7 hardback
ISBN 0 521 59887 7 paperback

Transferred to digital printing 2003

CE

Contents

Figures

Tables

Tables

Introduction: The supply-side in context

. . . it is their own will, their own ideas and suggestions, to which they will demand that effect should be given, and not rules laid down for them by other people.

J. S. Mill, *Principles of Political Economy*

International competition has squeezed profits in traditional commodity-based industries. Indeed, the fact that today commodities are available to everyone through market transactions suggests that they do not provide the same competitive advantage they did in the earlier twentieth century. The same can be said of finance and industrial processes. The former can be borrowed and the latter copied. Paralleling the dampening of traditional factors of competitive advantage is the rise in the importance of knowledge to the future well being of capitalism. Throughout the United States and Britain, and much of the industrialized world, we observe significant increases in knowledge-based industries. Thus, for many people work is being transformed: from the delivery of tangible products produced by manual labour to the delivery of knowledge-based products produced by the expertise of people. Consequently, the contemporary workforce is increasingly comprised of professional knowledge-based employees such as lawyers, accountants, managers, bankers, marketing and advertising executives, scientists, engineers, doctors, computer programmers and all those employees who support such occupations (see e.g. Silvestri and Lukasiewicz (1991)). Such knowledge workers are poised to play a leading role in the growth industries which include computers, biotechnology, robotics, telecommunications, pharmaceuticals, law and medicine. This transformation of the type of work performed, together with technological innovations which transform the workplace, suggest dramatic changes in the work environment of organizations, and the set of choices open to expert employees (see Ritzer (1989) and Reich (1993)). Increasingly, indeed, profits will be derived from knowledge which produces a continuous discovery of new solutions for a plethora of changing consumer tastes and needs, rather than from the advantages derived from economies of scale associated with high-volume production, (see e.g. Reich (1993)).[1] This scenario poses new challenges for employer/employee relations which can lead to new complications.

Many scholars have examined these problems in the context of organizational change which assists companies to cope with the new dynamics of employment and global competition. They tend to share the view that downsizing corporations, the increased use of atypical employment and numerical/functional flexibility characterize relations between employer and employee in post-industrial societies. For example, Smith (1994) shows how a large white-collar company, in order to sell flexible services, decentralized its organizational structure and used atypical employees. Davis-Blake and Uzzi (1993) use data from the US Department of Labor's Employment Opportunity Pilot Project employer survey. They conclude that externalization (the use of atypical employees – sub-contracted, part-time and temporary) is a means to increasing organizational flexibility, but is affected by the cost of externalizing work. According to Davis-Blake and Uzzi, if tasks require firm specific skills or are informationally complex, less use is made of temporary employees.[2] Colclough and Tolbert (1992), looking at high-tech industries, show that within organizations the employees linked with atypical employment are on one organizational structure and those related to the core are on another. Heydebrand (1989) links organizational form with the stage of political economy while developing new organizational specifications. Doeringer *et al.* (1991), while proposing that problem-solving education and employment security are means of increasing productivity, have tackled labour market turbulence in America. They point to downsizing via demand-sided influences including the use of contingent workers. Christensen (1991) specifically looks at contingent workers (in her terms, different from employees under flexible arrangements) and suggests that this group implies a two-tiered workforce in US corporations. Examining this change in manufacturing industries, Piore and Sable (1984) similarly emphasize 'flexible specialization' and suggest strongly that this (training, retaining core-workers) is based on the use of atypical employees. Colclough and Tolbert (1992), Block

(1990), Heckscher (1988), and Pfeffer and Baron (1988) also point, in some degree, to the gradual change of organization.[3]

Furthermore, descriptions and analysis of the flexible firm and global enterprises can be seen as an attempt to explain the changes in the workplace which are presently occurring due to technological changes in commodity-based industries. Lash and Urry (1987) treat technology as an exogenous cause of flexible specialization strategies. Freeman and Perez (1988) relate 'upswings' and 'downswings' in economic performance and conditions to changes in technology ending with a post-Fordist era of information and communication technologies. Hirst and Zeitlin (1991) discuss the relative differences in these approaches to changing workplace flexible specialization as well as to other theories. Ritzer (1989) demonstrates a 'Permanently New Economy' through changes external and internal to the United States, in technology and demographics .

Although these critiques yield many insights, such as the new precariousness of employment in commodity-based production, they frequently avoid discussing the impact of the preferences of employees in the emerging knowledge-based industries. According to this body of work transformation of organizations is a gradual process, engendered solely by the demands of firms to change; see e.g. Belous (1991); Storper (1989); Storper and Christopherson (1987); Magnum *et al.* (1985); Dale and Bramford (1988) and Abraham (1988). Again, this often involves organizations downsizing their permanent staff and increasing their use of contingent employees. The discussion of such phenomenon is usually historically limited and assumes a linear evolution of business organizations: from a permanent hierarchy to an organization which protects a core of well-qualified, privileged individuals who are offered security of tenure and relatively high renumeration, and does not protect a pool of less qualified people who are forced to accept unattractive casual employment and a precarious place on the periphery of the economy (see e.g. Burchell (1989) and Rodgers and Rodgers (1989)). This suggests atypical employment is peripheral to the more privileged case of permanent employees, and has given rise to what has become known as the dual or segmented labour market.

More recently, there has been a growing re-evaluation of the dual labour market literature which argues that single-demand issues cannot adequately explain the extent and growth of the casualization of the labour force by lumping all contingent employees into one category. Indeed, Hunter *et al.* (1993), provide some evidence that flexible manning policies are not due solely to a change in strategy by employers toward a core–periphery organization. Rather, they conclude that the observed increase in atypical employees is best described by 'traditional' reasons. Importantly, Hunter *et al.* also briefly report (p. 394) that employers feel that

> in some professional occupations where there was skill shortages, workers who might previously have worked as direct employees had become self-employed or worked through agencies in order to take full market advantage of their scarce skills and to command higher incomes. This was deplored by management, who had to cope with a degree of unreliability on the part of such workers who had no compunction about changing their allegiance in mid-contract if better opportunities arose elsewhere.

Cohen and Haberfield (1993) suggest that for temporary employees in Israel there is no evidence to suggest that they constitute a homogeneous group of 'secondary' workers. They draw these conclusions from statistical analysis on demographic, human capital, wage levels and wage regressions. Zeytinoglu (1992) supports this thesis through a study of part-time employees. In a similar vein Gerson and Kraut (1988) report on a small case study of home-workers who rated freedom from supervision as the most important reason for working from home. Together these studies augment the more traditional literature by espousing the preferences of atypical employees for different work arrangements. For example, Gannon (1984) shows that of 1,000 temporary nurses in the United States, 60 per cent chose 'freedom to schedule work in a flexible manner' as the most important reason for working as a temporary nurse, and Towers (1978) suggests that temporary work is associated with seasonal employment and prevalent in industries where labour shortages are durable features – thus, hinting at time-sensitivity and supply-side preferences. Our work builds from this relatively brief but consistent evidence.

We focus upon one influential group of employees – experts. One of our principal contentions is that the future roll of knowledge as a pre-eminent source of competitive advantage will significantly raise the importance of specific people who possess certain types of knowledge. People with knowledge crucial to wealth creation and an ability to manipulate it – experts – are at the heart of this book. Throughout the course of history different groups of experts (blacksmiths, wheelwrights, carpenters, cobblers, millers etc.) have always held a strategically important economic position (see Burnett (1994)). In the recent past, experts still relied upon tangible assets such as machines, natural resources and workshops. Today, in what is often called an information age (see e.g. Helvey (1971)), experts tend to be those with the ability to manipulate intangible assets. They include research scientists, engineers, a range of consultants from financial to architectural planners, journalists, musicians and film producers – people, according to Reich (1993), with an ability to manipulate symbols. This group is indicative of strategically located individuals who increasingly have the resources and opportunities to exert their influence over work and wealth creation. It is our contention that, in specific instances, the casualization of expert employees is more adequately explained by the desire of specific individuals to gain discretion over their work rather than the demands generated by specific organizations.

We examine the relationship of the preferences of expert employees to the growing phenomena of atypical work: freelance, temporary and part-time; see e.g. various *US Statistical Abstracts,* Carey and Hazelbaker (1986); Belous (1989a); Belous (1989b); Casey (1988); Marshall (1989), Appelbaum (1989) and Rodgers and Rodgers (1989). Our thesis extends traditional Labour Market Segmentation theories, as well as theories about flexible manning policies (both tend to place atypical employment in secondary labour market segments)[4] by re-examining atypical employment as a supply-side phenomenon in knowledge-based industries.

We hypothesize that experts, aware of their market value and wanting more discretion over their work, will attempt to achieve this through the use of atypical employment arrangements which will often involve some form of an agency system. Again, traditional labour market theories tend to suggest that the increase in employees working with atypical employment arrangements results from a strategic change in policy by business organizations to increase numerical flexibility: see e.g. Atkinson (1986) and Hakim (1990). While this might be the case for employees with skills abundant in the labour market and employees who work in commodity-based companies and jobs, it might not be so for individuals with scarce skills important in the emerging knowledge-dense industries. Accelerated changes in demographics, technology and product markets (see Ritzer (1989)), together with the consequent shift of market power to knowledge workers (see chapter 1 below), suggest that such workers, with a heightened awareness of their strategic importance, have an increasing set of opportunity choices likely to provide them with greater discretion over their work. Atypical employment could reasonably provide these workers with a means of achieving their objectives. To this extent, such experts constitute not a demand-led peripheral group but, a distinct supply-driven labour market segment which can influence overall productive efficiency and quality standards. The increasing use of agencies by knowledge workers is already impacting in some areas of the economy. In the future this is likely to be a significant trend which will influence organizations, wealth creation and employment (see e.g. Albert and Bradley (1995)).

The fact that technology and the rise in knowledge-based products allow contemporary experts to conduct their business regardless of geography increases their set of discretionary choices. To the extent that business organizations are unable to satisfy the demands of such experts, it seems reasonable to suggest that organizations run a risk of an exodus of skills which potentially reduces their competitive advantage. We argue that the more the knowledge-based employees recognize this, the more they will be in a position to exert greater influence over their work organizations. Increased power is provided to the expert by the increasing use and development of global communications. Indeed, statistics from the US Bureau of Economic Analysis, *National Income and Products Accounts, Volume 2, 1958–88*, and *Survey of Current Business*, August 1993 show that personal expenditure in the US on telephony rose from $41.1 billion in 1980 to $54.9 billion in 1990 and to $59.1 billion in 1992 (in constant 1987 dollars). Indeed, the number of lines offered by telecommunication operators world-wide grew 7.1 per cent between 1991 and 1992 reaching 242 million lines (*Financial Times*, 'A Global Scramble for Partners', 16 March 1994, p. vii). In 1994 the Internet nearly doubled in size as it has done every year since 1988 and now reaches nearly 5 million 'host' computers, each of which may connect several individual users. In 1993 a combination of special software and a way of connecting documents brought pictures, sound and video to the Internet and created a new medium, based on broadcasting and publishing with the added dimension of interactivity. This multimedia side opened the Internet to a much broader audience and further expanded its potential. These systems provide the infrastructure for experts to form their own formidable networks aided by agency systems. Today these are an estimated 30 million Internet users (*Fortune*, 'The Internet and Your Business', 7 March 1994).

It is our contention that one consequence of the exploration by expert employees for a work-life-style more in tune with their own preferences is the rejection of the nine-to-five life. The confidence of experts to reject traditional work patterns is predicated upon the relative ease by which they are able to reconstruct their work-life by way of a number of consecutive at-will contracts negotiated with the help of an agent. Bridges (1995) aptly reminds us that the nine-to-five job, undertaken in a business organization with others, is a relatively recent phenomenon in the history of work. Further, this pattern of organizational-based work might reasonably be viewed as historically specific, well suited to high-volume production but less so for the production of knowledge-based goods.

The consequence of experts working through atypical labour arrangements can also significantly increase their own productivity (and their income) as well as increase their career security. The achievement of these advantages (increased discretion, productivity and income) we refer to as a supply-side punctuated break from the traditional firm.[5] The significance of this break is associated with the importance of the people who make it. If they are employees with little market power then the impact they might have on a business or an economy will be minimal. On the other hand, if those who break with tradition in this way are those who are strategically important to emerging businesses and wealth creation, then such breaks can have economic significance beyond the expert employee group. This book describes new work environments and organizational change which results from the changing opportunities faced by expert employees and the changing nature of work. We augment the voluminous work on firm-directed change with a discussion of change and innovation engendered by the specific demands of people who supply expertise crucial to the future generation of wealth.

Beyond income and job security

In charting the demands of the expert employee we look beyond income and job security, and suggest that there is some evidence extending the evaluation of employment compensation. In the past, economists and policy makers have relied heavily on pay, national income and job security as indicators of how well a country is providing for its citizens. This makes sense so long as these indicators are accurate reflections of the aspirations of citizens and thereby tell us if employment is providing what the nation desires. We question the validity of solely using such indices as barometers of the well-being of contemporary employees. Such general indicators can not be ascribed to all citizens equally, and fail to adequately reflect the concerns of particular people. Besides pay and job security other elements of compensation may be ascribed greater importance by specific employees and their families. Indeed, Norwood and Klein (1989), discussing three examples of conceptual changes in statistical developments by US Federal agencies, recognize that a system 'if it is to remain relevant, must build on the past but also must be prepared for change'.

Can we still assume that for most people the way to a better life is through an increase in personal income? If not, how can a nation monitor how well it is providing for its citizens? Does it use those same indicators that were perfected in a time when what needed to be measured was something entirely different? Are the concerns of our parents the same concerns as ours?

We are provided with some insights into these questions from the findings of the US National Study of the Changing Workforce by the Families and Work Institute 1993.[6] The survey suggests that job security and salary levels are not the principal reasons for peoples' choice of employment. Indeed, from a list of extrinsic and intrinsic rewards derived from employment, these were ranked eighth and fifteenth respectively. Salaries and wages were eclipsed by such elements as 'family supportive policies' and 'control of work schedule' (the latter will be elaborated upon in chapter 5 below). According to the results from this representative sample of US employees the most important factor in choosing a job is whether or not there is, 'open communication' with 65 per cent of the participants choosing this reason. This is closely followed by the perceived effect their job will have on their family and personal life (60 per cent). And 59 per cent of all respondents feel that the nature of work was a 'very important' consideration in accepting their current job. Further, over half of all respondents strongly believe that job location, control of work content and the opportunity to acquire new skills were important considerations in choosing their present job. These results suggest that employee motivation, which for many corporations was once perceived to follow from compensation, has turned into a complex matrix which includes income from work, quality of life and control of work. These findings lead us to a re-evaluation of the position of pay and job security, which in the face of the evidence described above, can not necessarily be relied upon to provide growth and prosperity. This underlines the importance of understanding more fully the supply-side issues associated with employment contracts.

The company's response to new demands

One response to the demand for a more inclusive compensation package might be a change to employment contracts which provide expert employees with a means of balancing their work and home life and their personal growth. Such changes are occurring. Recognizing the importance of the personal side of individuals, the Kodak company in Rochester, US, permits leaves of absence not only for a 'compelling personal need or education', but also 'for a unique personal experience' (*New York Times*, 29 May 1994). American Telephone and Telegraph (AT&T) has provided an internal placement centre to facilitate functional flexibility and to provide employees with the flexibility they desire (this case will be discussed in detail in chapter 7 below). Deloitte & Touche based in Wilton Connecticut, US were concerned with the costs associated with their 25 per cent annual turnover. In order to reduce this they now support employees taking time off work in order to 'make time for a personal life'. In a similar vein, the Dentsu Institute for Human Studies offers its employees the freedom to schedule their work, allowing a greater balance between their home life and work. (S. Ganz, *The Japan Times*, 15 September 1994, p. 3). Such changes in the human resource policies of companies are found in many different cases and are a striking development from policies even of just ten years ago.

Other responses to new demands

The changes in the work environment found inside large corporations may not be enough for many of those who seek enriching employment. Alternative careers that encompass a life that has more than one career path or a work history that, at the very least, is associated with more than one organization may not be realizable within one corporation. A lifestyle offering significant discretion over work and personal life may be just too much for the traditional firm to handle. Where then will these people go? How will expert employees with strong personal aspirations find a suitable situation that provides income as well as personal growth and life enrichment?

Organizations may be adapting their employment policies to their employees' preferences. We argue that an organizational form may develop spontaneously outside the traditional firm setting. To show this, we draw on those marginalized work environments of home work, personal consulting businesses and temporary work, as well as others which provide the flexibility and agency systems that can increase discretion, productivity and income.

There is some evidence to suggest that these alternative forms of work outside traditional firms are providing advantages for individuals. For example, in Bristol, England an independent Informix database consultant is 'keen to find tele-workable contracts to avoid spending hours driving' (*Evening Standard*, 5 April 1995, p. 42). It has been reported in the *San Francisco Examiner*, based on a Stanford University career centre study, that MBAs in the area are 'shunning the typical climb up the ladder . . . seeking greater responsibility and control over their work and personal lives' (*San Francisco Examiner*, 2 April 1995, p.B-1). The Hebrides Islands to the north-east of Scotland are now attractive to such economically active employees – so much so that the Islands have appointed their own information technology officer ('High Tech Aids Turn Island Dream into Economic Reality', *The Times*, 16 January 1995, p. 5.). These anecdotal reports are representative of a trend towards more employees working in atypical employment settings.

In a 1993 report by the US Bureau of Labor Statistics, it was reported that approximately 20 million non-farm employees, about 18.3 per cent of the US workforce, work some of the time from home. Of this group, there are over 1.5 million managers and professionals which accounts for 41 per cent of all home workers. In a 1993 study by the US Department of Transportation, it was estimated that about 2 million people work as telecommuters and projects an increase to between 6.4 million and 10.9 million telecommuters by 2000. A 1992 survey by Link Resource estimates that in 1992 there were 2.4 million telecommuters which is broadly consistent with the US Department of Transportation's estimates, and is up from 1.4 million in 1991. This is a growth rate of 71 per cent in just two years. Furthermore, the survey reports that most of those who used their homes as alternative work-sites were self-employed, white-collar, knowledge-based employees (*Monthly Labor Review*, February 1994, pp. 14–20).

There are similar trends in the United Kingdom and other advanced industrial societies. Indeed, in the UK there is a movement away from work being undertaken outside the traditional *job-box*. In 1994, about 40 per cent of the UK workforce did not have continuous full-time employment and nearly ten per cent of these were multiple job-holders. A 1994 survey of long-term employment strategies carried out by the Institute of Management and Manpower plc suggested that UK companies are engaged in different types of flexible employment. Of the companies surveyed, 80 per cent employ temporary or part-time workers, 65 per cent are engaged in contracting out, 60 per cent employ flexible work patterns, 22 per cent use home-base workers and 11 per cent use teleworkers.

By the year 2000 the UK will have an estimated 10.5 million knowledge workers – experts – compared with only seven million manual workers. This reverses the situation of twenty years ago. Currently, there are 3.3 million self-employed in the UK, double the 1981 level. According to the Royal Society of Arts' (1995), 'as the balance shifts away from traditional labour markets, the competitive advantage to be derived from diversity – and from optimizing people's ability to contribute – will become increasingly important for UK companies' (p. 14).

The growth in jobs being undertaken outside the traditional job-box can be linked to the changing opportunities that experts face. One significant benefit of this is the increased discretion experts gain over their work and personal life styles. Working at home may not be the only labour market response, but it is an example of an abrupt break, which shifts the emphasis away from the traditional firm towards agencies.

Indeed, the demand for temporary work by both employers and employees is reflected in the number of temporary executive agencies developing in the US and the UK. Agencies such as Creative Options of Washington DC, The Traveller's Company and the scientific temporary agency LabForce which finds work for scientists across the US point to a trend of temporary work not only of nurse and secretary but of a much broader group of employees (Fierman (1994)) including those employees that are knowledge-based workers. This transformation is not solely organization or demand-side driven. Rather, it is also a consequence of demands by employees for freedoms that traditional hierarchical organizations find difficult to bring about.[7]

Flexibility: a historical context

To some readers a society based on home or temporary work may seem untenable. However, this is not the case if work is placed in a historical context. Indeed, it is only since the age of mass-produced products and large corporations that work has been constrained geographically into specific buildings and bounded by a specific range of hours. It was the advent of the coal-burning steam engine that first ignited the geographical dependency of specific mass-produced industries. The five towns of the Stafford Potteries in England were greatly influenced by the local availability of coal. There the potteries grew and the workers came because coal, the energy source, was geographically convenient. People worked in the factory because that is where the giant furnaces burned, capitalizing on the economies of scale. It is in settings like this that we first perceive the grouping of large numbers of employees in the confined areas of a factory producing a particular good. But this did not occur on a relatively large scale until the nineteenth century. The temporal constraints were laid down with the foundations of timed production lines that confined workers to strict schedules. It was incumbent upon the managers – a twentieth century phenomenon – to know exactly when employees were working and for how long. An absent employee in the middle of a production line could severely affect the whole production process. Regularity and consistency were the primary concerns for these organizations (see e.g. Buchanan (1994)).

Before the advent of mass production and the factory concept, much of the non-agricultural working population was based at home. Weavers in Scotland produced hand-woven tartan cloth. To their cottages was brought the raw material (wool) which was necessary to produce their final product. Knife sharpeners, potters, tailors, even shop keepers who lived above their shops and Inns can be said to be home-based workers. And the benefits of such work are recorded by them. Those weavers who worked just before the advent of the factory system and then just after recalled the 1820s and 1830s as a period when their work from home was a period of freedom in all senses (Hammond and Hammond (1920)). And the transformation of work from agricultural labourer to industrial factory worker can be viewed as a similar transition from pre-industrial control to industrial restrictions, from satisfaction derived by the nature of the work, like hedgerow cutting, to satisfaction derived from income (see e.g. Burnett

(1994)). The factory system, devised to reap the benefits of a mass-produced product and economies of scale, depended on a reliable, skilled work force to ensure its smooth operation; and the managers relying on Fordist-Taylorist concepts demanded a disciplined work environment that ran like clockwork.[8] Running like clockwork meant severe employee control (Taylor, 1947).

Viewed in a historical context, the resurgence of work undertaken outside the traditional job-boxes of a large organization in the late twentieth century is not as radical as it might appear. Perhaps it is the freedoms that experts now enjoy that will lead us not back (back to all of the discomforts of the pre-industrial revolution workers' worries about the inconsistent supply of food and clothing) but to a life style more aligned with those of the past. We can view these labour markets emerging as a response by those with scarce knowledge and skills away from the inherent restrictions that the hierarchical Fordist organization implies. The efficacy of such markets will depend crucially on agencies. And perhaps it is the freedoms that the expert employee gains that will allow them to enrich their lives and increase their skills and further their knowledge to make them even more productive – not necessarily in any one area, like accounting, but in a number of areas which just might include playing a musical instrument or retooling themselves to further engage in a rapidly changing product market and a changing technological environment.

Organizations and compensation packages directed toward the unique personal preferences of individuals will impact upon the analysis of the labour market, organizations and knowledge-based work. These issues will be addressed as we examine expert employees and their preferences in the new labour market process – a process we suggest crucially hinges on the use of agents and agencies.

PART ONE

Expert employees and their new organization

An economist thinks of the economic system as being co-ordinated by the price mechanism and society becomes not an organisation but an organism. This does not mean that there is no planning by individuals. These exercise foresight and choose between alternatives. This is necessarily so if there is to be order in the system . . . Within a firm the description does not fit well at all.

R. H. Coase, *The Nature of the Firm*

CHAPTER ONE

Trends in the labour market

The steam engine has relieved them of much of the exhausting and degrading toil; wages have risen; education has been improved and become more general; the railway and the printing press have enabled members of the same trade in different parts of the country to communicate easily with one another . . . while the growing demand for intelligent work has caused the artisan classes to increase so rapidly that they now outnumber those whose labour is entirely unskilled . . . some of them already lead a more refined and noble life than did the majority of the upper classes even a century ago.

Alfred Marshall, *Principles of Economics*

In the late nineteenth century, social scientists recognized the important effects that the changes in technology and the increased demand for specialized skills had on the labour market. In their terms, the new technology meant a real increase in the ability to purchase and consume an increased variety of goods and services, resulting in 'steady progress for the working classes'. This was seen to be accompanied by an 'emancipation from custom, and the growth of free activity' resulting in a special character of business. Just before and just after the turn of the century, business and labour markets had changed dramatically.

We argue that in the late twentieth century the character of business and of the labour market has also changed significantly on account of: (i) an increasing proportion of women in the labour market; (ii) moves toward a larger service industry sector; and (iii) a rapid development of information technologies. Although not always in accord about what these changes mean to organizations, industries, and economies, research in this area tends to share the assumption that the results will be driven by demand-side forces. However, a different conclusion is suggested if we examine these changes through their impact on the choices available to employees. We contend that supply-engendered changes have significantly influenced labour economies, re-organized labour markets and re-defined organizational boundaries.

In this chapter we use US national data to support our contention that the combination of specific changes in (i) the numbers of professional women (ii) the increase in the importance of knowledge-based jobs (iii) the new network-building capacities of information technologies and (iv) the increasing popularity of environmentalism, suggest an altered set of opportunities and choices to a larger spectrum of expert employees. These data also reflect a change in work-home life considerations. Later we will suggest that this different opportunity set available to expert employees releases different means of increasing their productivity, utility and income – means which result in a supply-side-driven transformation of labour markets. For the moment, we will outline these general trends and suggest some of their consequences for the labour market and the work environment.

The increase in professional women

One of the most significant changes in the labour market is the increasing numbers of women which are entering the workforce and therefore changing the circumstances of family and working life. In 1970 American women accounted for 37 per cent of the workforce, in 1980, 43 per cent and in 1992 they represented more than 47 per cent. In the UK in 1994, females comprised 46 per cent of the workforce. It is projected that by 2001 this figure will increase to 52 per cent. In all advanced industrial countries, the growth in female participation in the labour market is equally significant (*The Economist*, 5 March 1994).

More important for our thesis than this general feminization of work is the feminization of expert employee sectors within the workforce. As shown in figures 1.1 to 1.6, around 1970 in the United States there was a sharp increase in the number of women employed in the leading professions and a further increase by proportion over the ensuing years.[1] This trend of rising participation continues through to the 1990s where, in some professions, we see a slight drop due to recessionary pressures, and the practices of 'last hired, first fired'. The latest cohort of lawyers entering the profession is that with the largest percentage of women; the recession in the early 1990s thus tended to affect women more than their male counterparts. Notwithstanding, now that some of the recessionary pressures of the early 1990s have lifted there is reason to believe that the burden of adjustment will not continue to be borne by women. This is because the proportion of women obtaining qualifications and entering the profession is much greater than the proportion of women presently employed. Although there is some evidence that within professions women are not treated the same as men (see e.g. Spurr (1990), Cox and Nkomon (1991), Hagan (1990), Adam and Baer (1984) and Kanter (1977)),[2] this might be a temporary phenomenon given the trends reported in figures 1.1 to 1.6.

In conjunction with the increase of women professionals the United States between 1980 and 1990 saw an increase of 13.2 per cent of women enrolled in higher education compared with just a 0.3 percentage increase of men. In professions such as medicine and law, the number of women are quickly approaching 50 per cent of those who earn degrees; 37 and 43 per cent respectively in 1990 as compared to around 28 per cent for both in 1980. In 1991, over 35 per cent of all American MBA degrees were earned by women, up from 25 per cent in 1980. Figures 1.1 through 1.6 show that this increase is significant across a wide range of professional qualifications. Further, this percentage increase in qualified women suggests a future growth of the percentage of women in these fields. Our own conservative estimations using these data suggest that by the year 2005 women will represent 36 per cent of all lawyers, 27 per cent of medical doctors, 13 per cent of engineers and 35 per cent of all US architects.[3]

The increase in women as a percentage of the work force continues to rise but it is the potentially much greater change in the proportion of women to men in the knowledge professions (because of their presently fewer numbers in these professions as opposed to the workforce as a whole) that can provide the greatest impetus for future labour market changes.

It is our contention that labour markets are likely to change and, in some instances, change significantly because power is shifting to people who supply specific skills and management styles. Some scholars disagree and argue that women colonize professions which are in decline and that most professions operate a 'glass ceiling' policy which ensures that the career peaks for the overwhelming number of professional women tend to correspond to the career floors for their male counterparts (for example, see Hill (1981)). It is argued that women are systematically discriminated against and will never assume

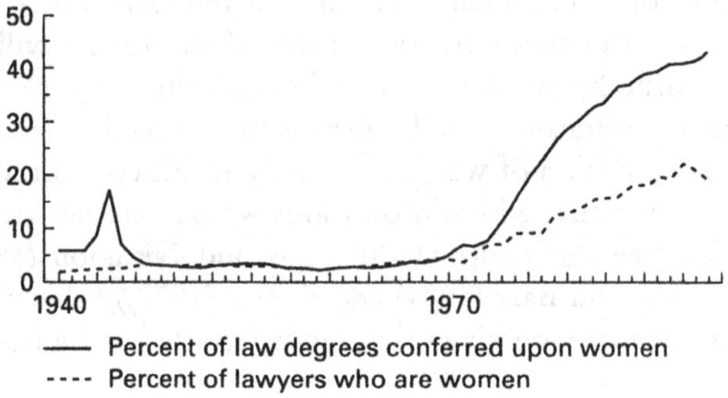

Figure 1.1 Women and Law 1940–1990

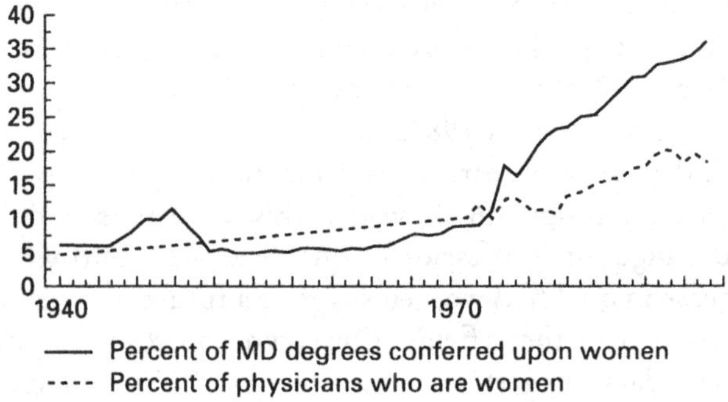

Figure 1.2 Women and medicine 1940–1990

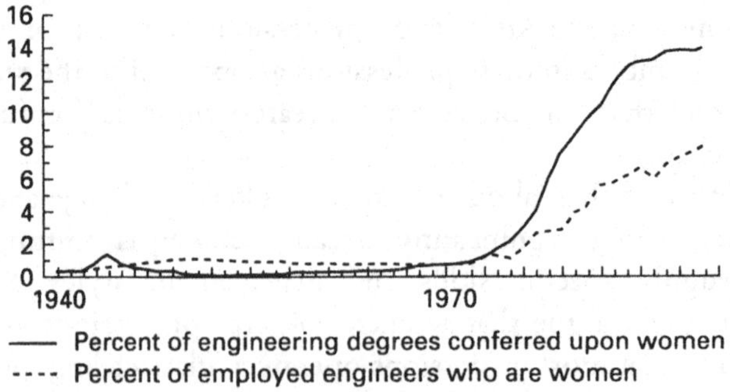

Figure 1.3 Women and engineering 1940–1990

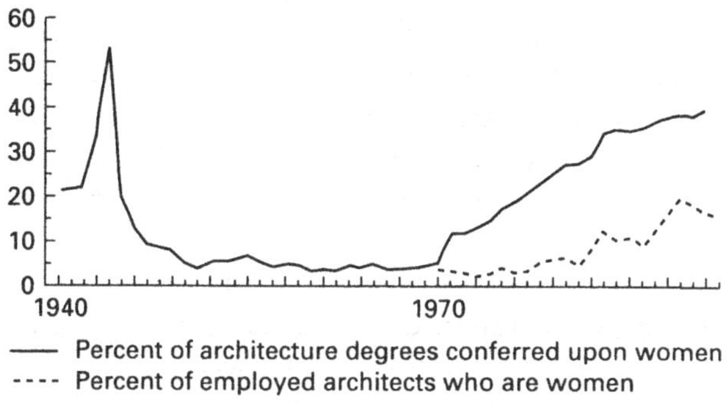

Figure 1.4 Women and architecture 1940–1990

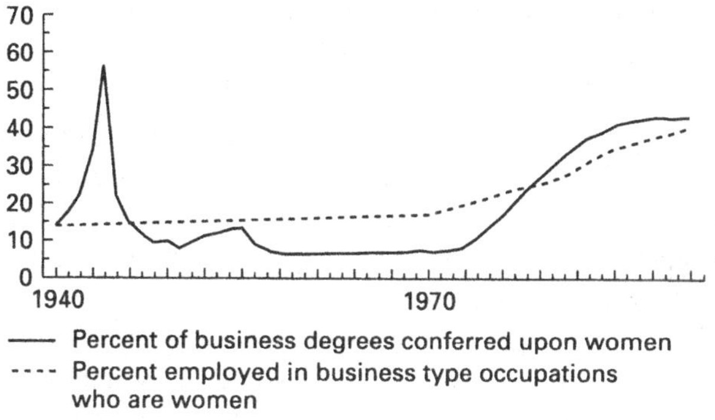

Figure 1.5 Women and business 1940–1990

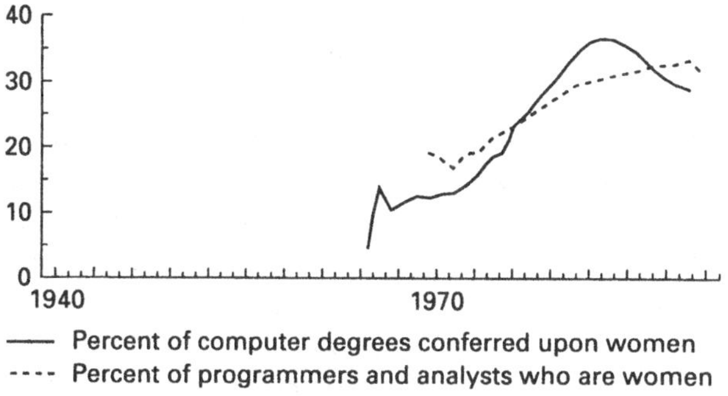

Figure 1.6 Women and computing 1940–1990

positions of management power and influence. But our evidence suggests that as competition for skills intensifies so gender will become less and less relevant. Further, given the rate at which women are colonizing the skill-dependent industries they are poised to have an important influence on these in the future, especially the emerging knowledge industries, in spite of current discriminatory practices and behaviour.

A brief input–output statistical analysis of our data presented in figures 1.1 to 1.6 suggests that there do not appear to be any significant reasons why women who qualify for a profession are not recruited into that profession. Time series data for previous years indicate there is a statistical lag in specific male-dominated professions which suggests that, for a time, a greater percentage of women will qualify for a profession than are actually employed in that profession. It is only when a male-dominated cohort has exited and been replaced with a more balanced male-female ratio of professionals that the cohorts of qualified women professionals and women actually employed in professions can be expected to coincide. This does not necessarily rule out discrimination against women once they are employed. Indeed, Spurr (1990) suggests that women lawyers generally take longer to be promoted than their male counterparts.

There is evidence to suggest, however, that gender influence in specific sectors, is already being recognized and in some instances appear to favour women. Indeed, Rosener's (1990) comparative study of male and female leadership styles suggests that, in some instances, women have an advantage. Men tend to reflect the command and control world congruent with large bureaucracies, while women tend towards an interactive style more appropriate to emerging knowledge-dense industries with flatter and more egalitarian organizational structures. This interactive style of management might be more effective in 'learning' organizations which operate more like teams than hierarchies where groups of people gather intelligence and knowledge which they use as foundations for advice and guidance. We argue that with the accelerated rate at which women are entering specific knowledge industries, the intense competition for skills in these industries, the role of such skills in wealth creation, and the facilitation management styles these industries require which Rosener (1990) describes, it suggests that women are poised to influence the emerging learning organizations. (chapter 2 below examines the learning organization more closely.)

In broader but related terms, the proportion of 'traditional families' – those in which the father worked year-round full time and the mother remained at home all year – in the US work force has continually declined since 1940. Indeed, by 1975 dual-worker families became the largest category of family labour force pattern and has continued to rise. Thus, in 1988 dual-worker families accounted for 40 per cent of the labour force family pattern and by 1992 only 20 per cent of two-parent families were traditional family structures (see e.g. Hayghe (1990); Hayghe and Bianchi (1994)). Sorrentino (1990) has suggested that throughout developed economies, 'the one-person household has become the fastest growing household type', and that most countries she studied showed a, 'rapid rise in participation rates of married women, particularly women who formerly would have stayed at home with their young children.' According to Sorrentino these trends will increase pressure for child-care facilities in traditional organizations. Fernandez (1986), meanwhile, shows that the lack of adequate corporate child care facilities continues to be a problem.

The consequences of an increasing number of women working as expert employees in knowledge occupations will also influence the notion of the traditional family. When women are offered jobs with pay and status substantially higher than their partners but in locations different from where they currently live, a non-traditional family migration occurs (see e.g. Yu *et al.* (1993)). Indeed, the increase of high-earning women may liberate many more married men to pursue jobs that provide intrinsic rather than monetary rewards since freedom from economic burdens provides freedom of job choice (see e.g. Martin and Shehan (1989)). Moreover, with two professional spouses there is pressure for each to play the role of nurturer and helper at home – a significantly different role for men and women and a different work structure as well (see e.g. Houseknecht and Macke (1981), Robinson (1988), Robinson and Gershuny (1988), Zick and McCullough (1991), and O'Connell (1993)).

To the extent that an increase in women in the workforce will alter the way in which home life and therefore work is arranged (child-care facilities, migration patterns, alternative careers, changing family roles),[4] the knowledge-dense areas, which now tend to be predominantly staffed by men, but show signs of increased participation by women, will be the sector of the economy most affected by these changes. The opportunity costs of working in an organization which provides compensation packages designed with this type of family in mind (when compared to the compensation package which might include flexibilities helpful for dual working and/or single parent families) may thus be high for those employees not in traditional family structures. Changes in the traditional family structure and the increasing proportion of women expert employees suggests a supply-side pressure for a change in labour markets and compensation packages. This is not just a women's issue. It is also because of changes in the family structure which exert increasing pressures on organizations, structures and compensation packages by both men and women who belong to the dual-worker family. Can traditional organizational structures be reconciled with new family structures? This constitutes a tug-of-war between demand-driven structures and supply-side pressures in professions. The significance of the increasing numbers of professional women, and the rise of the dual-worker family intensifies after examining the shift toward knowledge-based industries and occupations.

Trends in knowledge-based industries

The change in the type of work carried out is principally recorded by the evolutionary increase in the amount of professional employment. For example, the increase in industries of specialized business services which may arise from financial and administrative complications linked to the new global nature of trade, company structures and, for Europe, legislation (see Spence (1991)). This may largely be due to the developed countries shifting away from manufacturing toward knowledge-based industries.

In the United States, expert employee-dense industries such as biotechnology, robotics, legal services, accounting, management consulting and computer services registered large growth rates between 1980 and 1986, most near the 50 per cent rate. From 1983 to 1993 the number of lawyers grew from 612,000 to 777,000, an increase of 27 per cent. Over the same period the number of engineers grew 9 per cent to 1,716,000; the number of physicians grew 17 per cent to 605,000; the number of mathematical and computer scientists grew 126 per cent to 1,051,000; the number of financial managers grew 48 per cent to 529,000; and the number of natural scientists grew 49 per cent to 531,000. Overall managerial and professional speciality occupations grew 37 per cent compared with technical and sales administrative support which grew 18 per cent; service occupations which grew 19 per cent; precision production, craft and repair which grew 8 per cent; operators, fabricators, and labourers 6 per cent and farming, forestry, and fishing shrank 10 per cent.[5]

In Great Britain, between 1984 and 1991, there was a 12.5 per cent increase in service industries. This growth is marked by the higher growth rates in the professional expert employee-dense industries such as legal and business services, accountancy and computer services. Between 1984 and 1991, each of these knowledge-based industries grew more than 40 per cent. This is far above the total industries average of 3.5 per cent. Remarkably, computer services grew at a 97.5 per cent rate, and was the only industry to continue to grow at 20 per cent through the economic down-turn between 1989 and 90.[6]

The significance of these knowledge-based industries to the economy as a whole, and thereby the importance of experts to wealth creation is suggested by calculations of total payroll in these industries. In 1993 the average weekly earnings of US lawyers topped all other occupations with $1,079 per week. This is closely followed by physicians who earnt $1,007 per week, Engineers, computer programmers and business executives earnt $850, $799, and $650 per week respectively. All of these were well above the national average of $450 per week. In 1993, payroll for these five expert occupations alone amounted to $703 billion, equal to about 25 per cent of total compensation for all occupations which amounted to around $2,760 billion.[7]

However, it should not be inferred that the increase in experts necessarily leads to an increase in productivity or profit. In some instances the reverse is true. Indeed, specific services such as education and healthcare might be less productive as a result of a rapid increase in administrative experts as opposed to healing experts (doctors and teachers). But this seems to be a managerial issue which will resolve itself in time as these services restructure.

The future of employment growth in such sectors as engineering, computer programmers and business executives etc. appear to be assured by the projections of job growth. According to Silvestri and Lukasiewicz (1991), there is a:

> continuing above average growth rate for jobs that require relatively higher levels of education or training. This is reflected primarily in the increasing proportions of executive, administrative, and managerial workers; professional speciality occupations; and technicians and related support occupations.

These three major occupational groups . . . are expected to account for 41 per cent of the increase in employment between 1990 and 2005.[8]

Alchian and Demsetz (1972) in their seminal article, 'Production Information Costs, and Economic Organization', provide theoretical grounds for the view that the growth of knowledge-based occupations will change employer/employee relations. They submit that employees who primarily think or perform their tasks in their minds (our expert or knowledge-based employees) are, due to the nature of their tasks, very difficult to monitor. They conclude that, 'artistic or professional inputs . . . will be given a relatively freer reign with regard to individual behaviour' (p. 786). This hypothesis will not produce new behaviour among expert individuals but, it is proposed here, it will, in conjunction with an increase in knowledge-based industry jobs, change relationships between employer and employee. The increase in knowledge-based industries increases the costs of monitoring employees. Therefore, firms will be less likely to monitor, and discretion over work will probably increase as a consequence. Taken further, the firm with its highly structured monitoring functions (through management) might become less necessary as a result.

This freedom from monitoring eschewed by Alchian and Demsetz (1972) can be translated for our purposes into the change of compensation packages to include control: temporal and work-load control, and control over how organizations function – all influenced by the employee. Given the increases in professional women and the ramifications on family labour patterns, an increased demand for child care facilities is realistic (see e.g. Galensen (1991)). It seems reasonable to suggest that as expert employment increases, the changes demanded by experts may raise the expectations of other employees and this, in turn, might motivate them to demand specific changes. Thus, a multiplier effect might occur across a relatively broad area of the economy and could lead to the adoption of expert employee type work relations. Thus, the less easily monitorable work environment of knowledge-based work puts employers under pressure to provide an increasingly more open contract of employment. These new contracts make new forms of employment more typical and other employees follow. This increases the provisions of facilities at work for flexibility, as well as provisions in the community, so that new kinds of employment become ever more attainable for a range of employees.

Technology and networks

Over the last century, change for employees was significantly influenced by the infrastructure of the state (roads, canals, trains, planes etc.), and the tempering of working conditions by various employment, trade union and factory acts. Today, the infrastructure to move products is well established, albeit still improving, and the advances in automation technology have reduced the importance of people in manufacturing processes (see e.g. Braverman (1974) and Hill (1981)). In conjunction with the rise of knowledge-based goods and services critical to the work environment are the changes in technology that have established the information highway and its networks. Below, we provide a brief analysis of how well this information network is established and suggest some consequences of its development.

The modes of transporting information or knowledge from one person to another, one department to another and even one industry to another are the basis for the information infrastructure of a nation, a firm or an individual. Increasingly, information systems are configured in a person-to-person manner. The most important changes in the infrastructure of information, ultimately changing knowledge-based industries, are grounded in, but not limited to, the silicon chip and the information storing and retrieval capacity which it facilitates. Silicon chips are found in computers, printers, improved and more complex telephone services, satellite links, portable telephones, faxes, copiers, fibre optic cables, telephony and multi-media packages. Such devices have improved the infrastructure of communication and the delivery of information or knowledge. These changes are coupled with increasing standardization across trading blocks which significantly enhances the scope of these technologies to facilitate global information highways (e.g., see Gates (1995)).

In general, cable as a means of communication has seen rapid increases. In 1977 less than 200 cable systems receiving satellite signals existed in the United States. By 1983 there were some 8,000 systems, and by 1990 this had risen to some 9,900 operating cable systems. These basic cabling systems service about 53 million consumers and penetrate at the national level 57.1 per cent (see e.g. Calabrese and Jung (1992)). In 1994, in the United States, 2 to 4 million households were receiving digital television through cabling systems such as fibre optics. Such cables allow masses of information to move from household to household including digitized pictures. Within specific industries, there is rapid expansion of fibre optic cabling by telephone companies. Their aim is to transmit significantly more information over the telephone lines than is possible with the picturephone systems in use today.[9] Indeed, it includes such things as motion pictures on demand, where a consumer can choose a film from a long list. Rather than subscribing to one cable service and its programmers' choice of materials, a consumer can develop his/her own bespoke home channel, by selecting a desired programme. However, basic cable service companies are also attempting to put in place their own fibre optic cable systems. If the cabling of America and Britain continues, as is expected by Eugene P. Connell, president and chief executive officer of NYNEX Cablecomms Limited, most of the 25 million home computer users in the United States will have this capacity in the not too distant future. In Castro Valley California, Viacom Co. will set up a one gigahertz fibre optic cable system offering interactive and on-demand services. In other US cities as diverse as New York, Rochester, Hartford, Arlington, West Palm Beach, Omaha and Denver similar systems will be available with this digital capacity. For many Americans the ability to move pictures, sound and information in general, from household to household is becoming a reality.[10]

In conjunction with wired network access, wireless telecommunication services have also increased dramatically and show a great deal of growth potential. The Personal Communications Industry Association has suggested that the PCs market could have 60–90 million subscribers by the year 2002. Another report by Motorola estimates that these services will cater for more than 150 million domestic users by 2000. This expansion in service is reflected in the number of cellular telephone users in the United States. In 1984 there were less than 100,000, but, by 1994, there were 14 million users (see e.g. Frieden (1995)). Other countries have fewer users and the growth rate is not as dramatic, but with Germany, Japan, United Kingdom and France included in the tabulation, the number of cellular telephone users rises by another 3 million (see e.g. *Wired*, January 1995, p. 54).

This cable and satellite linkage is made more powerful by the increased availability and use of computers and computer services. Estimates have shown that the 'quality adjusted' real price of micro computers fell a staggering 28 per cent per year from 1982 to 1988. This fall in price corresponds with a rapid growth of computer use at work and the number of computers used from the home. In 1984, 24.6

per cent of the US workforce used a computer at work. This rose to 37.4 per cent by 1989, an increase over 50 per cent (Krueger (1993)). In the United States there has been a dramatic increase in the ratio of personal computers to desk workers. By 1993 there were 30 computers for every 100 individuals. For other Western countries the numbers are also significant: per 100 Australian citizens, 20 computers; Canadians, 20; British, 16; Swedish, 16; Swiss, 15; Dutch, 15; French, 14; Germans, 14; Japanese, 12; Spanish, 10 and Italians, 9 (*The Economist*, 11 February 1995).

It is the combination of cables, satellites, and the personal computers that forms the backbone of the new 'hard' technology. But as a 'technology' we also include the various network systems (e.g. the Internet and the World Wide Web) which this increase in hard technology implies. For example, the Internet's use has grown exponentially in the past few years, and continues to grow. Presently there are some 30 million users. The person who uses the network is no longer a scientist or academic or a computer hacker. The scope and breadth of the user continues to diversify (see e.g. Hart *et al.* (1992)). Software applications over the Internet become increasingly usable in 'real-time'. The rise in software patents suggests the degree of consumer response to new and innovative computer products and indicates the growth in what we consider new technology. The number of software patents issued in the United States has grown from about 350 in 1980, 2,500 in 1990 to a staggering 5,000 plus in 1994 (see *Wired*, January 1995, p. 54). Today, there exist some 14,000 software patents in the US alone.

The combination, cable and computers (and the substantial potential output of this combination) relies on a linkage between the broadband cabling that is offered by telephone and cable services, and the ability for computer users to use these services. But this linkage has its complications. Telephone and cable companies use the cable system primarily as a one-way cable service to their subscribers (videos on demand). This, it is argued, is their incentive in laying the cables. Broadband switches and cabling technology store vast potential for a networked computer user. Pictures and graphics with extra clarity will be transmissable from computer user to computer user. However, the growing competition between cable and telephone companies provides the cable in the first place. The question for national and international computer users is, how does this type of single switch (the computer user and network user demand a public switched broad-banded system) get transferred to a national broadband public switched system? See Hart *et al.* (1992).

These technologies alter the process of producing information-based products and services. Potentially, they can relax some of the production time constraints, change the way people learn and assist employees to retool over an entire lifetime. As a consequence, the user (in this case the knowledge-based or expert employee) would acquire a more flexible environment with a network which, by providing an increase in information and interconnection, would in turn increase the user's productivity.[11] For example, the Internet, with its World Wide Web, Gopher and Mosaic systems and the massively improved telephone exchanges, allows translators working with AT&T's Language Line to work with customers from around the world, translating conversations, meetings, and documents almost instantaneously, without the translator leaving his/her own home.

In a 1992 LSE Business Performance Group lecture, George Fisher, the former executive chairman of Motorola Inc., emphasized that the influence of these emerging technologies relies upon the standards-setting practices of firms developing and producing these products. Without universal standards the links could break down. The industry has recognized the necessity of standards and the equipment is becoming increasingly compatible across firms. These factors may reduce the importance of the central office and the working-time restrictions that office hierarchies impose (see e.g. Hakim (1984a and 1984b), Huws *et al.* (1990) and Kinsman (1987)).

The consequences of technological change do not have to be as severe as the abolition of centrally located places of work. The important fact is that within the workplace (be it the home or the centrally located office) the time constraints of production have become more relaxed due to advances in technology. No longer is sequenced production so constraining over working-time. If 'functional specialization requires synchronization of various parts' resulting in a fixed timed pattern (Hassard 1989b, p. 94), then knowledge-based jobs, a consequence of technology, with their more ephemeral functions may inherently require less synchronization, or specified sequencing.[12] This challenges the scaffolding of scientific management with its emphasis on simple repeatable routines.

In many ways, an organization's effectiveness as viewed by its employees will be determined by the extent and quality of its networks. Thus, technology is applying pressures, and providing competition to traditional organizations and their role as communications facilitators. The last decade has seen significant developments in the infrastructure of these knowledge-based industries. This is where changes in information technology may have the largest impact on expert employees. If such people can acquire a more inclusive network of individuals (through the technology changes outlined here) then their need to belong to an organization decreases and their demand to expand their own work environment to include these larger networks implies a different employment condition: one which is supply-side driven (chapter 4 below expands on the concepts of increased productivity and efficiency for knowledge-based employees working with networks outside an organization). It is the increased opportunities of external networks provided by the new technology which suggest a demand for expert employees to widen their employment horizons.

Expert employees and environmental issues

Measuring the change in attitude towards the environment may not be as easy as measuring the change in female participation, changing industries or changing technology, but this does not make it any less important in describing new opportunities and opportunity costs associated with contemporary employment. As Nobel prize winning economist F. A. Hayek said in his 1974 Nobel Memorial Lecture, 'Unlike the position that exists in the physical sciences, in economics and other disciplines that deal with essentially complex phenomena, the aspects of the events to be accounted for about which we can get quantitative data are necessarily limited and may not include the important ones' (Hayek (1975)).

We argue here that the threat of ecological destruction may surface in the form of a re-evaluation of what is considered valuable to the employee. Should an individual choose to purchase another or better car, and thus create the adverse ecological effects this purchase might have, or should a person choose intangible purchases to develop both professionally and personally? Opting for the latter results in supply-side demands for employment contracts which substitute increases in income with increases in control over work.[13]

Meadows *et al.* (1992) set out a simplified model (simplified from their complex computer model) of how present patterns of living and peoples' choices affect the future. Their model predicts the state of the world's resources and pollutants against material aspirations.

Meadows and his colleagues then alter the various parameters of the model and conclude that the choice is between either global collapse or a sustainable future. The results depend, of course, on the levels of the parameters.

A principal mechanism that the parameters pass through are the programmed delays in feedback systems. An extended delay causes the overshoot of production which turns into either an oscillating recovery of the system or a total collapse, as the system, unable to react in time, is unable to regenerate and then recover (oscillation alone can be devastating). The example given by Meadows *et al.* (1992) is overshoot due to delayed feedback mechanisms in the accumulation of chlorofluorocarbons (CFCs) in the stratosphere. Fourteen years after the possible link between CFCs and the destruction of the ozone layer, it was reported that Du Pont, the world's largest producer of CFCs had stopped production of those compounds. However, the production that took place within those fourteen years has not yet had its full effect on the ozone layer. Only time will tell if this particular overshoot has caused oscillation or collapse.

Even with the shortest feedback system Meadows *et al.* conclude that with liberal estimates of pollution control, yield enhancing, land protection, and resource-saving technologies, their model still yields a collapse scenario. This results in a world wherein pollution is high, consumer goods, services, and food per person are low, as well as a decreased life expectancy. The results of the combinations of changes in technologies and a structural change in the system are: (i) high life expectancy (ii) a generous amount of food per person is sustainable at a reasonable level (iii) ultimately falling pollution, and (iv) notably high services per person. Industrial output is sustained but decreases slightly and population is maintained by both increasing the standard of living and by a change in attitude. It is a far more attractive result than those predicted without structural change.

More importantly for our discussion is that according to Meadows *et al.* (1992) no combination of technology can sustain a healthy planet. They claim that in order to avoid global collapse, radical structural change is necessary. The change they programme for is a change in the 'cultural expectations and practices . . . that associates social status with material accumulation, and that define goals of getting more rather than having enough' (p. 192, this is programmed by restricting output *per capita*). According to Meadows *et al.* this does not mean a no-growth scenario, but a call for 'qualitative development, not physical expansion' (p. 210). This structural change in attitude may most likely be accessible to those groups of employees which have the most advantages in the labour market – employees that are comfortable at home and can afford the costs of being environmentally conscientious.

Some indication of the growth of employee concerns about the environment are reflected in the number of individuals who have joined environmental organizations like Green Peace who include some 400,000 supporters in the UK and over 4.5 million world-wide. Notwithstanding this, another significant indicator is the tone of the Rio Summit. At this world-wide ecological conference in 1993, discussion moved away from technological and conservation issues, through replacing highly destructive production with production that maintains consumption but replaces the products with low impact production, to a discussion implying a decrease in consumption. Or at least a transfer of what we should include in measures of Gross Domestic Product. Perhaps the inclusion of levels of clean air and the health of the environment will offset the loss involved in consuming and/or manufacturing fewer cars, for example. There is a significant difference between advocacy and actions; see Cagnon, Thompson and Barton (1994). But public policy has had an impact on recycling patterns; see Hong *et al.* (1993) and it has been argued that pollution may decrease steady state consumption; see Tahvonen and Kuuluvainen (1993).

It is not the task of this section to prove ecological conscientiousness has changed consumption. This is not the point. The point is that these are serious discussions in an accessible format, in books, on television, and in the classroom, therefore they may turn out to have a significant impact on influencing work attitudes and organization, compensation, and company structures. One need only look at the phenomena of Peters and Waterman's best-selling book *In Search of Excellence* (1982). This popular book has impacted upon management and management styles significantly throughout the United States and United Kingdom, and according to Guest (1992) has even altered the behavioural sciences themselves.

Trends and the supply-side impact

The four changes outlined above: (i) increase in professional women (ii) growth of professional occupations (iii) changes in technology and (iv) increased environmental concerns, combine to fuel the supply-side driven impetus for labour market restructuring and new relationships between employer and employee that results in an agency led labour market. An increase in professional women leads to altered family and work structures which implies a demand for organizations promoting temporal flexibility and flatter hierarchies. The increasing number of workers choosing to work in knowledge-based professional employment implies an increase in monitoring costs and a concomitant decrease in the effectiveness of managerial monitoring. This results in the reduction of organizational rigidities. Changes in technology facilitate the growth networks external to the organization, the use of which are demanded by expert employees leading to a rejection of organizational rigidities. These technologies also provide the ability for expert employees to work away from the confines of an organization. Environmental concerns are translated by the demands of employees, who are also consumers, into a work/compensation package which includes fewer work hours and/or increased control and flexibility, rather than increased income.

Each of these points is based on factual changes and trends with implications derived from theoretical discussions. Professional female employment is increasing. Rosener (1990), Yu *et al.* (1993) and others have argued that working women imply changes in organizational management and changes in work/family life. Knowledge-based professional employment is increasing. Alchien and Demsetz (1972) have argued that this type of employment is costly, if not impossible, to monitor. Technology changes include increased networks outside the organization and we argue in chapters 4 and 5 that this implies possible gains by employees in working outside the organization. Pollution is an increasingly significant problem. Meadows *et al.* (1992) and others, argue that a decrease in consumption is a necessary route to solving this problem. More importantly though, we suggest that there is room within the demand-side arguments which address changing organizational and labour market structures for these supply-side arguments.

The question remains – who will react to these changes? Will firms provide for the development needs of the expert employee within the corporate structure, and attempt to maintain control?[14] Or, will the firm relinquish its hold so that experts can pursue diverse activities, under conditions which yield the highest levels of satisfaction? On the other hand, external markets may begin to cater first for the needs of a workforce which prefers greater control over working-conditions. This could result in less restricting and new forms of organizational structures which also allows individuals to pursue personal development activities. Finally, there may be a combination of these influences.

In the next few chapters, we construct our argument by demonstrating that: (i) organizations find it difficult to cope with changes that these trends imply because of the organizations inherent defence mechanisms; (ii) traditional organizational functions such as control, monitoring and economies of scale are less relevant to expert employees working within these changing circumstances; (iii) the growth in networks external to organizations increases an individual's intellectual capital; (iv) temporal flexibility associated with external labour market arrangements can increase personal utility and productivity and (v) we link these concepts to social, political and economic discussions of the past. Following these theoretical chapters, we provide some case studies which support our contention that supply-side influences can have a dramatic effect on organizational structures and labour markets.

CHAPTER TWO

Adaptations in the labour market and the expert employee

A striking example of adaptive color change occurred among British peppered moths in the vicinity of Manchester. In the eighteenth century, all such moths collected were pallid in color; in 1849 a single black moth was caught in the vicinity, and by the 1880s the black moths were in the majority. Why? Because industrial pollution had blackened tree trunks in the vicinity, robbing the original moths of their camouflage while bestowing its benefits upon the few black moths there. Once pollution-control ordinances came into effect, the soot slowly washed from the tree trunks and the pale peppered moth population rebounded.

Timothy Ferris, *Coming of Age in the MilkyWay*

Historians did not generally accept the notion of an 'Industrial Revolution' until 1881 when Arnold Toynbee used the term in a series of lectures to describe a major transformation of society, see e.g. Beniger (1989) and Toynbee (1884). Since that time other labelled transformations have been introduced and made popular. For example, in the early 1950s Boudling introduced 'Organizational Revolution' (Boudling (1953)); in 1971 Helvey first issued the 'Age of Information'; more recently Piore and Sable (1984) popularized the term, 'The Second Industrial Divide'[1] and in an increasingly more prescriptive literature Hayes *et al.* (1988), Senge (1990), and Argyris (1993) made popular the 'learning organization'.[2] The works are similar; each frame a discussion on a particular aspect of organizations and labour markets at a particular time, and each tries to understand the associated phenomena by understanding the transformation process.[3]

Similar to the foregoing scholars, our work is concerned with the transformation of organizations. Important to this discussion is the nature of transformation. In brief, are changes best described in terms of a gradual transformation or in terms of breaks resulting in punctuated equilibriums? The terms 'gradual' and 'punctuated' are borrowed from the natural sciences because it is in this field that so much work has been undertaken on the description and analysis of differences and change.[4] We suggest that an examination of changes within labour markets and organizations benefits from the rich resource of terms and ideas of the natural sciences. An exchange of concepts and terms that dates to when those of the economist Adam Smith influenced the work of Charles Darwin, the natural historian. 'Darwin partly derived his theory of natural selection as a creative intellectual transfer from Smith's ideas' (Gould (1995), p. 8).

Placed in this broader context we see that recent social science literature on the transformation of markets and organizations assumes a demand driven gradual transformation. An understanding of this process benefits by a comparison with change processes within the natural sciences and approaching change as a supply-driven phenomena.

Gradual and punctuated transformations

Adaptation can occur along lines of a gradual change, as in the lengthening of the giraffe's neck over generations to exploit the niche of foliage high in the savannah trees, or along a punctuated equilibrium (Eldridge and Gould (1972)) like the abrupt change from the benefits of walking on four feet to those associated with walking upright on two. (For palaeontologists 'abrupt' changes mean millions of years. The same scale is not applied to our thesis.) This distinction between gradual and abrupt change is crucial to our analysis of labour markets, organizations and expert employees. Gradual change suggests a transformation of organizations with intermediate forms resulting in new species while an abrupt change allows for a rapid shift without intermediate forms.

Historical evidence suggests that labour markets evolve in both punctuated and gradual ways, and there are conflicting transformation theories based on both. A classic example of this is the change from slavery to feudalism which some researchers view as an abrupt break, while others see it as a gradual transformation. Let us examine this example in more detail.

Much of the discussion about slavery in the feudalism debate surrounds March Bloch's posthumously published articles on ancient slavery (see e.g. Bonnassie (1991)). He led the way in his investigation by pinpointing one of the debate's more intriguing problems; continuity versus the upheaval of the slavery system. Did the transformation between slavery to feudalism consist of an abrupt break or a gradual development? At the heart of the debate surrounding the change from the slavery driven mode of production to the feudalist mode is the debate surrounding the vehicles of slavery's demise. Was the cost of production through slavery too high (ee e.g. Duby (1974))? Did growth outreach slavery (see e.g. Parain (1979))? Or did class struggle signal its demise (Dockes, (1982))?

For Bonnassie (1991), it is clear 'the essential truth is of a discontinuity – the death of a very old social order (the slave system) and the forms of subjection associated with it, the birth of a new society (feudal society) and new types of dependence. The transition from one to the other constitutes what we may, with George Duby, call the 'Feudal Revolution' ((1974), p. 59): a punctuated break.[5] The struggle to explain the transition from slavery to feudalism is in many ways a debate about two questions. Firstly, how do we accurately define actual differences between the two systems.[6] For example, which elements, if any, of slavery are retained in feudalism. Secondly, what type of transformation is it – gradual or abrupt? In our discussion of the labour market similar questions arise. We answer the first by explaining the agency systems in the second part of this book. The second we examine in the next four chapters.

In chapter 1 we described the reasons for the changing labour market (women, technology etc) and now we enter a debate similar to that surrounding the move from slavery to feudalism. Do our reasons suggest a punctuated break or a gradual change?[7] Our answer is clear. The changing expectations of expert employees combined with changes in technology and product markets foster conditions for abrupt and radical changes in some labour markets and organizations. The debate between slavery and feudalism suggests that an analysis of change need not necessarily entail a gradual transformation. Indeed, it might include an abrupt change which results in the transformation of traditional institutions.

Evolutionary change and the US film industry

A classic example of an evolution from a traditional Fordist organization with vertical integration of tasks and mass production technology to a more flexible, dispersed organization is the Hollywood film industry (see e.g. Storper (1989)). The Fordist motion picture companies of the 1930s, such as Metro Goldwyn Mayer (MGM) and Columbia Pictures, embodied distinct departments each concerned with their own area of expertise. This included the pre-production activities such as script writing and casting, the actual production and then the post-production activities which included editing and sound effects. These all combined to form the production line for the hundreds of motion pictures produced in this Golden Age of Hollywood. In 1941 there were 504 films produced by large corporations compared with only 73 in 1989 (Motion Picture Association and *Screen Digest*, July 1990). In 1931 stars such as Clark Gable had long-term contracts and often appeared in some fourteen films a year. Today, by contrast, comparable actors are usually contracted for one film and their contracts nearly always include royalty fees, sometimes including a percentage of the gross sales from resulting merchandise.

Using Piore and Sable's (1984) industrial divide thesis, Storper (1989) and Storper and Christopherson (1987) describe the development of a new Hollywood film industry on increased product differentiation and vertical disintegration. They suggest that the Hollywood film industry encouraged a collaboration with independent producers in order to foster creativity. In this new industry,

> horizontal inter-firm networks begin to grow: product variety begins to supplement product differentiation and horizontal inter-industry relations offset some of the risks faced by supplier firms and encourage specialisation. As the efficiency of these networks increases – manifested in higher quality, lower prices, or product variation – the large firms increasingly turn to them in crisis. (Storper (1989), pp. 299–300)

Thus, Storper and Christopherson (1987) provide us with a demand-sided view of an evolutionary change. The large Hollywood, Fordist studios are gradually changing and combining with independent firms to form a new industry of flexible specialization. To some extent their analysis is correct. Between 1966 and 1982 the number of production-related companies in Los Angeles increased markedly (see table 2.1). The change is also exemplified by the success of independent productions. But, for some, this is not compelling evidence.

Table 2.1. *Companies related to the film industry: Los Angeles 1960–1980*

	1960	1970	1980
Production companies	563	709	1,473
Stage rentals	3	24	67
Properties	66	33	184
Editing	4	31	113
Lighting	2	16	23

Source: Storper (1989).

Aksoy and Robins (1992) argue that Hollywood's vertical integration constitutes a significant barrier to entry in the global market of film distribution. They conceptualize the industry as media production and suggest that 'already some of the Hollywood majors are among the biggest global entertainment companies. Hollywood is globalising . . .' (p. 16). Companies such as Warner Communications which now produces records, television programmes, and films are global in nature. And film-making in general tends toward a global production system. For example, Warner's Gotham City set was moved from its London Pinewood studio location to Mexico in order that *Batman* 2 could be filmed more cost effectively. By contrast to the Golden Age many contemporary US productions are filmed outside of Hollywood.[8] Further, today many of the large US production companies have significant foreign investors. One consequence of the globalization of the US film industry is the survivability of the smaller independent companies, both within Hollywood and in other countries. This has led to European film production companies, such as France's *Canal Plus*, negotiating firmly on their distribution strengths. During the 1994 World Trade Organization talks, negotiations stalled as the French film industry would not reduce specific trade barriers which it viewed as crucial for the maintenance of the independence of its film industry.

Here then are two distinct and conflicting views of the evolution of the Hollywood film industry. Although they compete with one another, they both emphasise a demand-driven post-Fordist organization – either flexible specialization or the globalization of the industry. The large Hollywood studios are organizations which have evolved directly from the ideal Fordist organization. Certainly, the motion picture industry has changed, and analysis along gradual evolutionary lines adopted by these scholars may be appropriate, and can be used as evidence for the emergence of flexible specialization or global firms. But other avenues of investigation, like our own, suggest an alternative explanation of change.

Because our analysis allows for a punctuated break we do not assume a gradual transformation of the Fordist organization. Nor are we making normative statements about whether a non-Fordist organization is better or worse than a Fordist one (recall in natural sciences it is not the 'survival of the strongest or best' but survival by random adaptation to those that fit into a niche). Our analysis includes the possibility of a new punctuated equilibrium of the organization of labour. This transformation includes what we may now consider as supply-side misfits but which might be forms appropriate to the expert knowledge-based employee.

The prevalence of demand-driven gradual transformations

In the following section we address a more disparate body of work, including examples of literature on the 'learning organization', which we believe addresses transformation as necessarily gradual and demand led.[9] However, we assert that the concepts of organizational defence mechanisms (a phenomena well discussed in the learning organization literature) inherently calls for an investigation into a supply-led punctuated break.

Our first example, Prahalad and Hamel (1990) in a *Harvard Business Review* article 'The Core Competence of the Corporation', applies demand-driven changes of employee utilization in order to improve core competencies. The demand-driven goal is to increase core competencies which Prahalad and Hamel believe will 'characterize the global winners of the 1990s'. They warn that 'the time for re-thinking the concept of the corporation is already overdue' and fear that 'managers are not only unwilling to lend their competence carriers but they may actually hide talent to prevent its redeployment in the pursuit of new opportunities'. According to Prahalad and Hamel the 'benefits of competencies, like the benefits of the money supply, depend on the velocity of their circulation as well as on the size of the stock the company holds'. Their call is for management to break its, 'adherence to a concept of the corporation that unnecessarily limits the ability of individual businesses to fully exploit the deep reservoir of technological capability that many American and European companies possess'.

What does this work contribute to our discussion? We can immediately see that those employees that carry the core-competence in the Prahalad and Hamel scenario are similar to our own expert individuals. We also see that the treatment of these individuals is unique. They are to be passed around and utilized throughout the company. Prahalad and Hamel have taken up an important position: that change is needed and that change must be generated from within corporate and company structures. In doing so, they deliver a recipe for a gradual demand driven transformation of organizations.

Another example, Drucker (1992) in his article 'The New Society of Organizations' describes 'the purpose and function of every organization' as 'the integration of specialized knowledge into a common task'. He defines employees as 'people whose ability to make a contribution depends on having access to an organization'. His concepts are explanatory but based on a demand lead transformation. For example, 'As more and more organizations become information-based, they are transforming themselves into soccer or tennis teams, that is, into responsibility-based organizations in which every member must act as a responsible decision maker. All members, in other words, have to see themselves as "executives".'

Drucker (1992) also calls for organizations to amend their 'narrow mission and vision' to include considerations of 'society and community'. The organization Drucker describes is a place where groups of knowledge workers consistently come together to achieve specific goals, each contributing their particular expertise. But the organization itself is retained, because contribution depends on having access to an organization. This is reflected in the transformation of organizations into soccer or tennis-like teams. Contributions from organization and/or knowledge-based workers (our expert employees) is organized by a group of 'leaders' who, rather than command, inspire.

Again, Drucker points to the modification and enlightenment of organizations. Although organizations transform, they continue to exist and alter such things as employment policies, community service participation and leadership roles. Drucker's prescription, similar to that of Prahalad and Hamel (1990) is demand-driven and critically associated with an organization which maintains a specific goal for a long period. After the transformation, the organization continues to be the place of employment for expert employees. Drucker (1992) contends that knowledge-based workers 'can work only because there is an organization, thus they too are dependent'. But, because they also 'own the means of production – their knowledge' – they are 'independent and highly mobile'. In this respect, organizations, for Drucker, 'have to attract people, recognize and reward people, motivate people and serve and satisfy people'. It is because of Drucker's belief that organizations must stay but transform that transformation to him is confined to a demand-driven gradual shift.

We do not discount the contributions and developments of Piore and Sable (1984), Drucker (1992) and Prahalad and Hamel (1990), but suggest that the thrust of their work tends to display a demand-driven concept of gradual organizational transformation with intermediary steps, and little or no consideration of a punctuated break resulting in a new equilibrium. By examining transformation as a function of the latter, we suggest that considerations of organizational structures and labour markets can be strengthened. In the organizational learning literature a similar refrain is revealed: a transformation of organizations from within to accommodate changing externalities and thereby retaining the basic elements of the organization. The organizational learning literature can be divided into two parts, that which describes the learning organization (see e.g. Levitt and March (1988); Nelson and Winter (1982); Huber (1991); Larson and Christensen (1993)) and that which prescribes plans and processes to achieve a learning organization (see e.g. Argyris (1993); Hayes, Wheelwright and Clark (1988); Senge (1990); Schein (1993)).

Descriptions of the learning organization highlight the problems with traditional organizations. Employees perform appropriate tasks (or what are regarded as legitimate) rather than learn or try new solutions. Structure and routine trap organizational behaviour so that work is performed on the assumption that 'what worked last time is best this time'. Thus, experience leads to 'competency traps' (see e.g. Levitt and March, (1988)) where current practices prevail over alternatives, resulting in little change. Theorists such as Huber (1990) define organizational learning as a mechanism which induces a broader spectrum of organizational solutions through the transfer of information. Achieving this is a complicated affair. Prescriptions range from the just-in-time production systems of Hayes *et al.* (1988) to the mental models of Senge (1990). And, in almost every case, the solutions mean leaping over the hurdles of some kind of organizational stagnation and/or defence. Once this has been achieved the transformation to a learning organization begins. Again, a demand-led gradual transformation of organizations and the labour market environment. It is these defence mechanisms that lead us to the influential work of Chris Argyris, who has made a significant contribution to action-orientated behaviour in organizations through his analysis of the learning organization.

Organizational defences and supply-side punctuated breaks

There is an extensive literature which suggests how 'political' behaviour within organizations can inhibit performance (see e.g. Allison (1971), Argyris (1993), Bardach and Kagan (1982), Brunsson (1989), Keggunder, Jorgensen and Hafsi (1983) and Stockman (1986)). Such 'political' behaviour is generally referred to as defensive routines and these are perceived to inhibit performance. One illustration of these defensive routines described by Argyris (1993) is David Stockman's experience as director of the Office of Management and Budget under the Reagan Whitehouse Administration in the early 1980s.

President Reagan's inability to understand the essence of some budgetary issues discussed at cabinet meetings was covered-up by Edwin Meese's (counsellor to the President) tight management of the meetings. This meant that some important issues were not discussed at cabinet meetings. Realizing this, Stockman adopted what Argyris views as a relatively common tactic in such a situation and bypassed the cabinet. He proposed to Meese that he create a committee called the Budget Working Group, which would review all 'big ticket' items before they went before the President at cabinet. According to Argyris, 'even though Meese and Chief of Staff James Baker would be members of the group, Stockman knew that neither of them would attend the meetings unless the President did. Meese agreed and Stockman selected his team. It was this group that made most of the difficult choices' (Argyris (1993), p. 18).

One member Stockman chose for his team was a policy analyst Martin Anderson who was given the task of educating new cabinet members and their staff about the importance and rigours of budget cutting. Stockman apparently supported Anderson because 'he knew how to cut the ministers down to size without humiliating them' (Argyris, (1993), p. 18). According to Argyris, however, this was wishful thinking on Stockman's part since people so treated would tend to cover up their humiliation. Thus, although there might be no overt signs of it, humiliation and anger accumulated within individual ministers and manifested themselves in dysfunctional retaliatory behaviour. According to Argyris the immediate effect of such defensive routines as those adopted by Stockman was to 'inhibit the detection and correction of error. The second-order consequence was to inhibit problem solving and decision making. This consequence led to a third-order consequence: less effective organizational performance' (Argyris (1993), p. 19).

Most studies on 'informal' and 'political' behaviour within organizations show that organizational defensive routines exist and few suggest ways of overcoming them. Those that do tend to prescribe bypassing defensive routines and how to cover-up the bypass. But this, argues Argyris, is counter-productive since it results in strengthening the actual defensive routines. Argyris makes a significant contribution going much further than his colleagues in suggesting solutions to the problem of defensive routines. One solution which is practised in many organizations and described in organizational literature is that of changing behaviour. But this, suggests Argyris, is difficult to carry out because of the multi-faceted nature of individual behaviour. A better solution, according to Argyris, is to correct the underlying 'master plan' or 'theory in action' which is responsible for the defensive behaviour. This is much more practical since such master plans 'are few in number throughout the industrialized world' and have few basic characteristics. This second approach Argyris refers to as 'double loop learning' which makes understanding and facilitating change and learning more feasible and durable. However, the change and learning which Argyris refers to is predicated upon a conventional model of an organization.

In a *Harvard Business Review* article 'Teaching Smart People How to Learn' (1991), Argyris calls for more productive strategies to enhance managers' learning capabilities. Managers, says Argyris, develop a defensive system to specific issues which deflects problems away from themselves onto other people within organizations. This phenomenon arises because new knowledge-based employees are likely to be highly educated and have experienced little or no career failure, 'They have spent much of their lives acquiring academic credentials, mastering one or a number of intellectual disciplines, and applying these disciplines to solve real world problems' (p. 100).

Again these are expert employees and Argyris has pointed out one of the problems they bring with them to the organization. He believes that

> more and more jobs – no matter what the title – are taking on the contours of knowledge work. People at all levels of the organization must combine the mastery of some highly specialized technical expertise with the ability to work effectively in teams, form productive relationships with clients and customers, and critically reflect on and then change their own organizational practices. And the nuts and bolts of management – whether of high powered consultants or service representatives, senior managers or factory technicians – increasingly consists of guiding and integrating the autonomous but interconnected work of highly skilled people. (Argyris (1991), p. 100)

As in Prahalad and Hamel (1990), we again encounter that important refrain of the corporation as a guide and an integrator of expert employees.

It is because of this that Argyris's organizations will need to teach the expert employee how to learn in new ways – to identify not only an external problem and solve it but to be able to identify a problem based within themselves or in a colleague and take action to correct it in a way which benefits the company. This again is an approach which calls for a change in the structure of a system that is already in place. The change will be driven by the needs of the organization and the organization is expected to benefit. There is much to learn from Argyris and his conclusions that organizations will need to change if they are to attract, retain and develop knowledgeable individuals, but we must not lose site of the fact that it is the expert employee that has caused Argyris to re-evaluate the learning process in the first place.

Others, too, have investigated organizations as stable structures that resist change. One such study is Lyth (1990), who examined nurses in a teaching hospital in London during the 1960s. She provides evidence that the organizational structure of teaching hospitals will not change and are designed for punctuality and strict adherence to a set of rules. There is an important reason for this. According to Lyth (1990), the strict unmovable organizational structure of a nursing teaching hospital is important to inculturate nurses with strict routines for specific tasks. This provides nurses with a shield which protects them from the anxieties that the nursing profession will necessarily bring, 'Nurses are in constant contact with people who are physically ill or injured, often seriously. The recovery of patients is not certain and may not be complete. Nurses face the reality of suffering and death . . . Their work arouses strong and conflicting feelings' (p. 440).

The strict routines nurses learn while training provide a defence for dealing with such stresses. Thus, the organization is designed for defence, it defends against change because change brings potential anxiety. This mitigates against an easy transformation to a more flexible organizational structure. Thus, if it ever was the intention of the originators of the modern organization to bring about a security against anxieties related to change (which may be the case as a reaction to economic depression and wars), then imbedded in those organizational structures will be a resistance to change.

If we accept the premise that due to defence mechanisms there will be difficulties in assuming that a significant change will occur, then it may be fruitful to look outside the established organizations to see some of the consequences of the new opportunities available to the expert employee. Because of defence mechanisms inherent in organizations, their ability to provide for the changing workforce, individual tastes and preferences and changing technologies may be limited. This suggests that rather than solely expecting a demand-driven gradual transformation of organizations, we might see in specific instances forms of a punctuated adaptation which occurs outside the organization. The potential for this abrupt change is highest among expert employees with their unique skills and opportunities.

Transformations

Our analysis suggests a wide range of employment opportunities which have at their heart the supply-side preferences of individuals rather than relying on one particular demand-sided structure. Some experts' lives will not be structured by one set of rules. Their increased opportunities will demand organizational flexibility perhaps beyond the scope of a gradual transformation of the traditional organization, more along the lines of a punctuated break. Current research continues to examine traditional organizational structures as the starting point of a potential transformation. Perhaps this is because there is much invested in this approach and therefore defences have built up over time which justify analysis of employee/employer relationships in this way. With this in mind we suggest that if employees are so important to wealth creation, then, in some key industries and firms, their preferences and demands will be influential.

Similar to the natural sciences, a punctuated break does not exclude a gradual transformation, both can co-exist. But natural scientists have generally accepted the important effects such breaks can produce, and the rewards that such theories have provided (like an alternative explanation to the incomplete fossil record). And it may be true that, 'the question of historical continuity or discontinuity simply cannot be adequately discussed in terms of such an either/or dichotomy' (see e.g. Huyssein (1986), p. 182).[10]

One cannot speak of the contemporary labour market with its expert employees as arising either solely from gradual evolution or solely from punctuated breaks. There is some evidence that both may occur. We contend that in a post-modern commercial setting, a plethora of organizations will be present, some gradually evolving with Fordist principles intact and others as mutations and oddities that find, in the contemporary labour market environment, that they are able to survive because they best fit the opportunities faced by some of the participants. Some of these mutated organizations will be formed by the employees themselves. This does not exclude those demand-driven gradual transformations any more than a gradual transformation in one species would exclude punctuated equilibrium from occurring in another.

However, one must be wary of the naturalists' powerful prediction that

> since there is a struggle for existence among individuals, and since these individuals are not all alike, some of the variations among them will be advantageous in the struggle for survival, others unfavourable. Consequently, a higher proportion of individuals with favourable variations will on the average survive, a higher proportion of those with unfavourable variations will die or fail to reproduce themselves. (Huxley (1974)

Whether a gradual transformation can adequately fulfil the necessarily rapid alterations in the external environment of the labour market is unknown.

Three conclusions can be derived from our analysis: (i) there is a difference between a punctuated break and a gradual transformation (ii) much of the literature on organizational restructuring tends to be linked to demand-driven gradual transformations, and (iii) inherent defence mechanisms call for an evaluation of a supply-side driven punctuated break. The last of these leads us to the next chapter where we explore other theoretical reasons for organizational change and examine why organizations exist. We also analyse some of the benefits of organizing labour through the modern organization and suggest that these tend to be defensive mechanism which foster specific aspects of organizations that do not allow for the changes that the trends described in chapter 1 suggest.

CHAPTER THREE

From the firm to the agency

It's quite clear to me that what you think of as a fault in yourself, your naturalness, your freedom, your spontaneity – that is precisely what people find attractive.

Turgenev, *A Month in the Country*

This chapter describes the results of a punctuated adaptation of the labour market which was suggested in the previous chapter. Recall that it was organizational defence mechanisms which inhibit change and promote the more radical punctuated break. In such a change it is the expert employee's compensation package which plays the key role. Indeed, supply-side demands for specific compensation packages tend to destabilize employer–employee relationships. New compensation packages and instabilities which arise from them are at the heart of the punctuated break from the traditional firm or organization (compensation packages that include elements indicative of changes in opportunities that we outlined in chapter 1). This initial hypothesis raises several questions. It requires a more precise definition of the organizations from which individuals break away and a description of where such individuals end up once outside the organization.

In this chapter we examine the consequences of expert knowledge-based employees with regard to four widely accepted theories of the advantages of organizations. These are: (i) co-ordination (ii) monitoring (iii) economies of scale and (iv) regulation of the speed of production. If organizations develop because of their inherent advantages (i) to (iv), then it is reasonable to assume that employees' demands which undermine these can not co-exist. To the extent that these demands compromise an organization's inherent advantages, that organization's *raison d'être* necessarily diminishes. Thus, firms tend to set up defence mechanisms which function to maintain their highly structured, traditional status quo. Increasingly, this results in a break by the expert employee from the traditional firm to an at-will contract, agency led, labour market.

The co-ordinating firm and the expert

The idea of firms as co-ordinators has long been at the heart of analysis of the firm. This fostered the debate about whether the firm co-ordinates by fiat or by firm internal market transactions. Coase (1937) in a seminal paper, 'The Nature of the Firm', suggests that employees within firms exist under contracts which determine that they agree 'to obey the directions of an entrepreneur *within certain limits*' (Coase's italics). According to Coase this is necessary because firms consist of a 'system of relationships which comes into existence when the direction of resources is dependent on an entrepreneur' (p. 393). This explains the existence of a firm outside any need or explanation of market transactions: the entrepreneur has special powers to direct and control employees. It is because the entrepreneur can do this better than the market mechanism that the firm exists. We have discussed some modern organizational theorists who suggest that it is the firm's job to co-ordinate employees, including experts. The assumption about the firm made by these theorists is one made clear by Coase over half a century ago, that the entrepreneur is someone with qualities who can direct employees in a more efficient way than the market pricing system. Entrepreneurs are said to be more efficient because they are specialists in particular areas and have information about many different prices of various inputs. Thus, they can reduce the cost of finding relevant market prices. The ownership and control of such information enhances their role as co-ordinators and makes the firm profitable. According to this thesis, expert employees seeking high wages, but not in full command of relevant information, will tend to accept a traditional firm setting under the stewardship of entrepreneurs. This suggests that entrepreneurship exists at the apex of a firm and employees are factors which fulfil the aspirations of entrepreneurs in return for some monetary compensation. It does not anticipate entrepreneurship more prodigiously spread among numerous expert employees, who might not be motivated entirely by monetary rewards. They, if organizations are unable to, satisfy specific demands made by the wealth creators – experts – for compensation which includes increased discretion. This reduces the advantages of the firm as an organization.

In the case of employing people, the Coaseian firm makes long-term contracts wherein employees, in exchange for remuneration, will obey employers. Obedience is a prerequisite for financial success and is a defining characteristic of a firm. According to such a model, the firm utilizes employees periodically during the life of a contract, and employees are indifferent as to what they are asked to do. To the extent that employers contract many people long term, they are in positions to co-ordinate employees without constantly renegotiating contracts. In effect, a number of different contracts are conflated into one which renders the employer more efficient than the market place that uses a series of contracts.

Is a firm, with its co-ordinating functions, a stable environment for knowledge-based expert employment? Firms tend to function optimally so long as remuneration of contracts are in monetary terms and all that employees desire can be converted into monetary terms. However, when compensation includes non-monetary elements the stability of the Coaseian firm is threatened. One element of compensation for an expert might be greater control over when work is performed. The greater the value an expert places on such non-pecuniary elements, the more difficult it becomes to trade them for income. Once such factors enter employment contracts, the stable co-ordinating function of entrepreneurs is weakened and power shifts to the experts. Each discretionary decision experts make potentially changes the employment contract. Under such conditions employers no longer co-ordinate the timing of employees' work because this is now, to some extent, in the hands of the employee. Given that expert employees wish to control non-pecuniary elements of their work it becomes increasingly difficult for the employer to distil a number of employment contracts into one.

Such trends tend to undermine the traditional Coasean model of a firm. One can imagine traditional employment relationships becoming strained as employers attempt to explain to employees the benefits of the conventional organization. If, however, one includes in an employment contract, such non-pecuniary elements as employee discretion over when to work, a stable organization is significantly compromised. According to the Coasean model, the firm loses both its control and its function. Thus, these seemingly minor changes in compensation renders the Coaseian firm unstable. To remain stable, therefore, a firm must resist contracts which include such elements. Such resistances – defences – will motivate some employees to abruptly break with the

Coase-type firm and seek alternatives in which to market their skills and satisfy their desires for enhanced discretion over their work. Successful employees in this regard will constitute a punctuated break from traditional organizations.

Team production and experts

Reducing transaction costs and the co-ordinating power of entrepreneurs may not be the only reason for a firm's existence. Alchian and Demsetz (1972) describe the firm in terms of its use of team inputs. They argue strongly that the firm has absolutely 'no power of fiat, no authority, no disciplinary action any different in the slightest degree from ordinary market contracting between any two people' (p. 777). This is opposite to Coase in that there is no need for employees to surrender their control to the employer. Instead, they define the firm as a place where co-operative production takes place. The existence of the firm relies upon its ability to provide a setting for co-operative production that is better than a market setting. This, it seems, could lead to compensation packages of the type that we are interested in, in conjunction with a traditional firm setting. But this is not the case. Again, as in Coase's case, problems arise between employers and employees when the latter demand more discretion over work.

To Alchian and Demsetz, much of employment within a firm consists of team production which is at the core of a firm's existence. For example, 'when two men jointly lift heavy cargo into trucks' (p. 779) the team production involves both men as inputs in the production of lifting the box. Without either of these men the box would not be lifted and therefore the product of the firm would not exist. It was Alchian and Demsetz' achievement to show what 'types of organization, contracts and informational and payment procedures' will occur when team production is a necessity for product formation. Their results essentially include the realities of team members shirking – a reality, since a shirker can still obtain rewards from the team production, but at a lesser cost than fellow team players. This shirking brings about the necessity to monitor each team member. The firm exists because the monitoring functions are taken up by a system of managers whose task it is to ensure that team members act fairly and are remunerated according to their efforts and productivity. Problems occur because the amount each individual adds to production of the output is not easily determined.

What most influences the possibilities available to managers is their ability to accurately monitor the actions of each team member rather than as Coase suggests, their ability to negotiate contracts with team members better than the market. The market place, on its own, will not have the expertise of the manager to know which of the employees is best at their job. For Alchian and Demsetz it is the 'shirking-information problem of team production' that gives rise to the classical firm (p. 783). And it is their contention that, associated with each form of information, associated with the different types of jobs, there is a different cost of monitoring, so that different types of firms will evolve with different types of monitoring and contractual arrangements (p. 785). Inherent in each is a disciplinary system to put in line the members of the team production in order to increase productivity. The monitor is remunerated by being given title to the net earnings of the team after payments to other inputs.

In light of knowledge-based employees and their new set of opportunities, is the system that Alchian and Demsetz use to distinguish a firm a stable environment for the employer/employee relationship? Alchian and Demsetz provide some clues to an answer. It is obvious to them that monitoring employees loading a truck is much easier than monitoring the inputs of knowledge-based employees. If much of what individuals do is in their heads and is not therefore easily understood by others, then monitoring by management might not be the most suitable route to increasing the productivity of a team. Professional inputs, they claim, will be given a 'much freer reign with regard to individual behaviour'.

For example, one can imagine the complications in monitoring the progress of a highly trained anthropologist as s/he works her/his way over a tray of bones. Each bone brings new information and might be the bone which links the skeletal structure with another species. How long should the anthropologist study each individual bone? No one fully comprehends what the anthropologist specializing in a tray of bones actually knows. It is almost impossible to make any clear set of rules as to what the product of this employee should be. Similarly, specific litigation is based on an analysis of specific evidence which often proceeds by an evaluation of each piece of documental evidence. The lawyer on a case makes a judgement, based on his/her knowledge, of which document should be studied for a long time and which should be studied for a shorter time – for that matter, whether a box of documents is relevant to the case at all. In the case of the anthropologist, exactly how much shirking and how much work is being produced is extremely difficult to evaluate. In order to monitor the progress it would take another anthropologist of similar training to provide an informed judgement as to the amount of shirking that may be going on. Probably even in this case there might be a dispute between the anthropologists about which bone needs to be studied longer. The same goes for the lawyer. Even if it was practicable to set up such monitoring, its cost would be prohibitive.

Alchian and Demsetz posit a response to these particular monitoring difficulties associated with professionals. They claim that professionals working in profit-sharing teams will be more productive than if they worked independently. Motivated by the potential profit share which is associated with the overall production of the team, individuals will tend to work with greater effort and thereby require formal monitoring less. Further, because individual rewards are dependent on team efforts, individual workers will tend to monitor their peers more closely. Thus, formal vertical monitoring is replaced with informal horizontal monitoring.

Because of the retention of the shirking problems that plague many firms, Alchian and Demsetz believe that self-monitoring partnerships will only occur among people who know each other well.[1] They must know each other well enough so that their work characteristics and their tendencies to shirk are also known by other partners. It is therefore their personal knowledge and the knowledge of the work habits of their peers that inform the professional employee involved in profit-sharing schemes that help individuals to monitor each other. Again, the problem of monitoring is at the root of the professional firm or the employer of expert individuals. It is not limited altogether by such profit-sharing schemes. This may be why large firms are distinguished not only by partnerships and profit-sharing but also by partners who serve for a time as managing partners or department heads who are involved in the general management of the firm of professional employees and perhaps in monitoring the product of individuals.

How does compensation in the form of control and freedoms effect relationships within professional partnerships? To the extent that experts include specific controls and personal freedoms in their employment contracts, partnerships are weakened. It seems reasonable to suggest that demands by expert employees for compensation, which includes spatial and temporal flexibility potentially, creates difficulties for partners to have sufficient information of their peers to establish the basis for effective team work. This suggests that partnerships might be less aware of how their employees work and therefore it becomes difficult to know how much shirking goes on. With these elements of compensation, partnership schemes might become unstable as the partners become wary of the shirking of others. Thus, non-pecuniary compensation serves to undermine the *raison d'être* of the firm as developed by Alchian and Demsetz, and partner demands for non-pecuniary compensation might be resisted. This resistance constitutes another form of defensive routines discussed above. The expert employee with strongly held preferences will more likely find such compensation outside the traditional firm structure. This encourages the expert to abruptly break from a firm.

Economies of scale and experts

Firms as co-ordinators and firms as monitors become unstable as expert employees increase their demands for increased discretion over their work. Similarly, organizations which capitalize on economies of scale are less important to the knowledge-based expert employee. Such organizations are relevant to the producer of a product that uses massive machines such as robotic assembly processes. This provides organizations with the advantages that they can produce their products more efficiently and thereby price competitively. This gives such a firm a distinct advantage over a smaller one or a group of competitors spread across a wide area. This is an often cited reason for the formation of large-scale production plants employing relatively large numbers of people. From an employee's stand point, there are advantages of joining a firm which capitalizes on economies of scale. Economies of scale and scope assists firms to win the competitive battle for customers by pricing their products lower. If they choose not to do this, their employees could benefit by capitalizing on the savings in the form of a higher wage. Furthermore, some products – motorcars and airplanes, for example – can only be efficiently produced in large organizations that can capitalize on economies of scale.

There will always be advantages to some large organizations which capitalize on economies of scale. It does not seem likely that, with the advent of knowledge-based work, a group of skilled knowledge-based workers will start up their own automobile factory and be able to produce an automobile with the quality and price of any of the major automobile manufacturers. Could not then the expert employee also see the benefits of working in a large office, which could then spread the cost of resources necessary to produce knowledge-based products? The cost of equipment like computers, libraries, administrative support and conference facilities would be spread across a large group of expert employees and the per employee cost would then decrease. The resulting price of the knowledge-based product could then be competitively cheaper than others.

Notwithstanding this, we contend that the most valuable asset in a knowledge-based product or service produced by an expert employee resides in the expert employee. Expertise is only marginally a product of the equipment we have outlined above. Indeed, computers are relatively cheap and data banks are easily accessed from computer terminals. More important to the expert employee with regards to economies of scale, is the size of the network that can distribute his/her knowledge-based product (chapters 4 and 10 discuss networks in greater detail). Presently, large organizations do not necessarily offer any more significant access to networking. It is not necessarily the largest firm in the conventional sense of size and scope which is advantageous to the expert employee. Rather, it is the firm with the largest knowledge and network base that can provide the greatest potential asset for the expert employee. Factors like computers and libraries are not as important to the expert employee, for these can be relatively cheaply purchased either as hardware or as on-line information services.

Still, the prestige of a downtown office or a building which at this moment in time cannot be cheaply purchased, provides a meeting place for peers to informally discuss and exchange ideas. This still has advantages which can benefit from economies of scale. However, such things as the Internet can offer expert employees greater scale and scope than a traditional headquarters which is not optimizing the use of such networks. Interestingly, the market place is already showing the impact of catering to the needs of these expert employees. Recently, in New York City, Chiate Day (a Los Angeles advertising firm) have designed a large office complex specifically for expert employees. In their design they have built a luxury office complex which has computer points where expert employees can plug into a leased space with all the amenities of a large office complex. It is an example of an alternative to the large organizational structure. This is not to say that production organizations do not capitalize on economies of scale by locating and building large production facilities. It is that those portions of organizations that produce knowledge as a product do not offer any great advantages to the expert employee through economies of scale.

The speed of production and expert employees

For knowledge-based work, the classic role of organizations to increase the speed of production is significantly less important. In the production of physical goods it is a matter of increasing the speed of the conveyor belt, arranging workers in a more efficient way, perhaps paying them more, or simply threatening them. The responses to these devices can be measured by the increased number of units that are produced. One is reminded here of Charlie Chaplin's attempts to speed up his use of the wrench in the production line in the classic film *Modern Times.* However, persuading experts to work faster or more efficiently is more difficult because their product is often difficult to quantify. Increasing their pay might produce more working hours, but whether they apply their tacit skills to achieve a qualitatively better output is uncertain. Therefore, because of the emphasis on knowledge-based work, another classic function of organizations is affected.

Timing is relevant in increasing the value of knowledge-based products. Innovation may strike at any time, but, if it is too late, then it is worthless since its moment on the market has come and passed. So that once a knowledge product has been produced it may be wise to speed up its delivery and marketing. The speed of production of knowledge-based work is different and can be separated into two distinct phases: the creation and the distribution. The creation of knowledge-based products and services may not easily be sped up (unlike in a factory line producing tangible products), but the delivery of the final knowledge-based product or service can, and this may be crucial to its value.

New organizations and the punctuated break

The problems which expert employees and their knowledge-based work bring to traditional organizational functions, like co-ordination, monitoring, economies of scale and speed of production, make the employment of expert employees in traditional organizations difficult. How then will these expert professionals with their specific compensation demands become employed? How will they integrate into the labour market in a way that they can contribute to team production, while maintaining their unique compensation packages? The answers lie not in a society dominated by large traditional companies, but in a society with a critical mass of exemplar organizations which satisfy the myriad of compensation demands made by experts through a system of at-will contracts and agencies.

Recall that our premise is that each knowledge-based expert employee will be uniquely compensated by a combination of pecuniary and non-pecuniary rewards. This premise implies a series of unique employment contracts. However, since the demands of the expert individual are in no way assumed to be temporally stable or of a predictable nature, it also implies a contract that is continually being renegotiated. This means contracts may be terminated at will if they fail to compensate an employee at a specific time. When a contract is initially agreed, the compensation may be acceptable for the expected future, but conditions may alter for that employee. This potential constant renegotiation of the employment contract is the essence of the at-will contract (a contract which can be terminated by either party at will). For the expert employee, the at-will contract is a logical answer to his/her inability to predict the future, and a developed desire for control over working conditions.

However, the doors of this contract swing both ways. To be an acceptable solution, the at-will contract must also provide the user of expert employees with benefits. There must be good cause for the user to apply this system or organization of expert employees. We have highlighted above the problems in monitoring the expert knowledge-based employee in a traditional firm setting. We also looked at the need to co-ordinate expert individuals. At-will contracts provide an arrangement which can satisfy these two demands. For example, if at any time, there is suspicion about the output of the knowledge-based employee, termination can occur without cause. The at-will contract works as a monitoring devise. Further, the expert employee can be co-ordinated in the sense that a number of employees can be hired and co-ordinated into a production unit and released at will. Let us examine these two dynamics a little closer.

Since monitoring and co-ordination are linked to an inability to forecast the future, at-will contracts embrace the two requirements of firm monitoring and team production. Monitoring of performance not only means the monitoring of the person with regard to his/her work and ability but also to the suitability of that work to the firm's needs. If an individual's product is expected to be important in the future, but it turns out this is not the case, then the individual will be less productive than expected. Monitoring productivity is associated with the unpredictability of the future. Further, co-ordination means moving and changing employees to future changing circumstances within the market and within the firm: as co-ordination needs change, employees change. Co-ordinating employees is linked to the unpredictable future. These are the endless marginal changes that are demanded when employing expert individuals. The at-will contract allows the firm or employer, or user of expert employees, to adjust to these changing conditions.

In a more general sense, the at-will contract provides the user of expert individuals with an ability to constantly upgrade. Upgrading in the sense that employers are more likely to have a knowledge base congruent with their specific needs. Personnel departments which have no trouble substituting their needs for qualified individuals often find individuals lack specific skills once they have joined the company (for example, see Kiser (1993)). At-will contracts facilitate a constant shuffle and re-evaluation of people within a firm and tend, therefore, to satisfy the changing needs of a firm.

As Epstein (1985) suggests, the at-will contract does not mean the necessarily harmful treatment of employees or of employers. In the first case, as an employee's contract is terminated, either because his/her knowledge or expertise does not yield the expected benefits to the team or because s/he no longer co-ordinates well with the employer's needs, another employee will be hired who is more appropriate to the employer's needs. So, as a group, the employee is no worse off. Further, if contracts are terminated by the employee because of unacceptable compensation the employer may expect better performance from people who are hired subsequently and appropriately compensated (see below). Thus, advantages arise from both the vantage point of the user of expert employees, and that of the knowledge-based expert. Our contention is that this constitutes one response in the labour market to the demands for unique compensation by expert knowledge employees.

A system of at-will contracts

In our proposed scenario, each expert individual who left the traditional firm would engage in a series of at-will contracts with several different users. This would allow the expert to renegotiate contracts frequently to include those freedoms that s/he requires. As discussed above, the risk to the user of granting these freedoms decreases because the contract can be terminated at any point in time. A system such as this requires, above all, a large supply of information. The expert employee needs to know the organizations which demand his/her skills. The users need to know where and how to contact these expert individuals and also in what capacity they might be available. In the best of worlds, this information would be perfect. An arrangement of this type would lead to a network which connects all available employees with all available positions, opportunities and their requirements. For example, if a knowledge-based individual showed a desire to work on a particular type of project, say a specific chemical process, and if s/he also demanded that the work schedule was such that s/he could work only Monday through Thursday, it would be a simple matter of seeing whether such a situation occurred. As for the employer of this person they need only find the person to fill this requirement.

In a more general sense, arrangements might occur spontaneously. As preferences, information and needs are passed from individual to individual, connections of work teams and co-ordination could be made that were not obvious in a traditional firm setting. Alchian and Demsetz speculate about such a market where 'teams of productive inputs, like business units, would evolve in apparent spontaneity in the market – without any central organizing agent, team manager, or boss' (p. 781). (They find this untenable because the monitoring of team members would be impossible, as boss's knowledge of who is shirking will be limited.) These spontaneous arrangements are intriguing, especially if there was a system which could provide everyone with the spontaneous and timely information necessary to produce the spontaneous markets, and which also could provide some form of monitoring.

In the current labour market, complications arise which make this perfect arrangement unlikely. An organization that needs specific skills may already have these in an employee who is idle. Such a person may not be as efficient as another who wishes to carry out the tasks called for. However, the firm is obliged to use its idle employee because of the long-term contract already negotiated. This tends to generate an inferior product and a less satisfied employee. The expert employee outside the organization who did not get hired is dissatisfied. Long-term contracts and search costs tend to be obstacles for the hiring of appropriate employees. In this situation we see the punctuated break failing. The main problem is that the labour market seems incapable of matching all the possible situations and their different compensation packages to the vast number of qualified expert individuals. It is very much a problem of information gathering and disseminating.

At-will contracts and agents

Where might we find a solution to this problem? Our first response lies within the computer and its capacities for information storing and retrieval. The development of networks, such as the Internet, provide the necessary framework for the information capacity and updating that a large-scale system of at-will contracts would demand. The capacities of computers to provide this have been well documented, but such systems have been relatively under-utilized by the labour market. With the advent of multi-media convergence (the combining of the telephone, television and data) the capacities of the different information media grow significantly. Recall that in the past technological revolutions the impact of one technology alone did not produce the radical change. For example, the agricultural revolution needed the harvesting tools and the irrigation capacities along with the changes in the labour market to bring about significant changes. The same can be said for the industrial revolution and its canals, trains, and engines. Such revolutions were driven by a series of innovations which, together, changed the social fabric of the labour market.

The computer revolution can be seen as a society-wide change. The personal computer industry is a $120 million industry and in 1994, 60 per cent of personal computers sold in the United States were sold into the home. This means that computerization is occurring as fast in the home as it is in the office. According to Gates (1995), 'the PC – its evolving hardware, business applications, on-line systems, Internet connections, electronic mail, multi media titles, authoring tools, and games – is the foundation for the next revolution' (p. xii). This combination, together with the growth of cable, can bring a plethora of information into the home and into the office and can send information between the two. Part of this information could be the availability of expert employees and the demands for them, and the combination of the two resulting in a multitude of at-will contracts.

But it is not just the total amount of information available that will characterize the information networks of the future, but the use of agents in analyzing this information to make it useful to the user. We suggest the agent who specializes in expert employment will be the key to the development of expert employment labour markets. A system where each expert employee, who has specific work preferences and unique skills, attempts to sell these to a vast number of firms will be inefficient. No one will have the time to wade through the mountains of information this would produce to find a suitable expert employee, nor will the expert employee be able to examine all the firms to find a suitable compensation package. Rather, we suggest, an agent with a subset of information will better market the expert individual's skills. And if the expert has skills that can be utilized by an array of industries, it becomes the agent's job to market these skills and to create markets for these skills. Perhaps the agent can produce combinations of employees and firms (or jobs) that neither side of the contract were aware of (akin to the Alchian and Demsetz spontaneous market discussed earlier). This is to the benefit of the expert employee and the firm.

Thus, the new firm (or agency) has as its main task the matching of expert employees' needs with their unique compensation packages to firms. Agents exist because they can filter and store information and make creative combinations that others, either firms or employees, find difficult. The fact that agents have access to a large group of experts allows a continuous supply of expertise to specific industries. The importance of an agency market for expert employees cannot be stressed enough. Look, for example, at the institutionalized agent of information, the university professor, who usually collects more in salary than his/her texts and articles (information) earn in sales.

The agent in the market place acts to streamline the decision-making process and provide information. With the advent of convergence, the availability of information concerning expert employees and their compensation needs will be great. However, it will be agents and their filtering and combining capacities which will make this type of labour market stable. It is the agent's ability to provide accurate information to both parties of an at-will contract that provides the stability and co-ordination, and it is the at-will contract that provides the monitoring device.

We suggest here that the traditional firm, with its co-ordination, monitoring functions and defence mechanisms, cannot provide a totally new environment because this will obliterate the original intentions of creating the traditional organization. We view responses by traditional organizations, such as techniques to engender greater commitment from employees, as attempts to stabilize the traditional firm/employee relationship. Because these contain so much of the traditional objectives to control and monitor, they may not provide the appropriate atmosphere and working conditions for knowledge-based expert employees to develop their market value. However, a system of information and matching made efficient by the employment agent will bring about a more stable expert employee labour market. It will be able to place skilled expert employees into production and knowledge-based sectors, while providing a suitable compensation package without diminishing the co-ordination of these employees (perhaps enhancing them) or diminishing the monitoring of these employees. Thus, the agency market, with its at-will contracts, is a good starting point for examining our hypothesized punctuated break from the traditional firm.

Our thesis concerning a punctuated break to an agency led labour market does not preclude traditional firms and/or their demand-sided gradual transformations. Traditional firms may well maintain themselves while providing a degree of discretion over working conditions for their employees (if not for other reasons, at least for the benefits of the economies of scales in production processes). We contend that this alone will not characterize the future labour market. Rather, the labour market will be a conglomerate of organizations which will also include the agency system providing levels of discretion that the traditional firms cannot, through a series of at-will contracts. However, we suggest that the changing circumstances of the supply-side opportunities for expert employees are a major source of change in both the firm and the labour market – a change pointing towards the at-will contract agency system.

CHAPTER FOUR

Expert agency employment as a facilitator of intellectual capital

In closing I should acknowledge that there are two kinds of knowing: knowing how, as in swimming and bicycling, and knowing that.

W. V. Quine, *Quiddities*

Agency employment, often thought to be atypical, can play an important role in the development of competitiveness for individuals, businesses and, indeed, nations. This is because of the strong links between experts, the transfer of knowledge and intellectual capital. During the twentieth century, capitalism built a strong foundation on physical and financial assets. Today, however, companies are in a process of retooling and developing new strategies which will assist them to be competitive at a time of unprecedented change in product and labour markets and technology. Recently micro-electronics created an Age of Information and, over the past ten years, there has been momentous advances in the science of bio-chemistry and genetics. Both bring the advent of another redefinition of our boundaries concerning knowledge.

In this chapter, we view knowledge as one of the integral parts to production and explore its consequences on the business and work environment with regard to the expert employee. We believe that in this evolving knowledge environment, individuals and companies will have one source of competitive advantage: intellectual capital. This represents an individual's accumulated knowledge and know-how, coupled with the ability to decant this into a system, predicated upon information technology, which will facilitate its speedy dissemination while protecting its quality.

The term 'intellectual capital', we believe, has its roots in a history of literature which views employees as assets in which to invest. Because of this, we have written this chapter in two parts. In the first part, we look at the history behind measuring and valuing human input: literature which uses terms like 'Human Asset Accounting' and 'Human Resource Management'. This work uses a demand-led approach and answers questions like 'How can the company alter its accounting practices to best benefit from the increasingly important value behind its human assets?' In the second part of this chapter, we flip this diagnosis of the increasing importance of intellectual capital by asking the question, 'How can the employee best benefit from the increasing importance of intellectual capital?' In the end, we suggest that agencies and agents are one way that expert employees can best exploit their own intellectual capital. For expert agency employment facilitates the use and development of one's intellectual capital. To start, we look at a few ways that intellectual capital can influence industry and society at large.

There are indications that intellectual capital will replace natural resources, commodities, finance, technology and production processes as the key strategic factor influencing competitive advantage. This is because, with the exception of intellectual capital, everything else is available to everyone on more or less the same terms.

Intellectual capital can create new industries and radically change traditional ones. According to Bill Gates, CEO Microsoft, 'within the next decade information highways will link most businesses to their customers and suppliers. Wallet and wristwatch PCs will be able electronically to transfer funds directly to shop cash registers, as well as store personal identification documents and even family photos' (*Financial Times*, 1 January 1995). Within the next decade this technology is poised to radically change the retail industry. Two knowledge-based concepts are currently competing for supremacy in the retail industry. One is home shopping and the other is the 'smart' department store. The former will allow people to shop from the comfort of their own homes with the aid of information on their television sets and remote-control handsets. In late 1994, Videotron, one of London's largest cable television operators, announced plans for an interactive shopping channel aimed at house buyers. The service was launched in March 1995 to nearly 300,000 cable TV subscribers across London and will offer 24–hour access to presentations on up to 700 properties on the market. In Canada, where the system has been running for about eight years, 57 per cent of Videotron subscribers use it as a first source of property information, 17 per cent use magazines and newspapers and only 12 per cent turn to traditional high street estate agents. Early in 1996, Virgin announced plans to launch an Internet-based shopping and entertainment service which will include live broadcasts, travel information and a virtual record store.

Among other innovations being developed to assist home shopping is the intelligent dustbin, which will be able to read bar codes on items thrown away and communicate this information to suppliers who will deliver replacement stocks whenever the dustbin senses that stocks are running down.

Competing with these home-based developments is new smart department store technology, which is designed to attract customers to stores where there will be no queues at check-outs and no congested aisles full of trolleys. Instead, customers will have hand-held devices, similar to those described by Bill Gates, which will allow them remotely to scan products. The device will not only give the price of the goods, but will relay other details such as the fat content, etc. It will also add up the total bill and can be programmed to provide other information which is specific to individuals: for example, information relevant to a particular diet. Once the shopper has chosen items, the device alerts the store's back office where goods are gathered and taken to the customer's car, or arranged to be delivered. Payment would be made remotely with the device debiting the customer's bank account or activating a debit card. These technologies, combinations of intellectual capital, are expected to fundamentally change the retail industry as we know it today.

These are just a few ways intellectual capital can influence an industry and, indeed, society at large. The examples emphasize the point that in the next decade competitive wars over know-how will intensify. Intellectual capital, the source of innovation and renewal, will be crucially important to future competitiveness. Despite the strategic importance of intellectual capital, accountants, analysts, markets and, indeed, managers, do not adequately value and measure its worth. At present, investment in fixed capital equipment is valued more highly than investment in human capital and networks. This means that intellectual capital leading to development opportunities is often overlooked and/or under-exploited.

Part 1 – Knowledge and business in an historical context

Conventional wisdom in management and economics has viewed the employee as one of the three factors of production: land, labour and capital. This paradigm views labour as an expense and sees its contribution to value-added as minimizing its cost. In traditional accounting, the implicit assumption is that those costs classified as expenditures are not expected to provide benefits beyond a defined accounting period. In the late 1960s, the notion arose that payments to employees should be viewed as an asset rather than an expense. In contrast to expenses, assets are that portion of a firm's costs that provide future investment, which are expected to render potential future service beyond the present accounting period.

The idea that labour costs are medium- to long-term investments provided the motivation for Human Asset Accounting, which was first developed in the late 1960s. This suggests that accounting practices which solely view workers as expenses result in a distorted measure of an organization's return on investment and could, therefore, lead to suboptimal decisions by management and investors. It is argued that, under traditional accounting practices, 'net income' is misconstrued because accountants treat all expenditures made to acquire or develop human assets as expenses during the period incurred, rather than capitalizing and amortizing them over their expected service life. Further, it is also argued that the balance sheet is incorrectly constructed since 'total assets' do not include an organization's human assets. One of the main motivations of Human Asset Accounting was to correct these perceived distortions by viewing employees as assets in which to invest and thereby adding to their inherent value.

During the late 1960s and 1970s, a range of research was conducted within the general field of Human Asset Accounting.[1] Basic models and measurement methods of the value of human assets were constructed and some empirical case studies undertaken. However, the development and widespread recognition of Human Asset Accounting was plagued by some fundamental criticisms: a substantial number of academics and practitioners alike questioned the underlying notion that labour costs were investments rather than one-off expenses. At this early period, the majority of research was undertaken in the United States by members of the Institute for Social Research at the University of Michigan. Much scepticism was voiced by people who believed that there were no significant accounting distortions associated with the classification of human resources as an expense and by the late 1970s the momentum to establish Human Asset Accounting appreciably slowed.

There are several reasons for this dampening of enthusiasm. People and knowledge were significantly less important to wealth creation in the 1960s and early 1970s when Human Asset Accounting was at its zenith. At this time, technology, particularly computerization, was relatively underdeveloped; jobs were predominantly in manufacturing and were relatively less skilled than service orientated jobs today, and businesses were reluctant to accept that there were problems with traditional accounting practices.[2]

However, by the mid 1980s, sweeping economic and structural changes created a business environment which challenged this view. As recession spread across developed economies, jobs were cut and training programmes reduced. Unemployment statistics soared in many Western industrial economies and productivity dropped in a wide range of sectors and across countries. As traditional values in the modern workplace began to be questioned, suggestions were made that conventional management accounting systems were becoming outdated and human resources as an investment once more gained ground.

This resurgence of interest in human assets was accentuated by an acceleration in the restructuring of economies away from manufacturing towards services dependent upon intangible assets, such as knowledge and quality of service. Accompanying this economic restructuring were the rapid development and widespread use of information systems. As more specialized skills were required from workers, the importance of training in the attainment of optimal productivity increased.

The changed conditions in the 1980s, largely attributed to a series of external global shocks which brought to the fore the importance of intangible assets, gave rise to renewed questioning of traditional accounting practices. This re-evaluation created the conditions for a focus on human resource management.[3] This did not see people simply as a factor of production which could be managed rationally and combined with other resources, such as capital equipment, to produce a more or less predictable set of outputs. Human resource management emphasized the unique characteristics of people and regarded managing people as analogous more to moderating the environment of a self-maintaining organism than to designing and controlling machines. It suggested that people are different, and raised questions of social dynamics and ethical principles which do not affect the management of other resources.

Human Asset Accounting can be viewed as the intellectual antecedents of human resource management. However, by the end of the 1980s, human resource management as an academic discipline lost ground. As a management practice, it failed; unable to deliver the promises it set out in the early 1980s (see e.g. Fernie and Metcalf (1995)). This failure concurred with a debate on new performance measurements which is steadily increasing in importance (for example, see Eccles (1991)). The difference between the current business environment and the earlier one, which gave rise to the debate on human asset accounting but failed to sustain it, is the significance of knowledge to wealth creation and the growth and impact of information technology.

Many of the questions raised by early researchers are relevant to the present business concerns. Researchers in the 1960s constructed some basic theoretical models for human asset accounting which continue to form a basis for present attempts at modelling the 'grammar' of human performance measurement.[4] Since the 1960s, the evaluation and measurement of human capital has been an issue of significant interest although this tended to subside in the 1970s and early 1980s. However, the appropriate place of these measurements in a company's accounts has always been a moot issue. Early researchers supported the complete synthesis of conventional financial accounts with less traditional measurement techniques for human assets. Researchers in the late 1980s and early 1990s advocated that traditional and modern measures of business performance should complement each other. The basic questions of interest have remained substantially unchanged since the early stages of Human Asset Accounting in the 1960s. However, changes in the international economic and technological environments have moved the debate about the status of human capital from the periphery towards centre stage.

The history of Human Asset Accounting follows three broad chronological stages: (i) the early development and motivation for analyzing people as assets – 1960 to 1976 (the ultimate goal, then, was the incorporation of human resources into companies' conventional balance sheets); (ii) a decline in the interest of human asset accounting – 1976 to early 1980s; and (iii) a period of revived interest in expanding conventional accounting techniques to incorporate intellectual capital – early 1980s to the present.

Early development of Human Asset Accounting 1960–1976

The development of human asset accounting was made possible by the economic theory of human capital, the (then) new human resource school, and organizational psychologists' focus on leadership effectiveness. At different times, and in different places specific types of resources have been associated with the growth and success of business. Acquiring and exploiting land has powered more than one period of economic expansion. The pioneer era of the United States and the British agricultural revolution in the eighteenth century are just two examples. Capital equipment arranged in highly standardized ways to allow mass production was perhaps a salient feature of industrial growth in Western countries during the first half of the twentieth century. By the 1960s, several writers had come to the view that people were an important resource which, managed better than their competitors, would confer on organizations the opportunity to outperform. This gave rise to a period of basic academic research in the 1960s which was aimed at developing and assessing the validity of models for the measurement of human resource cost and value. At this time, the potential use of Human Asset Accounting as a tool for managers and external users of corporate financial information was examined through a limited number of experimental applications in business organizations.

During this early period, academic research centred around the development of human resource value theory. This suggests that an individual possesses human value if s/he is capable of future economic utility, benefits or services. In principle, therefore, the value of people can be defined as the present worth of their expected future services. The basic theory consists of two primary models: one developed by Flamholtz (1969 and 1971) and another by Likert and Bowers (1973), which analyze respectively the determinants of individual and group values.[5]

1976–early 1980s

The late 1970s brought a decline in Human Asset Accounting research and its application to business organizations. Much of the earlier work was undertaken by a small group of researchers, mostly affiliated to the Institute for Social Research in the University of Michigan. Human Asset Accounting failed to become a generally accepted area of research and practice, and remained peripheral. Its decline can be attributed to a number of external factors. The economic environment during the 1960s and 1970s was such that businesses were not prepared to accept that there were problems with traditional accounting systems. Computerization was not as widespread and jobs were still less skilled than they are at present. Until fairly recently, there was a strong undercurrent in academic literature suggesting the classification of human resources as assets rather than expenses.[6] Further, the goal of including less traditional performance measures in conventional financial accounts may have been overly ambitious and infeasible. Two further factors may have contributed to the decline of Human Asset Accounting: (i) the need for more research to advance beyond the basic modelling stage; and (ii) the lack of organizations prepared to sponsor Human Asset Accounting applications, research and experiments. Despite the fact that human asset accounting systems have not been widely adopted by companies in the longer term, it seems reasonable to suggest that the value of companies' investment in people will be taken more seriously.

A major disincentive for companies to engage in training to develop their intellectual capital is the possibility that employees can leave and take valuable skills with them. If the chances are high that free-riders will poach newly trained employees, training becomes more costly to a firm so that it engages in less of it. Yet the fact that free-riding firms can poach expert individuals shows that a great deal of the expertise in industry is transferable and is not specific. It also underlines the fact that it is an investment in the individual that is being made. It seems reasonable to suggest that this disincentive might be significantly reduced through a system of transfer fees.

Such a system would turn poaching from being a vice into a positive virtue for an economy. Companies known for developing individuals could profit from this by making a profit on their experts which other firms are all too willing to buy from them. Companies might specialize in training according to their expertise in it and small companies lacking the economies of scale to engage in training can flourish by buying expert employees from efficient suppliers of them. Across the economy, the level of training would probably increase.

All this might be achieved by removing barriers and restrictions in the market. By making training and intellectual capital explicit, workers would see it more as an instrumental investment and fewer barriers to movement need be erected. Training could be seen as a true personal investment plan. A hostile reaction might be provoked by attempts to introduce transfer fees; a reaction which would at present conflict with the challenge of recruiting and retaining the best employees. There are, however, precedents: companies which sponsor managers to attend business schools typically require the fees advanced to be refunded if the manager leaves to join another firm. Attitudes change: if people come to regard training as investing in themselves and their intellectual capital, and if it becomes common practice for companies to buy employees from each other, then the prospect may become reality in the future.

Early 1980s to the present

Partly because of the debate about training and partly because of the growing awareness of the value of people and intellectual capital to competitive advantage, there has been a resurgence of interest in Human Asset Accounting and performance measurement over the 1980s. Some new research efforts have been instigated and there have been attempts by some major organizations to apply facets of Human Asset Accounting.

This has promoted some of the basic ideas of Human Asset Accounting which have become more widespread and thus have much stronger implications. This resurgence gained momentum from the seminal work of Johnson and Kaplan who, in 1987, argued that management accounting systems were inadequate for today's corporations, since they often date back to the creation of hierarchical organizational structures in the first part of the nineteenth century. According to Johnson and Kaplan, manufacturing processes have become more complex over the past 200 years, and the stagnation of management accounting leads to very aggregated and distorted accounts. The periodic financial statements prepared by most companies fail to provide accurate estimates of production costs, encourage myopic decision-making by managers, and provide little guidance in increasing productivity levels. As a tool for management decisions, Johnson and Kaplan (1987) encourage the return to non-financial indicators, which formed the original basis of management accounting systems.

Further, Johnson (1992) proposes the elimination of top-down accounting-based control, as it results in the manipulation of processes for financial ends. He argues that the present economic and technological environment, where global competition can be extremely fierce, requires bottom-up information which allows the employees to supervise their own processes.

In a similar vein, Eccles (1991) proposes that present management accounting systems are 'not only obsolete, but also harmful'. They encourage short-term thinking and 'are better at measuring the consequences of yesterday's decisions than today's performance'. According to Eccles, the change in competitive conditions requires a new corporate information structure, involving the definition of a new accounting grammar and vocabulary. He thus prescribes a new philosophy of performance measurement, where financial figures are not the only basis for decision-making by managers and external investors. Eccles proposes that financial figures should be supplemented by measures of customer satisfaction, quality, market share and human resources. Decisions should be based upon the broader set of measures, extending well beyond short-term financial reports and including intellectual capital.

Intellectual capital is not an easy concept for companies to grasp. According to Hubert Saint-Orge, a vice president of the Canadian Imperial Bank of Commerce (CIBC), 'organizations have been built and run to function in the relative stable and predictable environment provided by the industrial era. As a result the current speed of organizational renewal is too slow to cope with the velocity of change brought about in the market place by the knowledge era.' Saint-Orge believes that the credit industry needs new ways to assess risk:

> In the past, the most bankable asset was real estate, but with a 50 per cent devaluation of real estate all over the world, we have had to redefine what we mean by bankable value. Banks are already using cash flow lending and we are looking at knowledge-based lending to help the new companies of the information era, to help them thrive and make them good borrowers.
>
> (Saint-Orge, *Statement*)

The current debate on intellectual capital, like its predecessors, is predicated on measurement and contains definite traces of the debates on Human Asset Accounting of the 1960s and 1970s. The shift in emphasis is primarily due to the changes in economic and technological conditions over the past thirty years. The earlier researchers viewed the incorporation of human value measurements into conventional management accounts as their ultimate and ideal goal. Present researchers and practitioners, however, tend to suggest that human assets should be measured separately, but rigorously. Conventional financial accounts should continue to exist, but decisions should be based upon a wider set of pecuniary and non-pecuniary variables. This new approach will probably best be positioned to turn the new measurements of performance into a feasible goal. Key to these measurements will be the knowledge of the expert employees.

Part 2 – Agencies, experts and know-how

Tacit knowledge (Nonaka (1991)), which can be viewed as partly intuitive, is an important constituent of expertise. For example, an architect can have specific design capabilities in addition to technical knowledge, which distinguishes him/her from peers; Frank Lloyd Wright's flat concrete structures and William Rogers putting utilities on the outside of buildings are instances of this. Many knowledge-based occupations are influenced by such tacit knowledge: the diagnostic skills of a doctor, spatial awareness of a graphic designer, slogans of an advertising copywriter, and the talent-spotting activities of a casting director are some examples. Thus, tacit knowledge can add significant value and organizations often attempt to retain people with such abilities.

However, from the vantage point of an individual with tacit knowledge and abilities it might not be such an advantage to work for one organization. One reason for this is because organizations tend to pay such individuals the average marginal value they contribute, despite the fact that at different times this varies. Thus, some experts will be under-remunerated. Some organizations attempt to offset this by offering experts long-term contracts, but this is sometimes perceived to limit mobility and restrict freedoms. A further problem in this respect is that organizations are often obliged to conceal their information about their expert employees' market value, for fear that they might be poached by competitors.

It seems reasonable to assume that, at various times, different organizations will value an expert's tacit knowledge differently. This might be the result of specific projects or the marginal benefits a specific expert provides relative to his/her peers. Thus, given the losses that some experts could encounter from long-term employment contracts, they might reasonably view their optimum employment as a series of at-will contracts with a number of different organizations.

By contrast, explicit knowledge brings with it a set of more complicated circumstances. For experts, explicit knowledge is easily transferred to and from organizations. Once embedded in the firm's structure, explicit knowledge can be disseminated optimally. At first glance, from an expert's point of view, the value of having such knowledge might seem less important because they will have difficulties selling the knowledge again to the same organization. Once a firm has abstracted its knowledge requirement from an expert, reasonably it might cease paying for that expert's services. This presents a problem for experts if they rely on explicit knowledge as a means of professional worth. However, experts can reduce their risk of such occurrences by an association with an agency with a large external network (external to the firm they presently work with). This not only provides a network of organizations which might require such explicit knowledge, but it also provides experts with a number of potentially new work environments in which they might increase their own knowledge set, and thereby enhance their overall value.

Thus, agencies and their networks facilitate the flow of explicit knowledge between firms. This suggests that explicit knowledge as a source of value provides an incentive for expert employees to work through an agency or through a network of contacts. This network will arise partly because it is perceived by experts to provide them with benefits, such as enhanced opportunities to sell and increase their skills. Indeed, for the expert employee, networking and agency employment increases their amount of explicit knowledge (explicit to one firm) which, in turn, increases their own market value. Notice that it is nearly impossible for an organization, as traditionally defined, to provide such an inter-organizational network. Indeed, if the organization's value is partly defined by its intellectual capital, which is partially explicit knowledge, then it would be a disadvantage for that firm to provide a system that delivers this to competing organizations (see below). On a more basic level, the tacit knowledge of an employee which is learned in an organization can be thought of as financial investments in an employee's knowledge. This motivates firms to keep their employees, since there is the potential financial loss associated with search and training costs. This often proves to be an organizational defence mechanism which discourages an employee from selling his/her knowledge on the open labour market.

A simple example may help. Let us assume an architecture firm has developed a new software system which allows an architect to construct a computer model of an interior of a three-storey office building suitable for six tenant companies. Let us further assume that the unique advantage of this system is its ability to convey both to the architect and to the client the acoustics of the building before construction or final planning begins. Suppose the development of this system resulted from combining two existing software packages. This provides the architecture firm with a distinct advantage when producing plans and delivering presentations to its potential clients. The firm's architects are introduced to the system to ensure its efficient utilization. Other architecture firms lose business as potential clients move to the firm which has a more accurate acoustic representation of specific buildings.

For an architect within the firm which understands the technology and its use, remaining with the firm will only marginally increase his/her personal value. Others in the firm also have similar knowledge and therefore any one architect is of no particular extra value with regard to the application of this specific software. It is to the firm's advantage to retain any architect that wishes to leave, so that the explicit knowledge stays within the organization. Notwithstanding legal action arising over ownership claims, it might be to the monetary advantage of an expert employee to leave the firm and sell his/her knowledge to another firm. The rewards of this could be greater than, say, a rise in pay. Key in this scenario is our assumption that, along with the integrated software packages, it is necessary to provide know-how, in the form of an expert, to make the whole package work. To the extent that an expert does not perceive it to be in his/her best interest to remain in the firm for a long period, there becomes an incentive for the architect to move to another firm.

What stops the organization which originates an idea from selling its explicit knowledge to other firms? Nothing, except that an architecture firm is less likely than a specialist agent to have a network which is capable of such a transaction. The organization is in a dilemma: to retain or sell specific knowledge. Notwithstanding this, an expert employee associated with an agency and part of a broader labour market has a ready-made network. The importance of this example is that, because of labour market networks, the expert employee can capitalize on explicit knowledge as easily as, if not more easily than, an organization. This suggests that if labour market networks are constrained it is a disadvantage to the expert employee and an advantage to the traditional organization. Thus, we can expect the traditional organization to impede any type of inter-organizational employee network. Indeed, some organizations allow experts to become familiar with only one part of a total product system. This tends to keep experts tied to one organization and impedes the growth of inter-organizational networks.

However, a labour market designed around an expert employee agency will have refined its network to the point of greatest speed and knowledge. For any one particular firm to do so would be costly and prohibitive, unless it started to act as an employment agency (see below). Furthermore, the example we use brings to the fore the legality of experts selling or transferring their knowledge to other firms.

These are the basic financial advantages for the expert employee with his/her explicit and tacit knowledge in using an agency at-will contract system. However, on a different level the agency and at-will contract system may generally increase the value of expert employees by creating an environment which enhances the innovative process. Cohen and Leventhal (1990) claim that a diverse background and set of circumstances brings with it a more diverse set of knowledge. This raises the probability of linking innovation with an expert's personal knowledge and is therefore key to making novel associations and linkages. Thus, prior knowledge, which is viewed by Cohen and Leventhal as critical, gives the expert employee the unique ability to recognize which new information is valuable. With an increased system of information that the agency system provides, as well as a more varied and wide-ranging set of experiences, experts working through vast networks are more likely to innovate, thus increasing their own intellectual capital.

We have suggested that intellectual capital produces an incentive for the expert employee to use an agency or at-will contracts. We also suggest that traditional firms will impede such developments in labour market movements by holding on to their intellectual capital. The increased value of intellectual capital also implies the worth of networks which give a greater set and more varied range of information. These are applied to what the expert employee already knows to make novel associations and linkages. But this network, which increases market value and intellectual capital for the individual, is likely to include competitors of any one particular firm; thus we then have the same sort of tension between the firm and the expert employee, which could cause a break from the traditional firm rather than just a slow transformation. Indeed, it is unclear how this transformation could take place slowly and whether what results has any links to the traditional firm.

As another defence mechanism, the firm may configure its training investment in a way that contributes to the expert employee in a firm-specific way. This raises the possibility for the employee remaining with an organization in order to benefit from his/her specific knowledge. This, however, does not optimize the utility of intellectual capital and therefore can inhibit innovation, for firm specific investment is inherently linked to firm specified goals or individuals. For the expert employee, this does not provide the range of information or set of relationships that a fully fledged external-labour market network might.

The clogged brain-drain in Eastern Europe

The potential of agency work can not be over stressed. Its impact can be of significance both to Western labour markets and those of the world in general. Without agencies, the intellectual capital associated with experts can be clogged and under-utilized. A striking example is the intellectual capital locked-in in Eastern Europe. During the Cold War years, the flow of know-how was banned between East and West. This tended to deprive the world of the combined talents of Western and Eastern bloc scientists. One can imagine the extent to which space would have been explored with a collaborative effort of NASA and the Soviet Union's space agency.

Now, though, the barriers have come down and some of the intellectual capital is moving in both directions. But what should or could be a flood is a mere trickle. What can the Eastern bloc provide the Western world? According to John Kiser (1993), socialism and its shortages induced many Eastern bloc scientists to produce goods within their laboratories which cannot be readily bought from a catalogue – something which US scientists had no need to do. According to Kiser, this need led to specific and important techniques of synthetic chemistry, and enhanced the experience of Eastern bloc scientists relative to their US counterparts. They thereby represent valuable intellectual capital for many US organizations who experience shortages of specific experts. Derek O'Donell, a scientist from the Toxide Group in Cleveland, believes that these shortages are in the 'quality spectrum' (expert employees). It is the resourcefulness of the former Soviet scientists that is particularly valued in the West (resourceful because of the pressures to produce products that are in short supply for scientific research). Indeed, Eastern bloc scientists have been often obliged to use problem solving methods which their US counterparts did not have to face. It is not, however, the superiority of Eastern bloc scientists, but that within the Eastern bloc there is much intellectual capital that is valued in the West. Because the talents of these scientists are relatively more plentiful in the Eastern bloc, their value is not as great there. However, transferred to the United States, where there is a shortage of such expertise, its value would be heightened and the intellectual capital in the world significantly increased. What constitutes obstacles to flow from the East to the West?

There is some evidence that intellectual capital does, indeed, flow from East to West. Witness SUN Microsystems, which has contracted with selected research and development groups in Russia. Nordon, a division of United Technologies Corporation, has developed a microwave landing system using solutions developed in St Petersburg, where the most advanced operational landing systems exist. In the 1960s, the soft contact lens was developed by Otto Wichtele in the East, and its associated technologies have been used extensively by Bausch and Lomb in the West. Soviet surgical stapling devices are now used as state-of-the-art suturing methods in the United States. These are just a few examples; the list is impressive and the potential of the intellectual capital is even more staggering. However, transfers are inhibited by relatively rigid labour markets.

This is partly due to the lack of sophisticated agencies which can provide the information and networks that can combine the right expert employee with others to produce the intellectual capital. Moving finished products from organization to organization is a costly and patent-laden process. The movement of an expert employee can be produced much more efficiently if one imagines a system of international employment agencies with sophisticated methods of matching expert employees with the appropriate programmes. The problem for the Russian expert is the relative lack of agencies.

Kiser puts it succinctly:

> Corporations need to define clearly profiles of the kinds of people they are seeking. Working either through knowledgeable intermediaries or direct intervention in the countries of Eastern Europe, a system of recruiting can be readily set up. East European 'head hunting' is already an established market and desire to find employment in the West exists aplenty. The challenge is setting up effective and selective recruitment mechanisms. (1993)

Intellectual property law

All of these movements of intellectual capital have put increased pressure on lawyers and intellectual property law. Does the architecture firm that has developed an acoustically interactive virtual building own the rights to this knowledge? Is the simple use of two software packages patentable? Perhaps, but the ability to use such a system is not. Therefore, the expert employee, well versed in such a system, can still transfer this explicit knowledge across organizational boundaries. But discussions like this still cause significant problems in the employment of expert employees and their intellectual capital through agencies, and no two examples are necessarily the same.

Transferring explicit knowledge across organizational boundaries is more difficult when the person doing it is employed by one organization. It would be easier if the employee was working through agencies. However, agency work brings complications in intellectual property law in another way. Who is an employee? Due to the increase in agency employment and tele-working, there is a large amount of litigation concerning this question. Such atypical work causes problems in determining the status of individuals. Do teleworkers, for instance, work for an organization or are they sub-contracted by the organization? The importance of this question lies in the ownership issues which are associated with it. British intellectual property law suggests that an individual contracted to develop knowledge surrenders ownership of that knowledge unless otherwise stated. An individual who develops specific knowledge on company time, but outside the specific parameters of an employment contract, is usually owned jointly. Knowledge developed outside company time is usually owned by the developer of that knowledge.

In cases that are finally brought to court, judges attempt to understand exactly what the relationship is between the organization and the employee/subcontractor, agency employee or tele-worker. They assess agreements, income tax payments, incorporation status and job titles. In one case (*Harris* vs *Reiss Engineering*), a valve sales manager for an engineering firm developed an improvement on some of the valves that the engineering firm sold. The employee patented this improvement under his name and the company sued him claiming rights to the improved valve. But the court held that the manager's job description did not include invention and there was no 'special obligation' to the company, so his patent held. The point is, even under circumstances where there is an employment contract it is sometimes difficult for firms to retain intellectual capital. Imagine doing so when the employment contract is ill-defined and the developer of the knowledge is a citizen of another country thousands of miles away, with different language, legal and cultural structures. Notwithstanding this, the organization has an incentive to control and constrain expert employees in order to secure the intellectual capital they develop. This tends to restrict employee's personal growth and value and motivates experts to break away from traditional organizations.

Further, because of the relatively quick way in which a knowledge-based product is transferred and its relative timeliness (it perhaps has a short shelf or market life), the costs can be prohibitive to track it down and capture any escaped intellectual capital in a timely manner. Imagine a consortium of experts in three different time zones, working around the world on a specific project. Although geographically dispersed, they are able to work closely together since modern telecommunications technology allows information to flow quickly between computers. The software is packaged and marketed to businesses within, say, the United States. If, in India, one of the programmers decides to sell the software to Indian companies, it may take several months or years before the consortium discover this, by which time the product might have been preceded by a successor on the market. However, even if the illegal sale is discovered quickly, the national differences in legal, language and cultural structures could significantly impede the prosecution of the case.

This section is not comprehensive, but raises the point that laws surrounding intellectual property are complicated and often fuzzy, and that distributing work away from an organization and giving more discretion to expert employees causes problems for a structured organization in maintaining the intellectual capital within its confines. In the event, one response is for organizations to tighten up their controls and monitoring techniques for expert employees. To the extent that this is feasible, it is costly and potentially counter-productive, since such actions tend to alienate experts and motivate them to leave the organization.

CHAPTER FIVE

The temporal advantages of agency work for the expert employee

It is because I want to make economics more human that I want to make it more time conscious . . .

Sir J. R. Hicks, *Some Questions of Time in Economics*

We have suggested that an agency at-will contract system will develop for purveyors of specific expertise. This is because: (i) opportunities for expert employees have changed (chapter 1); (ii) organizations develop defence mechanisms which resist change and make them less attractive to specific expert individuals (chapter 2); (iii) some organizational functions such as control and monitoring are less relevant to knowledge-based employees (chapter 3); and (iv) intellectual capital is enhanced with an increase in networks associated with agency at-will contract systems (chapter 4). Together these conspire to encourage the expert employee to move away from traditional organizations towards agencies and systems of at-will contracts. It is from an economic theoretical approach that we add a fifth factor that encourages the punctuated break. This is that the temporal advantages of agency at-will contracts will result in an increase in utility for the expert employee and a qualitative improvement in the expert employee's product.

Temporal control is often reported in the economics of compensation packages as an element that would have little significance to employee/employer relationships. We take a different view and consider this aspect of work critical in the formation of new labour market arrangements. Interpreting temporal control as a marginal benefit for expert employees can, we suggest, lead to an inappropriate analysis of temporal control and the expert employee. We suggest that temporal control is an important aspect of knowledge-based work and make it central in our analysis.

In this chapter, we change gear and analyze a time-sensitive economic model developed by Winston (1982).[1] This describes rhythmical fluctuations within time and their effects on markets. Much of the time-sensitive theory briefly described below is derived from Winston's model. Our application of the model to our discussion of expert employees and punctuated changes in the labour market is new. The model is helpful for our thesis, since it facilitates a formal and more robust consideration of the impact of discretion over working time. (Of course, this is not the only element of the expert employee compensation package. There are others, such as discretion over work content as well.) Further, the Winston model suggests a break by the expert employee to a new type of labour market organization – the agency.

A time-sensitive economic model

The basic premise of the Winstonian model is that activities performed by an individual are dependent upon the time they are performed (here it is important to note that time is used in the sense of calendar time). A simple example of Winstonian time-sensitive consumption is that of sleep. Sleep is best performed when it is dark, i.e. when it is night time. So the production (consumption) of sleep is dependent on the time of day that a person (the consumer) sleeps. Sleep during the day may not be as useful or pleasant as sleep during the night. This characteristic is introduced by making the utility function time-sensitive. There is a constant flow over time of the potential utility from sleeping. Sleep during the day will give less utility than sleep during the night. This flow of utility within time can be shown also for activities other than sleep. Thus, an individual can choose between activities over time. For example, an individual lies out on the beach during the day (when doing so has a high utility flow) and sleeps during the night (when doing so also has a high utility flow).[2]

Figure 5.1 is helpful in understanding the Winston model. There are two flows of utility: utility from leisure, U_1 [home(time, income)], and utility from work, U_w [work (wage)]. These utilities flow over the time unit T where the changing environment over T, day to night for example, 'calls for an optimal temporal allocation of goods' (Winston (1982), p. 167). Since the wage over time is constant, then the utility derived from work is the straight line U_w. Utility from leisure, being time-specific, undulates and is represented by the curve U_1. If we

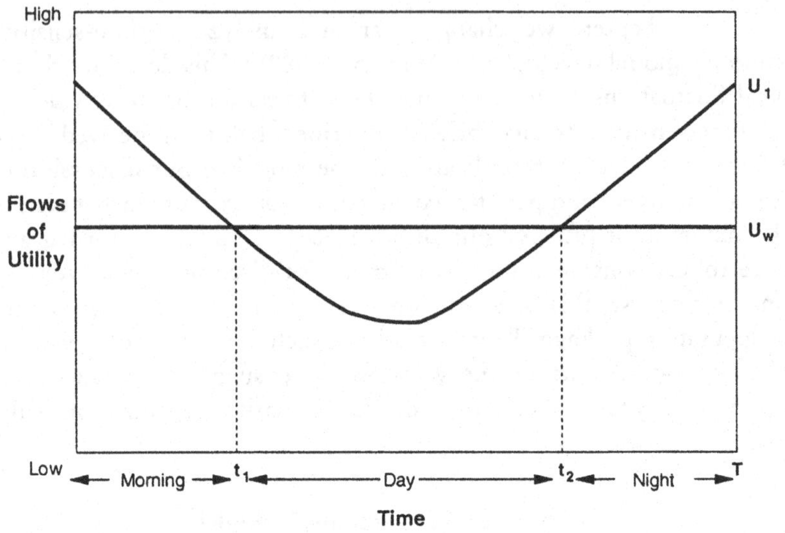

Figure 5.1 A Winstonian time-sensitive model diagram. This diagram reflects the preferences of a hypothesized individual who works during the day and performs non-work activities during the morning or night. It shows that during some hours of a 24-hour day, there are times when the indirect utility derived from work (U_w) is greater than the utility derived from non-work activities (U_1). There are also times when the utility derived from non-work activities is greater than the indirect utility from work.

assume T = one day, and leisure activities for this agent are better performed in the evening, as is shown, then this agent will work from hour t_1 to hour t_2 and perform non-work activities in the evening (t_1 and t_2 are the optimal switching times). Work is performed only when it derives (indirectly) a utility flow that is greater than that of the other non-work activities.

Figure 5.1 reflects the preferences of a hypothesized individual who works during the day and performs non-work activities during the morning or night. It shows that during some hours of a 24-hour day there are times when the indirect utility derived from work (U_w) is greater than the utility derived from non-work activities (U_1). There are also times when the utility derived from non-work activities is greater than the indirect utility from work.

The subtle difference of this model is its superior time-sensitivity. It treats time more appropriately for our discussion in that it does not treat it as a commodity, but allows analysis over time. It also does not hold time completely static, with equilibriums only for one specific unit of time, but allows analysis within a unit of time. This enables us to study the consequences for labour markets of the expert employee's demand for discretion over when to work. The model has the ability to expose the time-sensitivity of preferences *in time*, and therefore the time-sensitivity of different job forms in labour markets.[3]

The model is more formally described below and in more detail in appendix B. The mathematics are helpful to gain an understanding but not critical to understanding the concepts of this chapter and can be skipped by readers unfamiliar with such mathematical concepts.

For our example accumulated household utility is:

$$\mathrm{U} = \int_{t_o}^{t_i} u_1\Big(z_1\big(x_1(t);t\big)\Big)\,\delta t + \int_{t_1}^{t_h} u_2\Big(z_2\big(x_2(t);t\big)\Big)\,\delta t \qquad [1]$$

where flows of utility from activity 1, u_1, is a function of the intensity of the activity z_1 (which is function of timing) and the amount of goods used x_1. The same holds for activity 2.

This utility is maximized subject to the time constraint,[4]

$$\int_{t_0}^{t_1} \overline{p_1}x_1(t)\delta t + \int_{t_1}^{t_h} \overline{p_2}x_2(t)\delta t = \int_{t_h}^{t_T} \bar{w}\delta t + Y_p \qquad [2]$$

Where the price, p_i, is exogenous and goods, x_i, are time-sensitive. They are constrained by the resources, w, flow of wages and Y_p wealth.

From maximization and the resulting first order equations, Winston produces the optimal switching moment, t^*, between two activities (in our example sleep and awake). In each activity, time will have the same value,[5]

$$\mu_1(t_1^*) = \mu_2(t_1^*) \qquad [3]$$

Of course, other individual choices are more pertinent to our discussion. One can imagine a continuum of choices being made by individuals over a large set of possibilities. One possible choice is the decision to go to work or not. In Winston's (1982) model it is assumed that the utility derived from work is zero. The only positive utility derived from work is from the income produced, which can then be transformed into goods used while not at work – in leisure or home production, this is akin to Becker's (1965) home production model. An individual's decision to go to work, then, is time dependent, because s/he compares going to work with other non-work activities over time (for example, see Groneau (1986)). Since the perceived non-work utility derived from non-work activities is assumed to be time dependent, then the choice of when to go to work (t^*) is time dependent. Ultimately, work will occur only at those moments, over the unit time of analysis, that other activities have low utility flows.

The consequences of time-sensitivity – a punctuated break

Using a Winstonian framework, it is possible to compare the different employment solutions of two different groups of potential employees; those who do not value control over their working-time (time-insensitive) and those who do (time-sensitive) – our expert employees. When these two groups are faced with two different organizations their preferences, based on their changing opportunities, will drive them to one type.

The first group is distinguished by time-insensitive preferences, the second by time-sensitive preferences (expert employees). These two different types of workers, when maximizing their utility functions, compare the utility derived from non-work activities with the indirect utility derived from income generated by work. This is done in the manner described in the section above. It is first assumed that this occurs in a market place where the job form has a rigid set of time constraints that must be adhered to. Later this will be relaxed.

In general, because the first group of workers have preferences which are not time-sensitive, *when* they work has little bearing on their final utility. If the job form implies rigid work schedules, the effect on their final utility will be minimal. However, for a group of workers whose preferences are time-sensitive, the constraint of rigid work schedules will effect their final utility drastically. This difference between the two groups is shown in figure 5.2 below.

Figure 5.2 shows that under a time constraining job form, the demand for labour is absolute and set by the firm. In this case, the firm allows time off or does not need workers at week three. During week six, though, the time-sensitive employee (U_s) has a great demand for time off, since the utility of non-work activities is shown to be much greater than the indirect utility from work. However, they must work. The time-insensitive worker (U_i) exhibits an increase in utility at week three since it does not matter when the non-work activity is done for this type of worker.

The unit time of analysis T is assumed here to be two months, shown as eight weeks along the X axis. A representative of the first

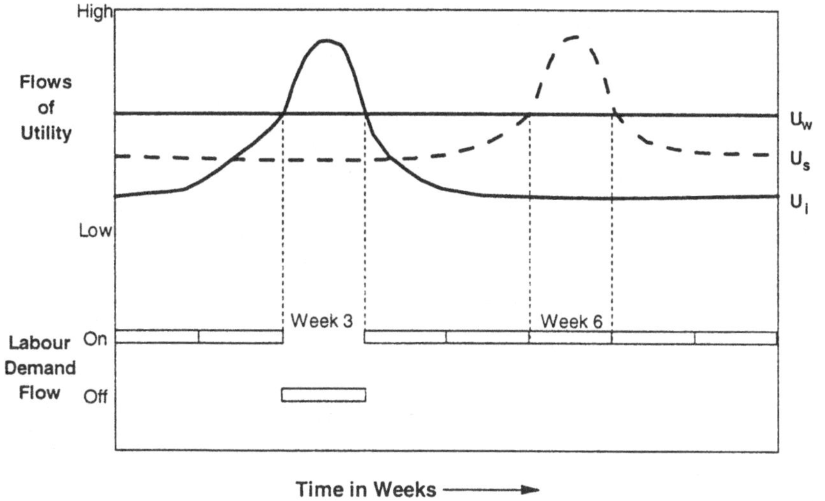

Figure 5.2 The expert employee in a time-constraining organization. The figure shows that under a time-constraining job form the demand for labour is absolute and set by the firm. In this case the firm allows time off or does not need workers at week three. During week 6, though, the time-sensitive employee (U_s) has a great demand for time off since the utility of non-work activities is shown to be much greater than the indirect utility from work. However, they must work. The time-insensitive worker (U_i) exhibits an increase in utility at week three since it does not matter when the non-work activity is done for this type of worker.

group of workers with time-insensitive preferences is shown by the flow of non-work utility as described by curve U_i. A representative of the second group of workers with time-sensitive preferences is shown by the flow of non-work utility as described by curve U_s. The indirect utility from work is given by U_w and is assumed to be identical for both individuals. The demand for labour is given by the dichotomous function D_1 where the demand for labour is either 'on' or 'off'. This is used to simplify the analysis and the diagram.

The time-sensitive worker exhibits an increase in utility from non-work activities in week six, otherwise at any other time the worker prefers to work, since the indirect utility derived from the wages earned is above the utility from non-work activities during all weeks except week six. There is no possibility of substitution. The employee's preferences for non-work activities (therefore work as well) are time-sensitive.

Formally this preference for control over working-time is felt through the *zi(xi(t);t))* term (speed of output) of equation 1. This term denotes the efficiency of production, and Winston suggests that this is time-sensitive, since the production environment (Winston uses *E*(*t*) to denote this) changes throughout the day (therefore the 'speed of output' will change). (Winston relies heavily on cyclical variations like day to night altering the production environment to change the relative efficiency of production.) So that we can rewrite z_i as:

$$z_i(t) = f_i(x_i(t), 1_i)E_i(t) = z_i(x_i(t), 1_i; t), \qquad [4]$$

Where z_i is a function partially explained by the production environment *E*(*t*).

In our application, we redefine the $z_i(x_i(t);t))$ term by redefining the effects of the production environment, *E*(*t*). Winston's production environment changes constantly via exogenous environmental rhythms, like the daily train schedule or the yearly weather conditions, etc. (Winston (1982), p. 159). We accept this influence over the efficiency of production but find it too narrow. Therefore, we include in our production environment *E*(*t*), personal preference aspects that individually determine the efficiency of production or the utility of work – elements like an individual's parents visiting, or an invitation to play tennis, or a preference to sleep late. Individuals who find the timing of their activities central to their utility (the expert employee) will have unique production environments, as represented in figure 5.2 by the U_s curve. A restrictive scheduling will decrease an individual's production efficiency (speed of production in non-work activities) and therefore decrease total levels of utility.

However, the production environment, *E*(*t*), of the time-insensitive worker is not a function of his/her own preferences, since the timing of activities is not a consideration. An individual's utility curve, U_i, shows a drastic increase in the utility derived from non-work activities during week three. This occurs just at the moment when the labour demand schedule D_1 is such that s/he is not needed (or not allowed to work). This is not by chance. It is because the individual's utility from non-work activities is time-insensitive that the utility from non-work activities will rise at exactly this point within the unit of time. It does not matter when the non-work activity is performed. It is merely performed when there is no work, as determined by the job form. So this increase is not showing the pattern of preferences of the employee, as much as it is showing the timing of non-work activities. The utility derived from non-work activities is independent of when it occurs. The time-insensitive preferences of this individual allows utility maximization while employed under this time constraining job form.

Because the time-sensitive worker must work during the week in which the flow of utility from non-work activity is greater than the flow of indirect utility from work, week six, there is a loss of utility (the difference in utility derived from non-work activity and the indirect utility derived from work). Furthermore, because the time-sensitive individual will not be able to work during the time when the utility flow from non-work activity is low, there is another loss of utility. It is the combination of an individual's time-sensitive preferences and the restrictions of this job form (rigid work schedules) that cause the decrease in overall utility.

In another job form, though, wherein an individual has control over working-time, the circumstance will change considerably. With control over working-time, the time-sensitive worker will be able to maximize the flow of utility from both work and non-work activity. This is shown in figure 5.3.

Figure 5.3 shows that, under an accommodating job form, the employee turns the demand for labour on and off. It is the employee who has control over working-time. If the employee is time-sensitive, as is shown here (U_s), then there will be a gain in utility from an accommodating job form.

In figure 5.3, the job form allows the workers to work when they prefer. Here it is clear that the time-sensitive individual will choose not to work during this week, since it is during week six that the non-work utility flow is greater than the indirect utility flow from work.[6] The decision to work is unconstrained. The employee turns the labour demand schedule on or off. This, of course, maximizes utility.[7] At the precise moment in time (t^*) that the time-sensitive individual requires 'time-off', this job form allows it. The utility that is lost in the time-constraining job form shown in figure 5.2 is recaptured by virtue of the control over working-time that is allowed in this job form. Faced with the two different organizations, the time-sensitive worker, in maximizing utility, would tend toward the job form that allows control over working time, since control produces a level of utility greater than the job form that is time constraining. This is the individual making the punctuated break.[8]

Adam Smith's (1976) 'equalising differences hypothesis', or theory of net advantages, suggests that the rewards of different jobs should

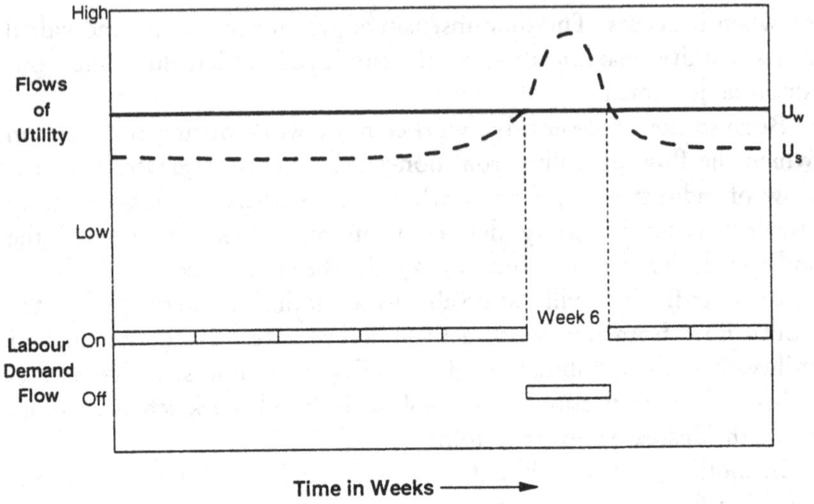

Figure 5.3 An expert employee in an accommodating organization. The figure shows that under an accommodating job form the employee turns the demand for labour on and off. It is the employee who has control over working time. If the employee is time-sensitive, as is shown here (U_s) then there will be a gain in utility from an accommodating job form.

tend towards equality – rewards in the sense of all the advantages of a job. In our discussion, it appears that for some individuals, those that prefer control over working-time, the calculations of net advantages of temporary work should include control over working time (at the expense of income), thus their selection of this organization.

For the time-insensitive individual, though, the choice may appear easier. Either job form will maximize utility. However, since there is no gain from choosing the job form that allows control over working-time, other characteristics of the two job forms may be considered, (these were implicitly held constant in the preceding analysis but are now relaxed). These may include promotional possibilities, job security, working peers and others. If the time constraining job form exhibits any more positive attributes, it will be selected (this may be the case as well for the time-sensitive worker, since only if the gain from control over working-time outweighs the benefits that the other job form has to offer, will the time-sensitive worker choose the job form which offers control).

Temporal control and performance

The preference for temporal control may play an important role in the compensation package (or set of working conditions) of the expert employee in their level of work effort or in the quality of their final product. This is because of the potential time sensitivity of knowledge-based employee work. If it turns out that groups of individuals within a firm have preferences for control over working-time that differ, their resulting working conditions may be attributable to these different preferences. Thus, if control is relatively unimportant to individuals, then the lack (or benefit) of control will have little influence over their final utility and therefore have little influence in the compensation package. However, if temporal control is valued highly, this may over-shadow pecuniary considerations of compensation and further discretion over working-time may engender greater effort. Let us illustrate this point with a simple example using the time-sensitive analysis.

Again the labour supply is distinguished by two different groups of individuals. The first has time-insensitive preferences and the second has more inconsistent time-sensitive preferences for activities. It is assumed here that the firm has a set standard pattern of demand for labour services over time. What are the consequences of this? In the traditional internal labour market the wage has been contracted in a prior arrangement for an extended period of time. This contracted wage then holds for the analysis over the entire length of the time unit. For those with time-insensitive preferences, the consequences are nil, since their expected patterns in non-work activity utility will be consistent with the firm's demand schedule. However, for individuals where non-work activities have time-varying non-work utility flows, discrepancies may occur.

If at a given moment within the time unit the non-work activity yields utility greater than the indirect utility gained by working, the individual is obliged by the long-term contract to work. This is because of the rigidity of traditional long-term contracts and the standardized patterns of work established by many organizations. The consequences are that an individual is being paid, for the length of time that his/her non-work utility is greater than the indirect utility from work, below what is necessary for the individual to work. This may yield inconsistent performance. It may also yield a decrease in effort. Clark (1992) among others has suggested 'that the perceived relative value of the reward will effect the level of effort'.[9] It is proposed here that the perceived relative value of the reward is time-sensitive. Thus, when non-work activities are valued highly, the relative perceived value of the wage decreases. Shirking could be a consequence, therefore a decrease in work effort may occur. This is exactly what organizations are designed to reduce.

This example can be shown diagramatically using the Winstonian model (figure 5.4). Consider the straight line U_i. This represents the flat utility curve of non-work activities for individual i. It is flat because individual i has time-insensitive preferences. The utility derived from non-work activities over time is the same for individual i.

Now consider the undulating line U_1. This represents the utility curve of non-work activities for individual 2. It undulates because individual 2 has time sensitive preferences. The utility derived from non-work activities depends upon the time they are performed.

The flat utility line U_w represents the utility derived from earning the wage, w, and for this example is considered static. This represents the total utility from work. If utility from non-work activities is greater than the utility from working and receiving wage w, then an individual can increase utility by not working.

If an individual is employed by an organization that adheres to a strict schedule, there will be moments when a time-sensitive individual is being paid a wage which provides less utility than if that individual were not working at all. In our example, individuals is under such circumstances and would be receiving less utility working from t_1-t_2 and t_3-t_4 than if s/he did not work at all. With the perceived rewards relatively less than usual, it is implied that the employee will decrease effort, resulting in a decrease in production. These circumstances present themselves in the real world when a time-sensitive individual accepts a job in a traditional organization with restrictive scheduling policies.

Of course, the selection of the unit of time in this analysis becomes very important. The selection here may be described as the ability to choose which weeks out of the year are worked. If one picked a smaller unit of time, say one day, the flexibility of working hours during the day would then be analyzed. The discussion would take place considering such questions as: if someone did not like to work on Wednesday mornings, or preferred longer lunch breaks. Still the consequences are the same. There may be a decrease in effort or a

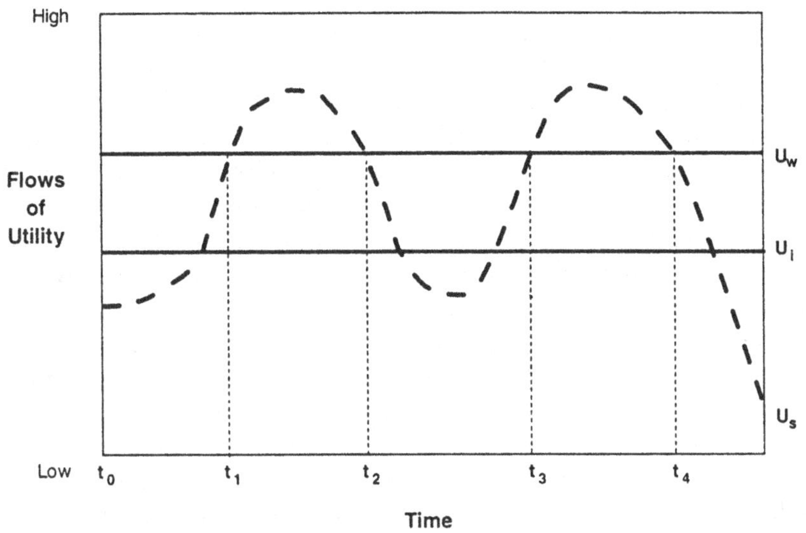

Figure 5.4 Time-sensitive worker in a time-constraining traditional firm. The figure shows that a time-sensitive worker's non-work utility fluctuates over time (U_s). There are some moments, from t_1-t_2 and t_3-t_4 that the non-work utility is greater than the indirect utility derived from work (U_w). However, in the firm the worker must still go to work because of the time-constrained work environment. This results in an overall loss of utility. The time-insensitive worker (U_i) does not suffer the same consequences, since as long as the employment structure wants them to work they are willing. It is only when the employment structure allows time off that the utility from non-work activities will rise for this time-insensitive worker. (This is not shown in the diagram.)

decrease in production. These time elements may be 'both physically determined and socially constructed' (Hassard (1989b), p. 80).

Figure 5.4 shows that a time-sensitive worker's non-work utility fluctuates over time (U_s). There are some moments, from t_1-t_2 and t_3-t_4, that the non-work utility is greater than the indirect utility derived from work (U_w). However, in the firm the worker must still go to work because of the time-constrained work environment. This results in an overall loss of utility. The time-insensitive worker (U_i) does not suffer the same consequences, since as long as the employment structure wants her/him to work, s/he is willing. It is only when the employment structure allows time off that the utility from non-work activities will rise for this time-insensitive worker. (This is not shown in the diagram.)

If a firm includes some control over working time in the compensation package, this could act like an increase in compensation to an employee who valued increased discretion and might motivate that individual to work harder. It facilitates this by allowing that individual to work when the utility from work (the utility from the wage) is greater than the utility of performing other activities. Overall work effort and efficiency increases for that individual. Such packages allow individuals to work when their opportunity costs are relatively low, or when it is easiest for them.

Not only will time flexibility act as compensation, but it could also enhance an expert's level of intellectual capital. This is simple, because it allows an individual to organize his/her time which could lead to that individual pursuing other self-enhancing activities when those activities are of most interest. This updates and/or increases that individual's know-how. Such pursuits increase the information flow and information variety which, as Cohen and Leventhal (1990) suggest, facilitates the innovative process and increases intellectual capital.

Some firms are implementing compensation packages which provide more flexibility to employees. Providing such benefits to individuals who really value this is a relatively efficient way of improving performance (see Orpen (1981), who suggests that flexitime has 'no adverse effects on production' – p. 115). Notwithstanding this, it appears that traditional organizations do not encourage a significant amount of working-time flexibility. In the long run this will render employer/employee relationships unstable.

This suggests that the driving force of creating flexible work patterns may not solely be competition for labour services. The competition argument suggests a battle for labour services being waged by offering different compensation packages – those which include flexibility and those which do not (the implication is that those which offer flexibility will be more attractive). Hill (1984) suggests that, with specialization and production process indivisibility, working hour flexibility is disallowed even if the pressures of competition for labour forces increase. Here, we take a different stance and suggest that: (i) working-time flexibility is only attractive to those who value it; and (ii) that working-time flexibility may not be detrimental to the production of knowledge-based products, but that flexibility may actually enhance employee performance. So, if Hill's suggestion is correct that traditional firms will not allow flexibility, in order to obtain flexible scheduling a break by time-sensitive experts from organizations will occur. Furthermore, the result of such breaks will improve employee performance.

Increased performance is also linked to the potentially time-sensitive knowledge-based product. Because many ideas and innovations produced by knowledge-based expert employees have a time-frame of opportunity (i.e. their timing is important), the flexibility of work scheduling may improve the expert employee's ability to time the knowledge-based product to the market place. If there is a moment in time when an innovation is particularly valuable, the expert employee realizes the greater potential market value and increases the speed of production (i.e. the delivery systems rather than the innovation). With time, inflexibility production takes place at regular hours, with time flexibility a greater number of hours can be worked, when production has greater value, and this is balanced by fewer hours, when production has less value. For example, the delivery of information on sugar beet yields during flooding will be most valuable when a hurricane approaches those areas that produce sugar beet. This knowledge-based product loses its value once the hurricane has passed and the market price has already found its equilibrium. In this instance, it is essential for the expert in sugar beet production pricing to increase hours of work to sell or supply the appropriate information prior to the hurricane. A time-restricted employee will clock in at nine and leave at five, no matter what the conditions. A flexible employee will be more likely to work through the night and deliver the information at whatever hour it is completed. Furthermore, such an expert employee with the know-how could work from anywhere in the world and send the information instantaneously, regardless of the time differences between countries. There is a distinct advantage in this case to the expert employee with discretion over his or her working time.

We also suggest that working-time flexibility may occur in various time units which includes flexibility of hours of the day, or days of the week, or weeks of the year. Each may yield significantly different results. This is why we prefer the phrase 'working-time control'. It allows for a greater range of time units than does the general term 'flexibility'. Again, a model constructed to explore work as an activity that takes place *within time* may be more suitable in exploring the consequences of working-time control for the expert employee, rather than a model that commodifies time. And a model that starts from the perspective of the expert individual, as opposed to the firm, may raise issues that have been previously neglected. Such issues as: can a firm exist and provide complete working time and job control? Does this imply a frequently renegotiated contract as we suggest? If so, what are the consequences of this to our definition of the employer and employee relationship?

As firms wrestle and negotiate with the demands of their expert employees, some differences in compensation packages may be currently observable within a firm. If there is a group of individuals who prefer working-time control, then they are more likely to exhibit working-time control in their compensation package, because of the increase in performance and the fear of losing these employees. The significance of this control to an individual's utility has already been suggested. If, as we suggest, the experts will increasingly demand discretion over their lives, it may be advantageous to both firms and individuals to organize increasingly diverse sets of compensation packages which include discretion over working-time control.

Conclusion

Along with the potential for increased productivity from temporal flexibility, the total enrichment of an individual may occur which, in turn, could have beneficial consequences on productivity and innovation. Whereas in the past a company leisure programme might have produced a well-rested and fit employee (hints of some kind of maximization problem), a more temporally liberal leisure programme may have proved useful to the expert employee's creativity. Freedom to schedule will allow an individual to create networks that were previously unavailable in the formal temporal structure of the traditional organization. This alone could increase intellectual capital and thus give a broader range of inputs into the tacit knowledge of the employee.

Thus, in a traditional economic analysis, the Winstonian model formalizes the influences of maximising behaviour in a labour market *within time*. We suggest that the consequences of this are the selection of one organization over another by an individual expert who exhibits varying time-preferences. In previous chapters, we have suggested some defence mechanisms and the problems traditional firms have in accommodating the expert employee. We use this here to emphasize the inherent difficulties firms have in providing the temporal freedom some individual experts demand.

Given the intensification of competition for experts and difficulties experienced by traditional firms to cope adequately with such individuals, it seems reasonable to assume that individual experts will increasingly reconcile their demands for work leisure and temporal control, by the use of agencies. An agency's use of at-will contracts provides some experts with the desired temporal freedom. This is one example of the punctuated break. The discretion over working time not only increases utility to the expert employee, but also can act to increase quality and value of the knowledge-based product.

CHAPTER SIX

Taking stock

Before progressing further, let us take stock. Expert individuals form the basis of our theories about new organizations and how they will develop. Experts are the catalysts, elements and structure of specific new organizations. Their opportunities, choices and lifestyles are particular. The power that they wield in both the labour and product markets suggest that they will impact on others as well. Organizational theory has tended to emphasize the importance of demand side influences on organizations. This has generally led to an under-appreciation of the influences of individuals on organizations and change. In contrast, our theory emphasizes individual preferences, networks and agencies which constitute the essence of the emerging structure for organizations.

Our examination of experts suggests that market and technological conditions encourage them to abruptly break with traditional organizations and seek employment by serial at-will contracts which are frequently mediated by agencies. In specific areas this has led to increasingly important agency labour markets. Such breaks and such markets do not prevent organizations from forming internal systems that also strive to accommodate experts. However, these tend to be defence mechanisms which resist change by certain forms of accommodation. Organizations in need of experts to maintain and increase their competitive advantage will, at some stage, be obliged to embrace the external agencies' labour market. The greater an organization's need to do this, the greater the threat to its traditional boundary conditions. In the future it might become difficult for knowledge-intense companies to recruit, retain and develop specific experts within a traditional organizational setting. If our theories prove to be correct, traditional organizations will be increasingly obliged to hire experts by way of a number of specific at-will contracts mediated by a number of agents. Thus, experts might be only tenuously linked to companies.

Let us now put our discussion in context by discussing some basic economic and social science concepts. This will provide an historical context to our discussion and show that our theorising is drawn from principles that have been fruitful in discussing labour markets and employee and employer relationships of the past. It will also highlight how we have added to the discussion by evaluating new developments in labour and technologies.

The expert employee and the economics of the individual

In Adam Smith's *Wealth of Nations* we have one of the first foundations for the systematic analysis of the economy and its workings, including its organizational structures. In all the sections of this seminal work, the preferences and attitudes of the people involved in these systems are thoroughly considered by Smith. This is often lost because people forget that *Wealth of Nations* is only one volume in a series which Smith regarded as a complete work (*Moral Sentiments* is another volume that looks closely at the activities of man and his willingness or unwillingness 'to do good'). Indeed, each of the areas is linked by common precepts, particularly with the psychology of man, and the way activities performed by humans control and may even help create particular social institutions. This is the crux of our argument: that expert employees, their opportunities and their choices will alter and create institutions.

Chief among Smith's contributions which are based on the psychology of man is his development of the importance of self-interest. His work can be said to have 'lent a certain sanctity' to the self-interested pursuit of gain. He showed that the self-interested pursuit was capable of elevating society as a whole. This annoyed many of his critics who believe Smith provided an intellectual legitimation for the ruthless pretensions of the mercantile and manufacturing institutions. And like Smith's self-interested man who provides, 'the invisible hand', the expert employee can be said to help create certain social institutions that will act to promote ends which are not part of their original intentions. Still, the point is that analyzing institutions and the emergence of institutions *via* individual preferences is rooted in the earliest of economic analysis.

If Smith brought individuals' preferences and their power to the forefront it was Marshall in *Principles of Economics* (1890) who highlighted the ever-changing organism of the business society. For him change was the essence of the short-run disequilibrium:

Thus one or another curves may be rendered false by such an event as a change in fashion, a war, a plague, the invention of new machinery, the opening up of a new market or of a new source of supply, the discovery of some new application of the commodity or the competition of a new rival. It must be distinctly understood that in any of these cases the old curves must be thrown aside and new curves drawn.

It was people who powered this change through their influence on all of his technical curves and calculations. It was their preferences and changing tastes that altered society and business. We admit to the same process but in a rather more subtle way. It is our contention that the change in technologies, education, gender equality, and demographics all impact upon organizations through the change in opportunity costs of working in a traditional organization for the expert employee. And because expert individuals have the power to choose where and how they work, their impact is critical to the future development of organizations. Although Marshall will be known for his refinement of the technical tools of analysis, we must remember that he also heralded an inter-disciplinary approach. He thought this necessary to 'capture the multi-faceted nature of the phenomena to be studied'. We subscribe to this as well.

Much of Marshall's technical approach is still used to analyze the behaviour of people, most notably in the work of the economist Gary S. Becker who studies, among other things, time and household production, marriage, fertility and the family, and discrimination. Becker (1976) suggests that economics is distinguished by three guiding assumptions: (i) maximizing behaviour (ii) market equilibrium and (iii) stable preferences.[1] Of interest to us is that preferences are assumed to be stable. This assumption of stability does not mean stable over goods and services and over the use of time. Stable is used in the sense of a stable set of preferences so that predictions can be made about responses to various changes. Thus, if opportunities faced by individuals change in an observable way, then we can expect the decisions of individuals to change.

We, too, apply this approach and used it in chapter 1. Here, we asserted that changes in the circumstances surrounding work and home of the knowledge-based expert provides changes in opportunities. This increases the choices available to specific experts concerning particular organizational structures more congruent with his/her needs. It is the very Beckeresque opportunity costs of, perhaps, higher earnings and greater security from a large firm as opposed to freedoms (that increase innovative output) provided by other organizations that could drive experts away from the rigidity of large firms to other organizational forms. Thus, the change in organizations is significantly influenced by the employee or the supply-side. We suggest that, like Becker, who approached all kinds of human decisions and their impact on the market using an economic approach, we too approach human choice, its underlying preferences, and changes in opportunities and apply these to their impact on the labour market and the organizations that arise from the labour market.

Thus, our approach is historically economic in a sense that, as Becker says in the introduction to *The Economic Approach to Human Behaviour*, 'the economic approach provides a valuable unified framework for understanding all human behaviour'. Our theories about experts and their impact on changes in the structure of organizations is consistent with Becker's strict rules of economic analysis. As we mentioned in chapter 1, for the expert employee the following has occurred: (i) the returns to employment have increased for all members of the family, including expert women. Thus, there has been a change in family roles and therefore the choice of family members away from a rigidly structured organization; (ii) recognizing the rise of industries whose products are based on knowledge and rely on innovation and tacit knowledge, the expert employee chooses an organization which monitors less frequently; (iii) the change in technologies makes the cost of producing a knowledge-based product from various locations and at various times much lower. This provides an opportunity for the expert employees to work away from offices if they choose. Finally (iv) ecological awareness may produce a shift in consumption patterns away from consumption of tangible things to the consumption of 'free-time'.

All of these changes and their consequences as we demonstrated in chapter 1 are rooted in a long history of well-structured social science analysis. We have placed the expert employee at the heart of our analysis since we believe organizations involving agents will appear because of the classic economic behaviour of these people when opportunities change. This will drive experts towards a system which compensates their work in a way that best maximizes their own utility and productivity, given the changes in opportunities.

Chapter 2 approached the problems of experts by firstly looking in a traditional way at the differences between two forms of labour markets. It compared how others have shown and described evolution from one labour market structure to another and thereby develops a new form of transition for our current labour market to the punctuated break. Many have shown the gradual transformation of the labour market in the context of a gradual evolutionary change from the Fordist/Taylorist organization, with its classic functions intact, to either a flexible or a global firm. This analysis assumes that expert employees have strong ties to traditional firm settings. By taking the view of transition as a punctuated break, we free ourselves from many of the ties to the Fordist/Taylorist systems. This allows us to approach at-will contracts and agencies as appropriate forms of response by expert employees rather than as aberration or the result of an organizationally driven labour market.

This has revealed much about expert employees and their benefits from such a labour market and chapter 3 described why the traditional organization will defend itself against this change or find it difficult to maintain its current systems when these break-away pressures mount. Organizations defend themselves because experts severely disrupt organizational monitoring and controlling functions as well as their anxiety-relieving structures. As most of what these experts do is linked to intellectual capital, we found in chapter 4 yet another reason for experts to use the agency at-will contract system with its improved and various labour market and information networks. Finally, chapter 5 considered the temporal aspects of the agency at-will contract system and illustrated the personal advantages of increased utility to the expert employee as well as the qualitative improvements in the expert employees' products. All result in the use of at-will contracts and agencies.

This is the point: there are a set of pressures which encourage experts to break away from traditional firm settings. No one reason may be strong enough in itself, but a combination of these factors lead to a general trend. This does not suggest that many of those who work in traditional settings will not continue to do so. However, those experts aware of their strengths predicated upon changes in product and labour markets and in technology, can be expected to become a vanguard for change. We have given some examples of how these pressures result in new labour market dynamics.

This leads us to the second part of our book. Below we show the impact of these changes on the definitions of labour markets and their segments and provide evidence as to the various forms of the agency at-will contract system. We look at its development using AT&T's Resource Link as an example of a firm internal system with its many external labour market characteristics. This is followed by a close examination of a London-based expert employee temporary agency which suggests that it provides temporal control, one of the many benefits of such a system to experts. After suggesting the relevance of temporal freedoms and agency employment we look at the break by Hollywood stars who began to market their tacit knowledge by breaking from the traditional large Hollywood studios. We then study the Internet as a potential advanced state of the external labour market system revealing just how far these systems can develop and how strikingly different that environment is in producing knowledge-based products and discretion for the expert employee. We conclude by suggesting that many of the past theories about labour market segments can be questioned when one uses the perspective of the expert employee.

PART TWO

The labour market and the expert employee

But when Scientists propose . . . comprehensive theories . . . they need particularly good support, and invented hypothetical cases just don't supply sufficient oomph for crucial conclusions.

Stephen Jay Gould, 'Hooking Leviathan by its Past'

CHAPTER SEVEN

AT&T's special employment policies for their expert employees

Our People are Our Competitive Advantage.

Robert E. Allen, Chairman and CEO, AT&T

American Telephone and Telegraph, AT&T, provides us with the first case of an agency-based system of at-will contracts in its in-house temporary agency Resource Link. It is the first example of our four examples of different types of labour market agencies. In the following chapters we look at (i) an external labour market temporary agency; (ii) the development of the Hollywood agency system and (iii) the Internet as a far-reaching expert employee agent. These examples are used to develop a more coherent understanding of agencies and what they do and do not provide expert knowledge-based employees. They are similar in some respects, but, as we examine the agency system, their differences become increasingly important. The differences, in the end, suggest that some agency systems can be more readily associated with a punctuated break from traditional labour markets of the past 150 years.

Because of its links to AT&T, a large traditional organization, Resource Link is the least radical of the agencies we examine. Many of the roles of a large firm, monitoring, co-ordination and team work, are left intact (perhaps due to organizational defence mechanisms we have outlined above). The case of AT&T highlights a basic dilemma. How can an organization uphold the organizational functions (monitoring, co-ordination and team-building) while supplying its employees with compensation packages necessary for their personal utility and their increased productivity? Not surprisingly, this is a familiar problem to the personnel and human resource departments of many large traditional corporations and has led to organizational adaptations towards structures which facilitate learning and greater flexibility. In examining one such US company, AT&T, we answer two fundamental questions. How is AT&T's response similar to those elements of expert employment labour markets that we have discussed and how is it different? And to what degree does AT&T's response imply a gradual evolution with links to the past or a punctuated break from the traditional firm and all of its intermediate forms?

Some might find it unusual that we look at employment policies of a large organization like AT&T when we propose a punctuated break away from those organizations. But it is because experts work for such large organizations that we must investigate such companies. Indeed, large organizations have played such a crucial role for the expert employee and their labour market that to neglect this aspect of expert employment would be to bias our response (for example, see Sampson (1995)). Furthermore, because so much of the discussion surrounding networks and agencies has been influenced by the demand-driven aspects of temporary agency and contingency work, it is crucial to describe the outward appearances of this development and then to evaluate its relevance to the evolving traditional firm. This is as important to our thesis of a punctuated break as are the expert employees and resulting networks and the agencies. AT&T's human resource policies prove excellent material.

For a long time, AT&T has been one of the classic examples of a traditional complex organization. With its research and development, customer service, marketing and a whole gambit of divisions that encompass many aspects of the product market, as well as the knowledge-based aspects of the company. AT&T, with its information-led technologies and services, is linked inexorably to the knowledge-based worker. The company employs thousands of expert employees specializing in knowledge-based work, and therefore must be aware of the problems expert employees pose. Thus, AT&T's response to expert employees is both relevant and informative to our discussion and theories. Indeed, AT&T represents an interesting example of a traditional firm coping with the challenges and opportunities created by the changing environment which surrounds expert employees and a knowledge-based industry.

New policies for AT&T

Traditionally AT&T's human resource policies have been predicated upon a strategy of hiring and retaining the best people by offering them essentially, life-time employment and career progression.[1] This policy resembles those that were so highly valued by people like David Harrison of Chevrolet, mentioned in our introduction: job security, relatively high pay and career opportunities within the firm. This held AT&T in good stead (along with its near monopoly on telephone services within the US) and it became one of the most successful companies in the United States.

However, AT&T's fortunes changed after the Reagan administration deregulated the US telecommunications industry in the early 1980s. This led to the break-up of AT&T in 1984 which triggered a significant change in the company's organizational structure. AT&T changed from an hierarchical monolithic structure to one which was dispersed with numerous independent business units. This eliminated many middle managers and increased the autonomy and discretion of local managers. The reduction of middle managers, although an abrupt change especially for those who lost their jobs, represented a gradual evolutionary step for the company as a whole. It was a shift away from AT&T's traditional organizational form which retained some of the firm's traditional organizational architecture. This evolution is congruent with some basic core-periphery models which dominated much of academic organizational debate in the 1980s (for example, see Piore and Sable (1984)).

During this transition, AT&T shed some 100,000 employees which led many of those remaining to become demoralized and insecure. This manifested itself in negative attitudes which were perceived by senior managers to be dysfunctional. It was incumbent upon AT&T's human resource specialists to halt the malaise by changing these attitudes which were widespread among employees. The company's human resource managers chose to address the issue by introducing new employment packages which were expected to change the attitudes of employees and increase their satisfaction for working for AT&T.

Thus, the company met a significant competitive challenge by attempting to change the attitude and work practices of its own employees. It viewed its employees as important consumers of company products, specifically employment and compensation, and sought to influence employees by changing these products. An expected outcome of this strategy was that AT&T could continue to attract and retain the brightest and the best, who would be committed and devoted to maintaining and increasing the company's competitive advantage. AT&T chose this strategy to enhance competitiveness rather than simply engaging in a price war.

AT&T is not alone in choosing such strategies. A US hotel group has successfully met competitive challenges with a similar strategy. The hotel chain was experiencing a high employee turnover rate and as a consequence its search and training costs soared and eroded its margins in an increasingly competitive market. Rather than simply increase wages to attract and retain staff the hotel management decided to tailor compensation to specific needs of individuals which the hotel wished to employ.

In addition to paying a long service bonus, the company provided a monetary incentive for employees to study part-time and purchase child-care facilities. For each dollar an employee was prepared to put to study at the local college, the company added another two; and for each dollar an individual provided for the purchase of child care the company gave another three. This strategy attracted to the company students and parents with small children. The former group tended to remain with the company until people finished their courses (3–4 years); the latter group until their children no longer needed child care (many years). This strategy significantly lowered the labour turnover rates and the costs of recruitment.

Similarly, AT&T was aware of the need to satisfy its employees while encouraging their continued commitment to the company. These are slightly different goals than the hotel firm, but, AT&T's approach is underlined by a similar premise of treating its employees like consumers. The company devised a compensation package which simultaneously facilitated downsizing while providing employees with job security in return for commitment. AT&T achieved this through a programme called Special Employee Leave of Absence (SELA). This enabled employees to take a special leave of absence of up to two years, during which time the company would provide employees with tuition fees, medical benefits and service credits. The only condition was that an employee did not work for a competitor during the absence.

The programme provided AT&T employees with an opportunity to pursue their own interests and enrol for educational courses. The overall effect was for a significant number of AT&T employees to enhance their skills and experience while increasing their commitment to the company. In addition, there was one further and important advantage to AT&T: it reduced their wage bill at a critical time, and facilitated a staggered and 'acceptable' downsizing.

This voluntary specialized leave has been introduced twice when it has been necessary for AT&T to downsize. In its first offering, 1,700 out of 84,000 eligible employees chose to take the leave. Experiences were generally positive, and most people who opted for the sabbatical eventually returned to AT&T. The programme became financially sound since it significantly cut the traditional costs connected with downsizing. It also retained specific AT&T employees and their firm-specific know-how.

This policy constitutes a significant move by AT&T toward a more flexible work arrangement (increases in numerical flexibility) but it is still demand driven. However, viewed from the perspective of an employee product devised by the company's personnel department another conclusion can be drawn. Because the programme was voluntary, it seems reasonable to suggest that it satisfied the 1,700 participants by providing them with a period to do what they wanted while still emphasizing their future job security.

The programme does not appear to have provided an opportunity for a punctuated break, since most of the participants in the scheme returned to the company after their absences. However, it did offer employees increased discretion over their particular life-styles while attempting to retain company loyalty by ensuring long-term job security for the entire employee population. Thus, it provided a break from many conventional responses to increased competition, but retained the traditional element of employee commitment. These are classic terms from which we can detect a gradual evolutionary process. An adaptation of AT&T's human resource policies to the circumstances of a volatile labour market while providing for employees' preferences.

Another response: AT&T's Resource Link

Underlying many of AT&T's new employment products is the principle not to rely entirely on competing for employees through the market pricing system. According to AT&T, in the long-run savings can be made by adjusting other elements of compensation to suit individuals and thereby enhance distributions to shareholders, consumers (in the form of lower prices), and employees. A further advantage is that this policy tends to evoke greater employee effort than does simply increasing pay. This highlights the advantages of temporal flexibility and compensation which includes discretion over work environments.

In 1991, with these things in mind, AT&T instituted Resource Link which acts as an in-house temporary agency. It supplies, to different business units, skilled expert employees at a time when those units need them (for example, when a project needs extra help or some expertise that the particular business unit does not hold). Resource Link treats AT&T's business units as clients and charges for the services it renders. The prices of its services vary according to the specific skills it provides. Indeed, the programme works much the same as an external labour market temporary agency. AT&T refers to it as internalizing an external labour market mechanism. Being an AT&T product, the billing system is ingeniously devised so that any Resource Link employee can call a specific number and tap in the hours worked on their touch-tone telephones.

Resource Link contracts with the various AT&T business units are temporary and typically last from three to twelve months. However, individuals who participate remain regular AT&T employees, with their salaries and benefits intact. Most assignments are for skilled management and technical jobs such as project management, account executives and financial and budget analysis. Of those working through Resource Link, two-fifths are in technical positions such as software development and systems analysis. In assessing Resource Link, many participants welcome the opportunity of working in different parts of the company and thus broadening their understanding. Thus, it is not the same upward mobility path described in a traditional AT&T career sense (or in the sense that labour market segmentationists have described). Resource Link employees move from project to project and gain experience in a wide range of areas and, thereby, increase their overall utility.

In 1991, Resource Link began with some thirty-three employees. By the end of 1993 over 500 employees had participated in the programme. Currently some 400 employees are on assignment, in some twenty-five AT&T business units and divisions. Initially, the overwhelming majority of assignments were located in AT&T's New Jersey head office, but over time other locations, such as Atlanta, Washington DC, Chicago and various cities in California, as well as locations in Europe and the Pacific Rim use its services.

Resource Link searches AT&T's employee pool to fill its staff with high performance, technically qualified, employees who are able to adapt to new and challenging business situations. These qualities allow individuals to immediately contribute to a specific business unit's needs. Resource Link is popular among employees with over 50 per cent of its staff volunteering to join as a career move since it is perceived to significantly enhance employees' exposure to the company and to increase their business experience. Furthermore, Resource Link assists individuals to increase their networks and enlarge their tacit and explicit knowledge. Some 25 per cent of Resource Link employees have used their increased network and know-how to re-establish themselves in a traditional permanent job within AT&T.

Resource Link: the flexible firm or an employee-demanded employment product?

Elements of AT&T's Resource Link fit into the core–periphery flexible firm model discussed earlier.[2] Employees working through Resource Link provide business units with increased flexibility. Crucial to our discussion is the amount of flexibility generated by Resource Link brought about by the company and the amount engendered by individuals. The former implies demand-driven flexible firms and the latter a supply-side adaptation or break. We examine some reasons behind Resource Link from both the firm's and employee's points of view. Recall, our earlier suggestion, that only examining the organization's point of view will give strength to a demand-driven core–periphery theory: not because it is the most accurate description, but because it tends to neglect supply-side influences discussed above. Here we attempt to redress this by including and examining employees' perceptions.

The demand-side

For AT&T the advantages of Resource link are numerous. One of the more concrete of these is the savings that AT&T can accrue from providing a buffer employment area rather than sacking individuals with specific company knowledge. In a purely financial sense, Resource Link can represent a significant saving for AT&T. It does this by providing a conduit through which it can influence employment levels from one business unit to another. In the end AT&T is able to reduce redundancies and its attendant costs, such as severance pay and exit bonuses.

For example, if business unit A has a momentary lag in its demand, it needs to reduce the numbers of its employees. Without Resource Link its only recourse is to sack people. This is not because the people are necessarily inferior, but simply because there is less demand for their skills at a specific time. Sacking a person costs AT&T the equivalent of six months' salary, which it is obliged to pay on severance. It is reasonable to assume that sacked employees are not predisposed to the company and take with them both tacit and explicit knowledge. Knowledge which is potentially useful to competitors and other AT&T business units. Resource Link prevents the haemorrhaging of important knowledge by redistributing underutilized employees to business units which require their skills. Further, if Resource Link is unable to immediately relocate an employee there are still savings to the company since it does not incur the attendant costs of redundancies. This provides Resource Link with a cost effective period in which to husband individuals and search for suitable placements throughout the company.

Further, it is financially prudent for AT&T to lease Resource Link employees for a finite period to specific business units at a price lower than an employee's wage and make up the difference. This is because Resource Link recovers some of the salary costs while the company avoids attendant redundancy costs. In addition, there are further potential savings to AT&T. Assume market conditions improve after the company had sacked certain employees, AT&T would be obliged to go down the relatively costly road of searching, recruiting and training people to replace those it had sacked. Thus, the financial advantages of Resource Link are increased.

Resource Link is marketed to AT&T's business units in much the same way as an external temporary employment agency. Resource Link makes itself known, stresses the quality of its people and the value they can add. Interestingly, it also stresses its contribution in creating within a business unit core-periphery employment policies: 'by partnering with AT&T Resource Link you can create a flexible, high performing team, with our associates working alongside your core work force' (*Resource Link* AT&T brochure).

The supply-side

If our discussion was to stop here then our conclusions would be that AT&T is developing a temporary agency service to provide numerical flexibility within its business units while saving money on its severance payments, and also possibly making future potential savings associated with hiring and training. However, let us examine Resource Link from the vantage point of an employee. This raises another dimension to the demand-type explanations we have thus far highlighted.

For the employee, Resource Link provides two essentials: first, continued job security and second, an ability to increase tacit and explicit knowledge. These represent important incentives for an employee to enter Resource Link. Recall that AT&T feels that in order to attract and retain its expert employees it must treat them as customers and provide an employment product congruent with employee desires. Further, job security reduces an individual's fear of failing and being sacked, and thus increases the possibility of employees not 'playing safe' with regard to innovation in the workplace. This increases the potential benefits to AT&T. Indeed, the company perceives this added potential for risk taking as an important contribution to innovation. This, coupled with the potential for increasing an employee's tacit and explicit knowledge, creates value for the organization itself. Such added value is further enhanced by the fact that Resource Link employees have frequent and broad exposure to numerous business units within AT&T.

These are all by-products of supplying some expert employees with what they desire. If individuals do not desire these aspects, their commitment to the company would probably decrease, as would the additional benefits to the company. Thus, we can view Resource Link as a means of satisfying particular demands of specific employees. This is especially the case when considering that at least 50 per cent of Resource Link associates are volunteers. This voluntarism does not rest easily with the core–periphery thesis which suggests that the cause for contingency employment such as Resource Link, is the need for firms to become more flexible. By contrast Resource Link stresses the need for AT&T to make specific provisions for its expert employees.

Further, the role Resource Link plays in increasing job security (in that the expert employee's employment prospects are not linked to one individual business unit but spread across several) is in direct contrast to the flexible firm's characteristics of decreasing job security by forcing employees into the contingent market. As far as providing an extended network for the employee, Resource Link has the advantage of exposing employees to a larger set of people, work environments and projects which can lead to increased explicit and tacit knowledge. Recall that explicit knowledge can be codified and acquired relatively easily, whereas tacit knowledge is difficult to codify, takes more time to acquire and usually means working closely with the holder of the tacit knowledge. By working for extended periods with new people the expert employee increases his/her potential of acquiring tacit knowledge. In the words of Jim Finn, an employee of Resource Link, 'it offers me the ability to increase my overall market value by providing an opportunity to continue to develop myself and my skill set, to work within many new and existing business units, to gain a better understanding of where these business units are headed, and to be a part of the overall growth of AT&T'.

Others, too, have enhanced their skill sets. One person qualified as a programmer and then was promoted to a supervisory role. It is clear that AT&T does not intend Resource Link to be the type of contingent work group that the flexible firm thesis implies. This would result in a relatively narrow set of advantages for AT&T, because employees grow less committed to AT&T as they feel more expendable: and with less commitment comes less firm-specific investment and/or productivity. This is associated with an expert employee's lack of interest in investing in firm specific skills because s/he does not know how long s/he can use these skills while at AT&T. As far as temporal control is concerned it appears that Resource Link provides very little of this; individuals are paid continuously as AT&T employees and, are generally expected to accept assignments regardless of individual temporal wishes.

There are several aspects of Resource Link which associates it with the flexible firm model; there are also aspects which link it to a supply driven employment product, driven by the preferences of expert employees – preferences of expert employees that AT&T want to attract.

Resource Link and the punctuated break

Does Resource Link constitute a punctuated break? No, it is more of a gradual adaptation within AT&T which helps to retain specific expert employees and increase organizational flexibility. However, there are aspects which can be associated with a punctuated break, in that the expert employee is demanding certain employment products that AT&T is providing. Through its characteristics, as well as its desired effects for AT&T, it can be firmly placed as a gradual evolutionary change. This is consistent with our theories in that we expect some organizational structures to adapt while keeping intact important traditional aspects of the organization. But, in terms of the world of AT&T, it can be viewed as a punctuated break.

Indeed, Resource Link is unlike any other employment product that AT&T has provided. Relocating individuals around the organization provides them with access to a much broader range of work experience than they usually would encounter. AT&T's goals are intrinsically those of a large organization of the past: providing increased job security in expectation for increased employee commitment and flexibility. Resource Link also adheres to one of the central functions of organizations as defined by Alchian and Demsetz (1972), that there are structures which monitor expert employees and their performance.

Once a Resource Link employee has been assigned to a particular business unit that employee still reports to a Resource Link staff manager who manages a broad range of associated employees. AT&T feels that this is important to the success of Resource Link: 'Associates who are constantly moving from job to job in the field must feel as if they are being supervised in the traditional sense and are being properly supported' (AT&T manager's interview with the authors, October 1993). Managers are responsible for such traditional human resource practices like performance reviews, coaching, and career counselling. In all, Resource Link attempts to capitalize on some of the elements of the external labour market, as well as perform the role of a traditional organization. This is because AT&T is still concerned with its role as an organization and the advantages that role can provide in creating surplus value. And this role is tied to past definitions of the organization, to both monitor, control and co-ordinate.

It also provides a function of reducing transaction costs in that it can better guarantee the expert employee from the agency a long-term role within AT&T. This means that the employee will be more likely to invest in firm-specific knowledge. In committing to the employee AT&T can reduce the transaction costs of obtaining an employee who will provide firm-specific intellectual capital. Without this commitment AT&T would have to pay the employee more in the short-term for investing in this training, since the employee would not be sure of his or her long-term return of such an investment, since such a return is tied to working within AT&T. But the commitment allows employees to invest while being compensated at a lower rate because they are aware that, in the long-term, the potential returns might be greater (the employee pays for some of the training costs). Overall, the transaction costs are reduced and therefore AT&T can capture greater returns on the transaction between it and the employee. This is another traditional role of organizations and Resource Link plays a part in that traditional organizational objective. Therefore, it cannot be associated with a break from the traditional firm.

Because Resource Link is, at this point, exclusive to AT&T's internal labour market it cannot, and does not provide the extended network that agencies developed outside an organization can provide. It is providing only AT&T specific knowledge of available employment and project opportunities. As we have noted, this restricts the network to participating AT&T employees. The goal of Resource Link is to provide people with general, tacit and firm specific knowledge. It attempts to engender commitment to AT&T while providing aspects of agency work that can improve an expert employee's intellectual capital which is closely associated to AT&T. But the vast size of an organization like AT&T makes it a large labour market in itself. And for an expert employee that has expertise in AT&T's specific knowledge, it functions much like the networks and agencies that we have discussed in the external labour market. Indeed, Doug Merchant, human resource manager for AT&T suggests that AT&T has essentially taken an external labour market system and applied it to the company's internal labour market. But one would be hard pressed to characterize Resource Link as an example of a punctuated break away from the traditional organization. Within AT&T it may be viewed as a punctuated break from the traditional form of working, but, because of its continued use of monitoring and team building functions as well as its role in reducing transaction costs, it can only be described by an outsider as a gradual adaptation by AT&T to provide for its expert employees.

In summary, AT&T and Resource Link provide an interesting example of a large organization capturing some of the positive aspects of expert agency employment. Resource Link is based on an attempt by AT&T to align the preferences of expert employees and their compensation packages. This provides some support for our thesis which suggests that the idea that labour markets are forced upon employees by way of monetary incentives is often misleading. There are aspects of Resource Link which are closely linked to the demand sided theories of the flexible firm. But, to overlook the supply-sided factors associated with it does not provide a complete description.

It is because we have been attuned to these employee aspects of organizations, like agency work, that some of these other aspects about Resource Link were brought to light. Indeed, we are not the first to think of Resource Link in these terms since it is similarly perceived within AT&T. As a transition it is interesting, but it still does not exemplify, in all respects, the punctuated break that we describe. To explore this side of expert agency employment we must leave the organization and look at the external labour market and examine whether what is being carried out there is more akin to the demand-sided movement of increasing numerical flexibility or akin to the supply-sided forces that suggest a punctuated break from a traditional firm and lead to an agency-type organization which is predicated upon serial at-will employment contracts.

CHAPTER EIGHT

An external temporary agency and expert employees

It was a sight to behold Tim Linkenwater slowly bringing out a massive ledger and day-book, and, after turning them over and over and affectionately dusting their backs and sides, opened the leaves here and there, and cast his eye half mournfully, half proudly, upon the fair and unblotted entries.

Charles Dickens, *Nicholas Nickleby*

The temporary agency as a different organization

In part I we argued that organizations, like temporary agency employment, possess features which will benefit the expert employee. For the temporary agency we proposed in chapter 5, the availability of, and preference for, temporal control were described as a necessary prerequisite for a punctuated break away from the traditional organization. For AT&T the agency concept was internalized and, for various reasons we describe, cannot be considered a radical break but more a gradual adaptation and transformation of the traditional organization. We also suggest that the over-emphasis of demand-sided transformations of organizations, in theory and in empirical research, tends to neglect other important elements of job forms as preferred by the employee (for this case study, temporal control). This implies that conventional analysis of the gradual transformation of firms may result in erroneous conclusions about contemporary organizations such as temporary agency employment. We contend that temporary agency employment is an important sector of the expert employee labour market. This is partly because of the potential temporal flexibility that it can offer these individuals and partly because of its potential for networking and cross-fertilization of expertise.

Whereas AT&T took centre stage in the previous chapter it is two

London accountancy firms that provide the data for this chapter's analysis.[1] In many ways the study we performed is a classic case study. One of the firms studied is a large London accountancy firm. The other is a medium sized London temporary agency specializing in accountancy. Being most interested in relative degrees of discretion over working conditions our study is comparative and purposely tracks two accountancy firms that have very different organizational foundations. We compare employee reactions, responses, and basic management characteristics of a traditional firm, in which there is relatively little discretion over work and to a less traditional temporary accountancy agency, which we suggest is a market leader in providing its clients with discretion over their work.

So, just as AT&T provided a distinguished example of a firm which provides a degree of internal flexibility for its employees in developing an in-house employment agency, a London temporary accountancy agency provides us with an example of external temporary agency work and thereby constitutes a good case of a general family of agency settings, the first being internal to the firm (AT&T) and the second external: a professional agency specializing in a specific sector in the external labour market (our London temporary accountancy agency). In delineating agency systems in this way we are trying to develop a more explicit vocabulary surrounding an agency system of employment – the system which, in the first part of this book, we theorized would provide many of the discretionary demands of the increasing population of professional knowledge employees (experts). We do this because we feel the flexibility debate can be more accurately addressed with a more detailed understanding of temporary agency employment and how increased discretion is achieved.

Our study in context

In the introduction we briefly stated that there is an increasing amount of popular literature attesting to the growing number of professional temporary agencies. In academic literature, this phenomena is mostly slanted towards a demand management perspective which suggests that temporary professionals tend to be the result of the demands of firms for an increase in numerical flexibility (see introduction for appropriate references). The temporary use of professionals can, just like non-professionals, provide an adjustment mechanism that will allow for seasonal and/or business-cycle fluctuations: the number of

Table 8.1. *Levels of Income: agency versus large firm employment (in percentage)*

	£ per annum (thousands)				
	<9	10–18	19–36	37–60	Total
Agency	14	38	46	2	100
Large firm	11	45	35	10	100

$n = 224$

temporary staff increasing during boom periods and the number of staff decreasing during periods of economic downturns.[2] In some instances this may be the case. However, there is some evidence to indicate that specific professional employees work through temporary agencies because this labour market can provide them with enhanced discretion without any significant lose of wages.

In our study there are no significant differences (x^2 = 5.04413 significant at 0.1686 with 3 degrees of freedom) between traditional large firm and agency in terms of wages earned (see table 8.1). Thus, income is not a reason for expert employees to choose agency work.

Accountancy and temporary agencies

We have chosen a London temporary accountancy agency since accountancy represents a bottom line marker for professional temporary agency expert employment and it is a field which relies heavily upon knowledge-based work. Accountancy demands the explicit knowledge which Nanoka (1991) defines as the forms of government tax and accounting regulations as well as systematized in-house accounting practices. These can be learned either through experience and or education, and some are also testable in forms of professional qualifying examinations (the means by which the profession ensures that each certified accountant has had some basic level of accountancy education and or has some basic level of accountancy knowledge). In this form, accountants distinguish themselves as experts by providing information across industries and applying basic accountancy standards and regulations to a vast number of firms.

In our study all of our accountant respondents had passed several professional examinations regardless whether they worked for the large firm or the temporary agency. These are the routes to the qualifying credentials, and they are the same for temporary expert employees as they are for the large firm employees. High percentages in both groups of experts had received formal university education although this was significantly higher in the group associated with the large accountancy firm: 55 and 80 per cent respectively.

Our choice of accountancy as a case study of expert employment was further influenced by the fact that the profession is a good example of tacit as well as explicit knowledge. Indeed, a skilled accountant will not only apply the rules, regulations and systems of explicit learned knowledge, but will also tailor these explicit skills to individual situations in specific companies. Without digressing into a detailed discussion about creative accounting, our point here is to stress the fact that accounting is not simply a matter of applying rules, but within general principles and regulations there is a margin for creative interpretation which employs tacit as well as explicit knowledge, and this can result in significant savings for companies and enhance the presentation of financial situations. For a stockholder, the employment of this tacit knowledge implies a positive benefit. And, of course, the expert's tacit knowledge-based skills are purchased in the labour market. In this way, accounting fulfils one prerequisite (to the statistical trends we have gone over in the introduction), that knowledge plays a key part in the expert employee's occupation.

Another important reason for choosing accountancy as a case study is that the accountancy market provides us with a relatively traditional occupation of expert employment. It is a knowledge-based industry which has a long tradition of employment and labour practices (note the short extract from Dickens' *Nicholas Nickleby* at the beginning of this chapter). It has a foundation in more traditional enterprises like textiles than some of the newer expert occupations such as computer programmers. If an occupation such as accountancy feels the effects of, and, or exhibits characteristics of, our theorized supply-side transformation, then we may expect an even greater response from expert knowledge-based employment that comes from less traditional sectors such as software development and university research. In this sense the accountancy labour market probably provides one of the least likely areas where one would expect to find expert professional employees seeking, and therefore exhibiting, supply-side pressure for greater discretion over their work. An employee training to enter a profession ensconced in traditional management structures like accountancy would find it more difficult to appease his/her discretionary goals and therefore would find it less desirable to enter such a field. If there are such individuals attempting such a transition in this field, then it makes our theory more robust.

A third reason for studying accountancy is that it was our intention to examine a field which had a robust labour market. To the extent that accountants are in demand contributes to the negotiating power of individual accountants for a more flexible labour market. However, as the study started the industry fell into a recession (along with London in general).[3] If anything the prevailing economic conditions of the time we conducted our survey weights the evidence against our theory since the more precarious the labour market, the greater the relative value of a permanent job which has traditionally been perceived to provide greater job security. Thus, an accountant, during a recession would tend to seek increased job security rather than discretion over his/her work.

Despite the prevailing recessionary conditions we found no statistically significant differences between the two groups regarding job security. Respondents we asked rate their perceived level of job security as an advantage. They were also asked whether they thought they would be made redundant in the future and whether an increase in job security would improve their current employment situation. Having run various regressions on these and other variables (and combinations of these responses), we found no statistically significant difference in responses between the groups. This suggests that job security is related more closely to the specific industry rather than whether an accountant works through a large firm or through a system of agents.

Thus, similar to income levels, the desire for job security does not explain why some people prefer permanent employment in large firms and others, with similar expertise, choose to work through temporary agencies. This finding encourages us to search for other explanations. It is our contention that expert employment, with its increase in professional women, changes in technology (the accounting industry has been transformed by the personal computer and software package developments) and its general growth, will lead to accountants rejecting organizational rigidities of a large bureaucratic firm and satisfying their desire for discretion over their work by using employment agencies.

Our final reason for choosing accountancy as a case study is to provide a contrast with the Hollywood film industry we discuss in the next chapter and which some readers might feel is idiosyncratic. Their juxtaposition is used to provide an example of the scope of our organizational break.

A temporary agency and a large organization compared

It is important to remember that although much of the temporary agency literature pays tribute to professional temporary agencies as providers of employee discretion, this mostly amounts to peripheral remarks within the wider context of temporary employment. Although the number of temporary professionals is relatively small compared to the labour force as a whole, it is significant. This is because there are indications (see chapter 1) of an increasing proportion of the labour force becoming professional knowledge-based expert workers. We have also suggested that some of these professionals appear to be abruptly breaking with traditional organizations and seeking employment through temporary agencies. Although it is the long-standing labour markets which will be considered historically significant, it is also important to investigate apparent anomalies; in this case temporary agency employment. This may hold important clues to stresses and strains within the labour market or may well be the beginning of a labour market that is better able to cope with contemporary circumstances.

Notwithstanding the potential economic significance of relatively small groups of expert individuals to specific companies and industries, there has been relatively little sustained study about the people who supply important expertise and how they might be influenced by different compensation packages with varying levels of discretion, and by large traditional organizations as opposed to professional temporary agencies. Our study of the London accountancy market was designed to reduce this imbalance in the academic literature. We set out to study the effects on accountants of different compensation packages and also the effects of people on compensation.

In some respects the London temporary accountancy agency market resembles the AT&T internal temporary agency. Temporary employees work in a variety of different areas and are retained for the length of a particular project. But, in the case of London accountants, temporary employees are marketing their skills, through agents, to a variety of employers. Agencies provide the series of at-will contracts which earlier we discussed theoretically. Thus, an agency is a venue from which accountants can be hired and fired quickly and without any significant penalty. The employee, if dissatisfied with a particular project, can leave and immediately seek an alternative. Flexibility for the company and increased discretion for the employee – facilitated by the temporary agency.

Experts' temporal discretion and agencies

Is it the employer or the employee who wants increased flexibility? Temporary agency literature often uses terms to distinguish between 'involuntary' and 'voluntary' participation in temporary work. The former is instigated by the employer and the latter by the employees. This distinction is too broad and may veil important aspects of temporary agency employment. Our survey was designed to shed new light on this by probing for intangible differences in working conditions (what many, in the past, have relegated to a secondary importance in compensation or felt were almost unnegotiable in labour contracts).

Because of the changes taking place in labour and product markets and in technology, some individuals are motivated to make an abrupt break with traditional organizations. To the extent that this is the case, what previously was perceived as marginalized labour market issues (like temporal control) may become important factors in the evolutionary process of the labour market. In the case of AT&T, there was little evidence that temporal control was obtained by those employees who worked through AT&T's Resource Link. In our study of the London temporary accountancy agency, we find that this is not the case. Indeed, temporary agencies provide some accountants with greater temporal control which is valued by respondents who use the agencies.

There are several different statistical procedures available to assist our analysis of the differences in the job characteristics between accountants in permanent employment with large firms and those which obtain employment by the way of temporary employment agencies. Each procedure allows us to identify true and significant differences rather than those which occur by chance. In order to test for significant differences we employ logistic regressions, wherein we can test the capacity of independent variables in predicting participation in a group.

In order to find the distinguishing characteristics we grouped

Table 8.2. *Working conditions as predictors of temporary agency participation*

Independent Variables	Coefficient B	Wald Statistic	R	exp(B)
Temporal control	0.8298*	22.4224	0.2927	2.2928
Mobility	−1.0239*	30.6551	−0.3467	0.3592
Other control	0.2481	2.4569	0.0438	1.2817
Job security	−0.0450	0.4185	0.0000	0.9068
Income	0.0044	0.0008	0.0000	0.9956

* Significant at <0.05
$n = 222$

questions which measure similar things into indices.[4] This is important since it increases the reliability of employee indications about their working conditions. Our analysis starts by comparing responses to five key elements of work: (i) temporal control (ii) availability of job mobility (iii) control over other aspects of work (iv) job security and (v) income. From the responses we calculate respondents' general tendencies. For example, if one group of respondents is paid more, then we could use the level of pay to predict which group any one respondent works for. In general, we are locating differences in working conditions between agency employment and large firm employment. Our results are given in table 8.2.

Data reported in table 8.2 suggest that there is a significant difference in the levels of temporal control between agency and large firm respondents. Agency employees have greater control over when they work (temporal control). This suggests that there are advantages for expert employees to find work through temporary agencies. As we argued in chapter 5, such advantages can prove to be important in the development of tacit and explicit knowledge as well as improving performance by allowing expert employees to work when they are best able to, or prefer to.

A more conventional segmented labour market approach might consider this result either an aberration or relatively unimportant. The crucial factor differentiating our approach is that we have demonstrated that there is a significant correlation between people who derive greater temporal control over their work and the use of temporary employment agencies. Recent figures released by the UK's Department of Employment and published in the Central Statistical Office Report show how over 6 million people in Britain's labour force currently work part-time; of these, many are career minded professionals. Our findings, together with this official trend data, suggest that temporal control and temporary agency employment cannot easily be relegated to a residual category as it has tended to be in the past.

Our evidence supports the idea that there is a difference in working conditions between agency and large firm employment: an issue which is sometimes overlooked by organizational behaviour analysts who tend to concentrate upon the relative number of people either working in large firms or employed through temporary agencies.

Data reported in the second row of table 8.2 (mobility) show that there is a significant difference in employees' perceptions about whether their jobs provide opportunities for advancement. Large firm employees perceive that they have significantly greater opportunities for career advancement than do their counterparts using temporary employment agencies. This supports traditional theories about the flexible firm which argue that the absence of conventional promotion opportunities and traditional increases in work-related responsibilities characteristic of temporary agency work makes professional employees favour working in large firms where such things are available. Our survey did not probe the perceived advantages of lateral, as opposed to vertical, mobility among London accountants. This may be an important feature and will be an issue in further work.

Preferences of agency versus large firm employees

For our work, the availability of different compensation packages between temporary agencies and large firms is a necessary condition to explain a punctuated break. Thus, the employee must be offered something at the temporary agency that s/he does not receive in the large firm. However, we would like also to show that the respective employees actually prefer these compensation packages. Measuring preferences is notoriously difficult since questions of cognitive dissonance arise, as do temporal problems, such as employee preferences might be specific to one point in time. This raises questions of interpretation and validity. Aware of these difficulties, we asked employees in both firms for their opinions about which parts of their extended compensation package were most important to them (which they valued the most). Results reported in table 8.3 suggest that there is a significant difference between the two groups.

Table 8.3. *Preferences for working conditions as predictors of temporary agency employment*

Statistically significant variables	Coefficient B	Wald statistic	R	exp(B)
I value control over . . .				
Which weeks of the year I work	1.0559*	9.8736	0.1817	2.8745
Choosing who I work with	−1.0076*	5.8295	−0.1268	0.3651
The location that I work from	−0.4550	0.4890	0.0000	0.6345
The types of tasks that I perform	0.1611	0.2494	0.0000	1.1748
The amount of work I must complete	0.8958	1.8059	0.0000	2.4492
The setting of deadlines	0.1771	0.1425	0.0000	1.1938
Which hours of the day I work	−0.5251	1.8102	0.0000	0.5915
Which days of the week I work	−0.1427	0.0458	0.0000	0.8670
The total number of hours I work in a week	0.5931	2.2727	0.0336	1.8097

* Significant at <0.05
$n = 223$

These results, when combined with earlier ones on what agencies provide for their employees, suggest that discretion over temporal aspects of work is provided for and preferred by agency employees.[5] This is an important aspect about agency or at-will contract employment, highlighted in our theoretical discussions in chapter 5, and suggests that agency work can provide an abrupt break from traditional organizations for some employees and provide them with enhanced temporal control. Interestingly, there is not a greater preference for control over working-time in all of the time units.[6]

These results suggest that temporal aspects about agency employment distinguish agency employees from large firm employees when comparing job characteristics: it is neither pay nor job security. Mobility too helps in distinguishing jobs. We can even be more specific, in that it is which weeks of the year are worked. Even though all forms of temporal control are greater for the agency employee, it appears that this one unit is most important.

When we combine control and having control over which weeks of the year are worked (in statistics this is called the interactive term), we get similar results (see table 8.4). Again, this suggests that agency employment is providing temporal control for its employees. This is the situation needed to induce a punctuated break from a traditional organization.

Table 8.4. *Interactive terms as predictors of temporary agency employment*

Independent variables	Coefficient B	Wald Statistic	R	Chi-square improvement
Weeks	1.9928*	22.8891	0.2960	26.214*
Hours	2.0557*	11.1597	0.1960	11.562*

* Significant at < .05
n = 223

Temporary agency work as a punctuated break

It is always difficult to generalize from a case study. However, we specifically chose to analyse accountancy firms because we thought it was reasonable to suggest that situations pertaining to them with regard to work and working conditions might be applicable to other professional firms which employ expert employees. Although our evidence suggests an environment for a punctuated break, it does not show that agency work actually increases productivity. An understanding of productivity increases would require a longitudinal study. The fruits of working in several firms over time is difficult to gauge from a sample taken at one specific time. However, our results suggest that further work in this area, especially longitudinal and embracing a number of firms, might be a logical next step.

Further, it is important to note that 65 per cent of the temporary agency employees in our study were female, as opposed to only 40 per cent of the large firm employees. This reflects one of the traditionally assumed aspects about temporary agency employment, that it is performed predominantly by women. The feminization of the workforce generally, and especially the vast increases in female participation and education in the professional knowledge-based occupations, supports our argument for a punctuated break. As women enter the expert employee labour market in increasing numbers (see chapter 1), there will be an increase in forms of work that provide temporal control and discretion over working conditions like temporary agencies. This is not because they are marginalized, but because this type of work provides them with the flexibility they desire and the possibility for growth. Perhaps it is a response by women to circumvent some of the traditional barriers and discriminating attitudes often assumed to reside in large traditional organizations which will accelerate the punctuated break. It is often assumed that women are forced to work through temporary agencies, but the contrary may be increasingly true. Women could be leading the break away from traditional careers in conventional firms because these firms do not provide the desired compensation packages.

Thus, the temporary agency we studied shows signs of a punctuated break. The agency facilitates a series of at-will contracts over time which are continuously renegotiated. The agency further provides a network and temporal freedoms that the agency expert employee demands. The characteristics of the temporary agency we have studied are congruent with our theories for a punctuated break towards an agency at-will contract labour market. We did not study all of those aspects about the break but focused on just one that we felt was seminal to that particular labour market (temporal control). For other elements which suggest a clearer punctuated break we look at another example of agency work, the US Hollywood film production industry. Here we investigate the lure of the freedoms to explore areas of tacit knowledge. The lures which engender breaks from the traditional Hollywood film studio to agencies.

CHAPTER NINE

The Hollywood agency system

I rebel against any force that threatens to overwhelm me as an individual.

Robert Redford, Hollywod star, from *Films Illustrated*, July 1976

The United States film industry displays many of the attributes characteristic of the experts who break employment ties with traditional organizations in favour of an association with a network of agencies which offer a form of economic security and greater discretion over the nature and timing of work. Notwithstanding these similarities, the Hollywood agency system which, among other things, co-ordinates and develops the lives and careers of experts like leading actors, differs from AT&T's in-house agency, Resource Link, which provides alternative employment for underutilized company employees, and the London based temporary agency for accountants, whose development appears to have accelerated as a result of pressure from accountants who wish to have greater control over the timing of their work.

In this chapter we argue that the recent organizational changes experienced by the US film industry has been influenced by Hollywood experts – stars – parting company with the large film production companies in order to obtain greater control over their work and personal lives. This abrupt break results in individuals entering into at-will employment contracts and, in time, a sophisticated agency system. Hollywood's experts severing their employment ties with the major studios and the rise of a network of agencies has shifted some power away from the major studios to an élite group of actors, directors and technicians, and their agents.

This, however, is not the conventional explanation described by Storper (1989) – see chapter 2 above – when he used the United States film industry to illustrate a gradual transformation of an industry from traditional hierarchy to flexible specializations. His explanation of change drew heavily on Atkinson's (1986) and Piore and Sable's (1984) core–periphery model of organizational change. This suggests that large, 'core', firms cushion themselves from market fluctuations by sub-contracting work to a number of independent 'periphery' firms with significantly inferior pay and working conditions. Encouraging competition among periphery firms assists core firms to lower prices and production costs, increase productive diversity and maintain relatively generous pay and working conditions at the core. This is a variation of demand management, where specific demands at the core are met by the judicious management of the periphery. Storper (1989) invokes this to suggest that the large Hollywood production companies have encouraged and exploited smaller independent companies at the periphery to provide a cushion from market fluctuations so that relatively smooth transformation of their core business can take place.

Aksoy and Robins (1992) take a different view of the importance of small peripheral film production companies in organizational change. Contrary to Storper, Aksoy and Robins argue that there has always been independent film producers in Hollywood and their impact is relatively unimportant. Hollywood in the 1990s is an 'extension of vertical integration into the new media markets, the deepening of the power of a handful of Hollywood firms across a whole set of new image markets, and the expansion of the new image business on a global scale' (Aksoy and Robins (1992), p. 16). In this extended scenario they argue that Storper and Christopherson (1987) underestimate the nexus of power located in film distributors.

Although reaching distinct conclusions, both explanations neglect the influence Hollywood's experts might have on the changes taking place in the US film industry. According to both theses, the change in organizational structure of Hollywood's production companies oblige actors, directors and technicians to change their work patterns to fit the new order. In contrast, we suggest that the Hollywood film industry, similar to other knowledge-dense businesses, relies on experts to create wealth and therefore is susceptible to the supply of this expertise and therefore cannot be fully understood by only demand management explanations. Indeed, we suggest that the sudden departure of a critical mass of individuals who are key to a knowledge industry and difficult to replace in the short to medium term, can have a dramatic effect on organizations. Hollywood and the US film industry is just such a case.

Hollywood as a demand-driven phenomenon

In the 1920s and 1930s, during Hollywood's Golden Era, a relatively small number of production companies such as Paramount, Universal, RKO, and Warner Brothers, controlled the entire American film industry. These corporations (studios) also owned the motion picture theatres which gave them a virtual monopoly on what audiences could view. During this period most large businesses were controlled by powerful leaders and the large Hollywood studios were no exception. The people who controlled the studios became known as 'moguls' and they made motion pictures in a way similar to how Henry Ford made cars. Essentially films were produced in Hollywood like cars were in Detroit: on an assembly line (Staiger, 1980). The final product was compartmentalized into discrete elements; each of these were associated with a specific task to which people were organized. Once completed, the discrete elements were assembled and distributed through a network of theatres owned by the production companies. Speed and quantity of production were important aspects of this process, and everyone involved was an employee of a large film production company.

At this time motion picture technology was in its infancy but it benefited significantly from its relative newness and the fact that it was the only visual media available to a mass audience. The industry also enjoyed advantages emanating from the palatial nature and comfort of their theatres which offered people momentary escapes from the misery of recession and later from the aftermath of war. It is not difficult, therefore, to see how motion pictures attracted huge audiences in the United States and Britain. The film industry took advantage of developments in sound and colour processing but was unable to sustain itself when challenged by the development and spread of television (see figure 9.1).

Indeed, after the Second World War a combination of television, convenience foods and economic boom created an environment for a vast home entertainment industry to grow and challenge the monopoly of Hollywood. This competitive shock was compounded by the fact that at the same time the large film production companies lost their hold on distribution by allowing independent producers to

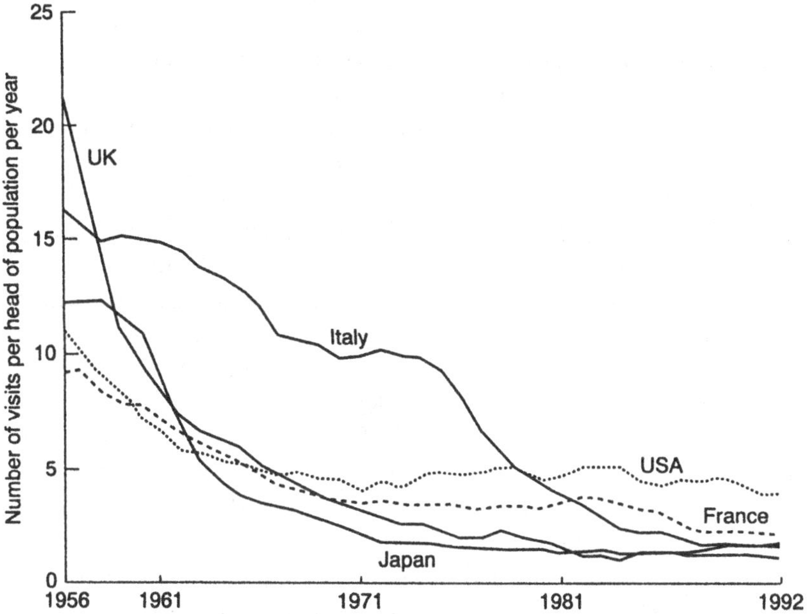

Figure 9.1 Cinema attendance in selected countries. From Centre National de la Cinematographie.

distribute their own products. No longer would efficient mass production techniques, a generic star and an original story attract the audiences necessary to sustain the industry. Hollywood organizations would have to change to survive.[1]

This is the juncture where Storper and Christopherson (1987) and Aksoy and Robins (1992) begin their respective arguments about the US film industry. According to Storper and Christopherson, the competitive shock we have described above resulted in the demise of the vertically integrated Hollywood corporation and the rise of flexible specialization within the industry. By contrast, Aksoy and Robins (1992) suggest that the impact of the competitive shocks have been exaggerated and the Hollywood moguls still control media production and all the important distribution networks. It is not important for us here to adjudicate between the relative merits of the opposing conclusions. More important from our perspective is to underline the fact that both arguments are variations of demand management and both neglect to consider the potential impact of supply factors such as the impact of the experts.

While not denying the influence of competition on traditional

Hollywood organizations and the fact that their scale and scope impact also on the change process, we argue that the Hollywood film industry and its incumbent organizations are influenced by the decisions of experts comprised of leading actors, directors and technicians. The decision which appeared to have the most significant impact on traditional Hollywood organizations was for leading actors, directors and technicians, holders of Hollywood's expertise, to abruptly break their employment ties with the large studios and enter into serial at-will employment contracts with a number of organizations. These breaks tended to coincide with the entrenchment in the US film industry which was principally triggered by the competitive challenge from television. The early initial breaks of these individuals with the large Hollywood studios, and their freedom to engage in at-will contracts with a variety of film producers, can be reasonably understood as an important first step in the supply-side influence on the Hollywood motion picture industry.

In time, individuals who had severed their employment ties with the studios turned to agents whose *raison d'être* was to vigorously represent their specific and varied interests. In this new environment, agents leveraged the talent, branding appeal and strategic importance of individual actors, directors and technicians. Employment negotiations with a number of production companies broadened to include conditions of work, structure of remuneration and the nature and choice of project. This was in stark contrast to Hollywood's Golden Era, when actors, directors and technicians were 'owned' by large studios who controlled much of their personal lives, paid them a salary and obliged them to make a number of films each year. After breaking with studios, individuals, through their agents, gained control over their crucial decisions which had previously been the preserve of the Hollywood moguls. In a sense, power had shifted away from the traditional production companies to Hollywood's experts.

Increased competition significantly enhanced the public's exposure to a variety of visual media and, over time, audiences became more discerning. This dented the traditional Hollywood star system which was sometimes more the result of successful advertising techniques than acting ability. Studios, too, retreated from the broad star system as they responded to competition by cost cutting and differentiating their products which called for more specialized inputs and family entertainment: Universal with horror films and Paramount with spectaculars, for example. This, in turn, increased the pressure on actors, directors and technicians to develop specific aspects of their skills and tacit knowledge.

Hollywood stars and punctuated breaks

On 12 June 1969 in Manhattan's Plaza Hotel, Paul Newman, Barbra Streisand and Sidney Poitier announced that they were starting their own production company: First Artists. Barbra Streisand stressed how necessary it was for her to be free to play the roles and to sing the songs she wanted and added: 'I know that my new associates have the same desire for artistic individuality and total commitment. [First Artist] will fill that need' (*Film and Television Daily*, 12 June 1969).[2]

The artists' views were stressed by Pat Kelley, President of First Artists, who said that the company was set up to create 'a climate in which these people (leading actors) can create and manufacture those pictures they might never have been able to make under more conventional circumstances . . . First Artists allows actors control to select working conditions which best suit them.' This was soon to be borne out when Steve McQueen, who joined the company, was able to choose the director and producer for his film *The Getaway* (*Hollywood Reporter*, 12 September 1972).

This break with custom and practice is a manifestation of our punctuated break thesis. First Artists constitutes a concerted effort by leading actors to break with tradition and significantly increase their control and influence over their work. At about the same time, other leading actors broke away from the studio production to form their own independent production companies (Albert (1996)). Clint Eastwood started Malpaso Productions and other independent companies were started by Robert Redford, Burt Reynolds, Dolly Parton, Jodie Foster, Robert DeNiro and Goldie Hawn. The companies had mixed results, but together they represent an important institutional challenge to the traditional Hollywood production companies. Over the 1970s, First Artists made over twenty films. An early success of an independent production company was Eastwood's *Every Which Way but Loose*, which cost a reported $3.5 million to make, but grossed $87 million in sales revenues. Malpaso products were also artistic successes: *Unforgiven*, for example, received seven Oscars. Notwithstanding this, Eastwood used Malpaso to produce films which satisfied his own individual interests rather than specifically for financial and artistic success.

Similarly, Robert Redford used his production company, Wildwood Enterprises, to pursue his own interests. In the 1970s he took advantage of the procrastinations of the large Hollywood studios and purchased the film rights of the book *Ordinary People* which he made into a financially and artistically successful film. Redford also managed to purchase the rights to *A River Runs Through It* when the traditional studios failed to do so. Further, similar to Eastwood, Robert Redford and his company produced films which reflected his personal concerns and interests concerning environmental issues.

The motivation for Goldie Hawn to break with the major production companies was her concern that they did not produce enough films for leading female actresses. She perceived this as a major obstacle to her career and set up her own company to provide her with more leading role opportunities. Although these small independent companies use finance and technical staff from the large studios, they represent a significant break with the Hollywood tradition. They do not have the same hierarchical structures of the larger production companies and they also provide individuals significantly more choice and greater control over the content and nature of their work.

The impetus for the growth and increasing importance of relatively small independent production companies can best be explained by a number of expert individuals who demand greater control over their work and personal lives. This, coupled with the reluctance of the large Hollywood studios to change, provide the conditions for abrupt employment breaks. Together these breaks accelerate the growth and development of agencies which, over time, gain significant power and control over the US film industry.

At the moment, the influence of agents is significantly associated with leading actors. An agency's strength is, in large part, derived from its on-going ability to please its clients. Without bankable clients an agency's influence is seriously diminished. Increasingly, Hollywood agents include a number of specialists concerned with such things as finance, public relations and legal issues etc. These different agents tend to work in concert to promote specific clients.

Consider a brief stereotypical example in which an agent represents a leading, but ageing actor. The preference of film audiences for relatively young actors sometimes makes it difficult for Hollywood agents to secure appropriate work for older clients, despite their distinguished acting careers. Let us suppose an agent finds an appropriate script for such a client. The actor and the script alone might be insufficient to secure the all-important financial backing. With this in mind, the agent might reasonably solicit the interests of a leading younger actor and a high profile director from other agents before attempting to secure some initial finance. With the support of two contrasting stars, a well-known director and some seed-corn financing, the agents, acting in concert, are better poised to attract further funds and a distributor. Generally, such *ad hoc* teams only exist for the duration of specific projects, and each agent involved would negotiate contracts with specific obligations, rights and rewards for their clients.

It is reasonable to assume that within the bureaucratic structures of a traditional Hollywood studio the scale and scope of such deal-making would be more difficult, since each studio would be obliged to use the expertise of it own in-house employees. Further, it also seems reasonable to assume that under the conditions prevailing in the traditional large film production companies, older actors, regardless of their skills and tacit knowledge, might find it more difficult to find work than under an agency system.

Indeed, the agency system does more than respond to demands for employment. Agencies, as in our stereotypical example, are proactive and can engage in innovative activity to foster new work and to develop new career possibilities. This potential is partly derived from the relationships between the different interest groups. For example, agents and clients are mutually supportive. It is in the interests of agents to represent the preferences of their clients and to provide them with counselling and guidance. Failure to provide this might lead to an agent losing a prized client. According to Clara Hacken, an agent who represents Annabella Sciorra, the star of Spike Lee's critically acclaimed film *Jungle Fever*, an agent's job, 'is to help her client put together a diverse body of work . . . we do not want people to think of her only for dramas' (*The Hollywood Reporter*, Starmaker special report 'Star Power', 1992).

Hollywood actors, directors and technicians are attracted to agents because of their networks and their ability to develop projects from scratch. Indeed, some projects are specifically started to satisfy the needs of valued clients. Thus, agents can create environments conducive to individual growth. With regard to the film industry, this does not always mean securing the largest role in lucrative film projects. Indeed, many actors, directors and technicians, at certain junctures in their careers, have an eye to the long-term and prefer roles which potentially bring them critical acclaim. Agencies, rather than large bureaucratic organizations, are better placed to achieve this. The facility to develop careers, provide income and offer significant freedom of choice attracts experts to agencies. Thus, a virtuous circle is established which helps perpetuate and develop the agency system in Hollywood.

Bolstering the rise in the importance of agencies are regulatory and technological changes. Regulatory changes allowed television networks to own their own television studios and programmes and encouraged competition between telephone and cable companies. The legal changes reflected developments in technology where the visual, data and audio signals were merging. This brought together the telephone, entertainment and computer industries into one huge new communications industry.

At the confluence of these industries are agents who act for different interest groups. One of the most successful is the Creative Artists Agency (CAA), run by Michael Ovitz, which represents some 1,200 leading Hollywood actors and has been a catalyst for many of the largest deals in the US film industry. CAA was started in 1975 by Ovitz, four partners and $100,000 raised by a second mortgage. It distinguished itself by offering a one-stop-shop, from script to finance which was made possible by Ovitz's networks of the business advisers, lawyers and studio executives representing leading actors. Thus, CAA 'shifted the balance of power in Hollywood from the studios back to the talent, packaged and nurtured and represented by Michael Ovitz' (*Guardian*, 14 June 1995).

It is reported that in 1995 Edgar Bronfman jr., owner of Seagram, a drinks conglomerate, had offered Ovitz $250 million and an annual salary of $35 million to run one of the worlds largest film production companies, MCA-Universal. Bronfman's offer came after he secured an 80 per cent state in the studio for $5.7 billion. Earlier, Seagram had sold its interest in DuPont because they strongly disagreed with the strategy of Conoco, a subsidiary oil company of DuPont, to join forces with Iran's national Oil Corporation to revive and modernize Iran's devastated offshore wells. At about the same time, Matsushita, a Japanese electronics corporation, was looking to divest itself of its stake in the Hollywod studio. In 1990 Matsushita had invested $6.5 billion in MCA when the yen was strong and there appeared a good opportunity to unite their electronics hardware with the studio's software. The weak yen, relative to the US dollar, had cost the Japanese dearly and they were looking to sell. Bronfman, having divested his interests in DuPont, bought MCA-Universal and asked Ovitz, who had previously brokered the MCA-Matsushita deal for $6.5 billion, to run the studio. Michael Ovitz surprised the industry by turning it down.

The reason Ovitz refused is suggested by Congressman Sonny Bono, who runs the Republican task force on the entertainment industry: 'If you're a big player like Michael [Ovitz], do you do the conventional old thing and run a traditional studio and work for someone else? Or do you take a big chance to develop a whole new industry?' (*Guardian* 14 June 1995). This view was supported by Michael Ovitz himself, who saw the choice as 'pretty simple'. 'On the one hand was the Seagram corporation (which owns MCA-Universal), run by a nice 40–year-old guy called Edgar Bronfman with eight billion bucks in his pocket . . . . On the other is Bill Gates, with maybe 20 billion bucks in his pocket and three of the biggest communications companies in America (Atlantic Bell, Nynex of New York, and Pacific Telesis) who are going to spend 20 billion bucks putting fibre optics in home telephone lines so they can pump all the movies in the world straight into 50 million homes' (*Guardian*, 14 June 1995).

By the year 2000, Atlantic Bell, Nynex and Pacific Telesis will spend some $16 billion to facilitate 500 channels, interactive capabilities and telephones for domestic computer users. This, according to Ovitz, is an important staging post for a huge new communications industry. Michael Ovitz, by refusing MCA-Universal's offer, has positioned his agency CAA to play a leading role in this new industry. The rise and the growing influence of agents tends to be underemphasized by the traditional demand led analysis of the US film industry.

Agency, at-will contracts and demand concepts

With regard to the Hollywood film industry, two fundamental sets of questions need addressing: Who or what is driving the changes in the industry? What are the consequences of such changes? In addressing these questions a consideration of the supply of expertise to the industry is instructive.

The demise of the powerful Hollywood Production studios is associated with: (i) the reaction of production costs in the face of increased competition from other visual media (Storper, 1989); (ii) the large production companies tightening their control over distribution (Aksoy and Robins (1992)); and (iii) the increased power and influence of experts and their propensity to use at-will employment contracts rather than to choose a career with one of the major Hollywood studios.

Until now, explanations (i) and (ii) have tended to overshadow alternative explanations which emphasize the supply of expertise. For example, Aksoy and Robins contend that the power of distribution remains in the hands of the major Hollywood studios. At first-glance this might appear to be the case. Indeed, most of the popular mass audience films are usually produced or distributed by one of the Hollywood studios: Warner, Goldwyn Mayer, Disney, etc. However, on a closer examination it is not altogether clear whether the entire power of distribution is with these companies or, indeed, shared with particular leading actors and directors.

For example, where films are distributed often has an important connection with leading actors. Some actors have specific appeal in certain countries. For example, Dépardeu in France and Brannagh in the United Kingdom. Other actors have had more universal appeal, like Sylvestor Stalone world-wide (*American Film*, June 1989). Thus, in some indirect way, the power of distribution lies with specific actors. In a more direct way, the failure of certain actors to join specific production projects might either jeopardize them altogether or affect the extent of their distribution.

Further, according to Aksoy and Robins, a film's success depends on how well senior managers from the production companies have, 'anticipated, nurtured and channelled' the cultural and aesthetic preferences of consumers. They suggest that this is achieved by controlling distribution which allows them to take risks. This argument underemphasizes the fact that specific distributors will only become involved in a project, providing specific actors are associated with it. Even then, the magnitude of their involvement is proportional to the perceived earning's potential of specific actors. Indeed, Mark Johnson, producer of *Good Morning Vietnam* which starred Robin Williams, says that 'Katzenberg [Chairman, Walt Disney Studios] is famous for putting figures on films. He'll say it makes sense at $13 million but not at $15 million. If *Good Morning Chicago* [the proposed sequel to *Good Morning Vietnam*] gets made with Robin Williams, it can arithmetically be worked out to do $12 million to $13 million in its opening weekend – whether it is a good movie or not' (Natalie

(1989)). Thus, the earning capacity of specific films is associated with the involvement of particular actors.

We suggest that the changes in the Hollywood film industry are partially the result of the environment of experts (actors, directors and technical film staff, all knowledge-based and skilled employees) and the rise of agencies which nurture and develop the interests of experts. These factors, together with changing technology, have created a new terrain or network which has the capacity to create and extend production projects. Thus, we suggest that there has been a shift of power away from the traditional large Hollywood production studios to specific experts and their agents. Content, production and decisions about which motion pictures are made often resides in the hands of experts and their agents. Their power began with their abrupt breaks with the major studios.

CHAPTER TEN

The Internet as an agent

The foremost bird in a v-shaped flock is the one in charge . . . [This is] not so. The orderly formation is the result of a highly responsive collection of processors behaving individually and following simple harmonious rules without a conductor.

Nicholas Negroponte, *Being Digital*

Introduction

In the Hollywood film industry agents have become increasingly powerful, especially in recent years. This is because of their knowledge, networks and abilities to combine expertise. Evidence discussed in previous chapters suggests that similar potential exists for agents to grow in other spheres and industries. In the past, agencies have tended to operate most effectively in either concentrated geographic areas, such as Hollywood or London, or when dealing with a relatively small number of individuals who share similar expertise such as sport, music or management. More recently, however, advances in technology, especially the combination of telecommunications and computing, has brought a new powerful dimension to bear on agencies and their potential.

In the mid-1980s it was generally thought that the combination of electronic systems with modern computers would promote the control of more complex systems, in a more complex way, from a smaller number of centres.[1] This forecast of the concentration of power failed to foresee the influence of personal computers and the development of the Internet which began life in 1969 as a Pentagon-sponsored initiative called the Advanced Research Projects Agency. This was a relatively loose confederation of interconnected computer networks which used leased telephone lines to enable people working on military contracts throughout the US to share large data sets and expensive computers. In essence, the system split data into small packets and transported these over different telephone lines to their destination where, on arrival, they are re-assembled. This made the network safe and robust. It was safe since the means of transporting the data made it difficult to eavesdrop on messages. It was robust since it had no centre or headquarters, and therefore could withstand large-scale destruction, even a nuclear attack. Further, if specific routes were destroyed, data would simply travel along routes which were intact.

In the early 1980s the Internet was relatively small, comprising about 500 host computers which were largely military. Over the 1980s the Internet was colonized by universities and research laboratories, and by 1987 it comprised some 28,000 host computers. At this time, although the Internet provided a flexible and global network it was difficult to use and tended to be 'inhibited' by computer technologies. Thus, over the 1980s access to the Internet remained relatively restricted.

During the late 1980s changes in the business world were taking place which later would effect the Internet. Many businesses had exchanged their mainframe computers for personal computers (PCs) and began to create local area computer networks to enable PCs to share data, printing and e-mail. However, because these local area networks were not standardized, it was difficult for businesses to develop their computer networks. At the end of the 1980s, when the US government relaxed its hold on the Internet, businesses seized the opportunity to link up with it in order to create wider and international computer networks. This was helped also by some Internet users writing software to make the Internet more user-friendly. This was freely available from the Internet. In 1994 companies overtook universities as the dominant users of the Internet.

A third influence on the Internet was the plummeting prices of personal computers and the consequent rapid expansion of the home computer market. Modems provided a simple and inexpensive means for home PCs to be connected to commercial 'on-line' services and bulletin boards. In the UK, Internet services are offered to individuals for as little as £10 per month. This provides users access to a range of software, international connections and a number of other services. This easily accessible format is poised to become a catalyst for an explosion in the growth of individual users of the Internet. This suggests an even greater network of information, ideas and people which can be leveraged by experts geographically dispersed around the world.

The Internet has no centre. It has no substance and uses established telephone lines which means that the large telephone companies carry most of the costs. It is similar to a spider's web with many ways of getting from one point to another and operates like a virtual network running in parallel with the physical networks of the telephone companies. Since 1988, the Internet has doubled in size and now reaches an estimated five million 'host' computers, each of which may connect several individual users. Internet analysts put the number of users at about 35 million. In mid-1993, advances in software and a way of connecting documents allowed the Internet to become a multi-media forum using pictures, sound, video and data. Thus, the Internet has been transformed from a way of sending data and e-mail to a place to visit which is full of people and ideas. Indeed, in the early 1990s the Internet became a new medium based on publishing and broadcasting, with the added advantage of interactivity. In 1995, remaining curbs on commercial use of the Internet were lifted; the US National Science Foundation began to phase out the last direct federal subsidy of the network: the Internet has come of age.

> The Internet already offers . . . most of the services and technologies that cable and telephone companies are still a decade from delivering. You can make a telephone call on the Internet; watch a video; listen to an audio broadcast, or broadcast yourself; shop; learn; and, of course, communicate. Every day, the Internet delivers more of the features of the fabled super-highway. It may be doing these things clumsily, unreliably and slowly, but it is doing them now.' *The Economist* (1995)'The Internet Survey', p. 4

It is our contention that the Internet has a significant potential to act as an agent or to provide phenomenal advantages of scale and scope to traditional agencies. Personal computers and software developments have put extraordinary communications power in the hands of individuals who choose to use it. Encoded within the Internet is an agency format with the potential of encouraging people to break abruptly with their traditional employment and develop a uniquely flexible work pattern.

The Internet as a super-agent

Agencies tend to be prescribed systems from which individuals find employment. They may free individuals from some time restrictions common with the most traditional organizations. Conversely, agencies might, in some forms, also constrain employment practices. For example, an agency operating within a well-defined arena such as AT&T, the London accountancy market or Hollywood, generally has information which is both abundant and limited. Abundant in that data are often rich in particular areas of opportunity, but limited in that such data are usually restricted to a specific sector or area. Thus, agencies, although more liberal than their hierarchical predecessors, still have constraints.

Notwithstanding this, Hollywood agents exert significant power and influence across a number of industries, and thereby provide a significantly greater range of opportunities for their clients. Consequently, leading actors can be seen endorsing particular brands of merchandise and providing voice-overs for acustaguide tours for art exhibitions. We contend that the Internet can work in similar ways as an agent but with the added advantages of increased scale and scope. A distinction of the Internet is that it is not constrained by a cognitive capacity in a similar way that a traditional agent is. Thus, the Internet can reasonably be viewed as a super-agent which has a vast network of individuals throughout the world with an immense range of interests and know-how. The millions of Internet users determine its range of interests and know-how. They also determine the Internet's role. There are no pre-described areas of interest; no limits on working relationships, no geographical boundaries, and no red-tape. The Internet is an arena which can provide individuals with boundless freedom and absolute discretion.

Information versus communication

Underlying the historical developments of the Internet is an important division between information and communication. Let us consider briefly both in turn.

Information storage and retrieval is a service which the Internet performs well and it works similarly to a large filing cabinet. The information characteristics of the Internet provide the basis for emerging commercial activity. For example, Mecklermedia, a US software company based in Westport, Connecticutt, was one of the first to explore the commercial potential of the Internet. It developed software called MecklerWeb, a menu-driven description of various services which individuals can access and purchase. For example, MecklerWeb provides information about the law which it obtains predominantly from Cornell University's Legal Information Institute, and includes information on specific legal services and their process offered by US law firms. Thus, MecklerWeb provides individuals with an opportunity of comparison shopping. Such systems, which can be easily accessed by millions of people, will create stresses and strains on traditional firms and organizations. At the very least it seems reasonable to assume that some traditional methods of advertizing and marketing services will be transformed by the Internet. Already large consumer goods companies, such as Sony, Virgin Records and Reebok are now using the Internet to market their products, as they complement advertisements on information services.

Publishers view the on-line world both as an opportunity and a threat. It is an opportunity because on-line publishing has no distribution costs which some entrepreneurs are already taking advantage of. One entrepreneur taking advantage of this is Laura Filmore whose online book shop operates from Rockport, Massachusettes. For a fee, an individual linked to the Internet can have sent electronically entire volumes or specific chapters. Filmore essentially uses the Internet as a consumer marketplace in cyberspace where there are no taxes and no red tape. The November 1995 Interactive Investor was launched in London. This uses the Internet to market retail financial services. Potential investors can find out detailed information about specific products and purchase them straight from the Internet. On a larger scale, MCI, an American long-distance telephone company, has created a virtual shopping mall called Marketplace MCI which is accessed via the Internet and sells a variety of unrelated items.

Thus the Internet as an information provider has the potential to transform established industries by providing relatively low cost easy market entry by new businesses in specific sectors. For these emerging companies, the Internet serves as a personal printing press, radio station and billboard all in one and reaches some 35 million people. Interestingly, although some large companies are beginning to use the Internet, it is the smaller, newer companies which have been more commercially successful. For example, Netscape Communications, started in 1994, commands the Internet software market.

At the moment estimates of the Internet market suggest that it is relatively small but its potential is enormous. In 1994 the Internet market was estimated to be about $100 million. Commercial users now dominate the Internet with more than 80,0000 companies worldwide connected. Between them there are some 1.4 million Internet hosts, each supported by a number of individual users. Analysts point to the existing \$53 billion catalogue and the £2.5 billion global shopping markets.

The other aspect of the Internet is that of communications. Rheingold (1995) describes the Internet's origins as a facilitator of computer mediated communications (CMC). This aspect of the Internet has greater importance for agents and agencies. According to Rheingold the Internet's communicational aspects have created virtual communities in which conversations, friendships and understandings take place: 'wherever I have travelled physically in recent years, I've found ready-made communities that I met on-line months before I travelled. Our mutual enthusiasm for virtual communities served as a bridge, time and time again, to people whose language and customs differ significantly from those I know well in California' (Rheingold (1995), p. 10). Earlier, Keiser (1985) suggested that computer users tend to capitalize on this aspect of the Internet. 'One of the surprising properties of computing is that it is a social activity. Where I work, the most frequently run computer network program is the one called "where" or "finger" that finds other people who are logged onto the computer network.' According to Keiser, CMC provides a means to 'break down hierarchical and departmental barriers, standard operating procedures and organizational norms'. This appears close to our suggestion of the Internet as having the capacity to be a flexible agency that averts some of the defence mechanisms inherent in organizations.

The dichotomy – between information and communication users of the Internet – provides a basis for a struggle for space on the Internet (cyberspace) and/or its regulation. Many original users who used the Internet as an efficient means of communication would like it to remain so. These people tend to be critical of its commercialization which uses the medium as a way to access and retrieve data and information at cost. This, say some users, tends to ignore the Internet potential as a sophisticated communications network.

However, perhaps the future is a combination of information and communication. Indeed, the importance of the current technological changes owes as much to the personal computers as it does the Internet. The former put computing power in the hands of individuals and the latter provided these individuals with something to do with their new found power.

Internet as an agent

People beginning to use the Internet quickly become familiar with electronic mail and Network News. The former allows users to send, receive and store messages, and the latter reports news under various headings. Together they provide the networking capacity and flow of information and ideas between experts regardless of geography. One small example of the benefits of this is a book entitled *The Whole Internet*. Its authors, Knoll and Loukides, met through the Internet, and wrote the book from their respective terminals. They used the Internet to gather information and electronic mail, share data and drafts of chapters.

Whereas electronic mail demands commitment to an on-going conversation between specific users, Network News is a looser conversation among a group of individuals who can drop in and out of the conversation at will. Users find groups via 'bulletin boards' from as wide-ranging areas as 'word processing software' and 'the poetry of Tom Waits'.

Electronic mail and Network News together function as an agent for Internet users. They can link vast numbers of people together in a way which no organization can, and they provide the means to communicate and gather information and ideas. Let us briefly illustrate the point. Suppose a person working in a New York Law firm wishes to further his/her interest in, say, the pollinating aspects of wild flowers specific to the Judean desert. S/he believes the best way to do this is to begin a discussion group with a number of like-minded individuals. It is possible, though unlikely, that he/she will find these within his/her firm or by advertizing in the *New York Times*. There is a greater chance of finding such people on the Internet. Indeed, starting a discussion with people interested in the wild flowers of the Judean desert might be simply achieved by logging-on to the Internet and posting a request. This might connect the New Yorker with individuals in Jerusalem. It might also be the case that one of these Israeli users has a need for a New York lawyer. Thus, connecting on one issue leads to a development in another and so on. This epitomizes the Internet as an agent. The Internet and its users thrive on diversity and the free flow of ideas and information. This tends to fuel innovation and provide a continuous stream of opportunities which do not always exist in traditional organizations.

Thus, the Internet works as an agent for experts in various ways. It brings together people regardless of geography and at low cost and it provides them with information and, increasingly, services. The nature and extent of this agency characteristic is, as yet, not altogether known. However, the acceleration of the development of technology suggests that the Internet's agency role will significantly expand in the not too distant future. Indeed, with the transmission of information increasingly digitalized, the distinction between telephony, television and computing is now blurred. Experts will soon have at their disposal, or at the click of a mouse, the visual and educational impact of television, the memory and brain of a computer and the two-or-more-way human interaction of a telephone. Further, the growth power and impact of the Internet as a form of agency will be enhanced by the increased capacity of the telephone and its mobility. In the next decade, telephone density in Asia will increase as countries like China and India become more important players in world trade and increase their wealth and wealth-creating capacities. Today the global population is almost 5.5 billion, and there are some 600 million telephones, the majority of which are in the rich countries. As telephony becomes cheaper and less developed countries become wealthier their consumption of telephony will increase and the Internet will grow even larger.

At the moment the advantage of the Internet requires time and familiarity with specific software. 'Cruising' or 'surfing' the Internet can be perceived as an end in itself. But 'cruising' can also be a means to an end: to provide an extra-agency service for Internet users. This, according to Nicholas Negroponte, head of MIT's Media Lab, is one of the major growth areas and is also potentially extremely lucrative. Already software agents exist that assist the user to navigate the Internet. However, the Internet still is an embarrassment of riches which can be daunting to an individual user or a company wishing to use it. It has an overwhelming abundance of data and an insatiable capacity to make a vast number of connections. Agents are forming to help people further filter and organize the reams of data available on the Internet. It seems reasonable to suggest that in the near future agencies emphasizing speed, relevance and quality of data will emerge to provide an extra filter for the business user of the Internet. Thus, its function as an agent will be significantly enhanced. Traditional organizations, especially those whose wealth creation relies on knowledge, will be obliged to engage such agencies.

CHAPTER ELEVEN

Labour market segments re-examined

And to live in agreement with a theory for any length of time is like what Americans call a common-law marriage; you and it are wedded by habit and repute. A man wedded to a system is less and less able to apprehend contradictory realities. He becomes like the dogs and pigs people in the South of France specialize to hunt truffles; he can at last discover his system at the merest hint of evidence, and all that does not countenance it ceases to interest him, ceases to exist for him; he thrusts past it heedlessly, scornfully.

H. G. Wells, *The World of William Clissold*, vol. 1

In certain instances experts have voluntarily and abruptly left their employment and used a series of at-will contracts to establish alternative employment. Sometimes this shift has resulted in enlarged networks, knowledge enhancement, increased discretion over work and greater job opportunities for the individual. In essence it constitutes new forms of work which are different from the segments of work described by labour market theorists. For this reason we need to re-evaluate some of the traditional labour market concepts.

Conventional labour market theorists tend to argue that people employed full-time for life in large corporations are 'advantaged' while people employed in atypical (part-time, temporary, etc.) employment who use agencies to secure work tend to be 'disadvantaged'. We question this and suggest that a life-time commitment to a company might not be so highly regarded by experts who voluntarily seek employment through a series of at-will contracts. People who choose this form of employment tend to assign greater weight to greater control over their work and personal development. Many large organizations, where security and length of employment have been the hallmarks, have either been unable or unwilling to provide this.

Abrupt breaks from traditional employment and the transition to an agency-driven labour market can be examined by using a segmented labour market approach. However, in order to do this we need to construct a 'new' segment characterized by experts and their desire for discretion, variety, enhanced networks and increased knowledge. Experts who inhabit this labour market segment tend to believe that their pursuit of these objectives through at-will contracts is more likely to bring them security, income and stability than the promise of long-term employment by a corporation.

Our objective is to emphasize the importance of personal attributes – such as tacit knowledge and personal preference – and the potential impact they can exert on labour markets. To ignore or under-emphasize personal elements may have been possible when work was predominantly a series of mechanical tasks, but it is difficult to do so in today's environment of accelerated technological change and rapidly changing product and labour markets.

Let us develop our thesis by starting with a description of traditional labour market theories since these have significantly influenced our understanding of labour markets.

The dynamics of Labour Market Segmentation theory

Labour Market Segmentation (LMS) theory was initially based on the belief that segmented labour markets are distinguished by a 'primary' and a 'secondary' market. The former exhibits all of those 'good' traits of employment, such as job security, high pay, mobility and interesting work, and the latter exhibits all of those 'bad' employment traits, such as job precariousness, low pay, repetitive and tedious work. Particular attention is paid to income and job security. Thus, segmentation was defined by the working conditions of a particular job or occupation. Ultimately, segmentation theorists believe in a compartmentalized labour market with barriers and obstacles between different compartments. Labour Market Segmentation theory has been described, most notably by Caine (1976), as a direct attack on neoclassical labour market theories which assume that market forces will efficiently distribute the workforce and, more importantly, that market forces will do so in such a way that if there were forms of segmentation, they would be abolished through competition. The theory contends that this has unsatisfactorily described the labour markets in North America and Europe.

As LMS theory developed, the definitions of the different segments varied according to size and basic working conditions. Although this imported into the theory a degree of complexity and sometimes confusion, it was valuable since it enabled the theory to adapt to a variety of labour market conditions. This allowed the theory to account for certain aspects of working conditions to become more significant while others became correspondingly less so. With this adaptability it may be appropriate periodically to reassert different labour market aspects which may be segmenting the labour market. One such aspect is the growing importance of experts within this labour market and for agency network systems which seem to be emerging to accommodate this.

Most LMS studies have attempted to determine whether segmentation exists at all. From this broader question, however, other studies have tackled questions pertaining to labour market segmentation specifically. These studies endeavour to resolve issues such as what to include in the primary segment and the secondary segments; whether there is a high or a low level of mobility between the two segments; whether the segments are characterized by gender or nationality, industry or occupation; the extent to which institutional arrangements like unions have been active in promoting or breaking down the barriers between segments; and whether social institutions such as discrimination play a part in segmentation.

To us, expert employment constitutes a new kind of labour market segment. This does not have all the same features or characteristics which have distinguished labour segments in the past. Thus, there may be some benefit in combining opposing labour segmentation theories and examining whether together they may be able to coexist with some neoclassical ideas. This becomes important when discussing new labour market segments, such as the expert network-driven agency employee who has often been relegated to the vague classification of a secondary level job form.

Historical depiction of labour market segments

Labour market segments, at the outset, were described by the relative size of the labour market they covered. These levels of classification are described in table 11.1. Level 1 represents some of the first theories of LMS, such as the Piore (1970) model. Here, labour segments are defined by the people which inhabit them. This is partly because the

Table 11.1. *Progressive Levels of Labour Market Segmentation*

Level 1	Divided by class, gender or nationality
Level 2	Divided by industry
Level 3	Divided by occupation
Level 4	Divided by mobility chains
Level 5	Firm internal division

theory was developed to explain the persistence of urban ghettos and poverty in the United States. It argued that the inferior characteristics of the secondary labour market relative to those of a core market explained by secondary market workers were unable to graduate to the primary market. This emphasizes traits which are developed by secondary employees because they are the most rational course to follow when living in secondary market circumstances. It was the pursuit of this 'rationale' which ensured that workers in the secondary labour market remained secondary citizens. Cain (1976) states that 'this model has the aspect of the "vicious circle" or the "self-fulfilling prophecy"'. This is the broadest of terms in segmentation theories in that it can encompass whole classes, nations, and groups of people.

Table 11.1 shows the five levels of Labour Market Segmentation theories. There is a general progression towards smaller units of analysis as one moves from level 1 to level 5. Much of LMS debate is trying to determine where the segmentation between primary and secondary segments occur.

From this broad segmentation theory we move to level 2. At this level, discussion takes place on an industry scale where certain industries are seen as either being primary industries, which provide the good jobs and secondary industries which provide the bad jobs. Oster (1979) found evidence from the US, using census coded industries, that reflect industry segmentation. Whereas level 1 yields only two segments, this second level of definition can give rise to tests over many industries. The divisions can be numerous.

Level 3 is a division of the primary and secondary segments by occupation. There is some evidence which suggests that this may be some of the best uses of LMS theory. Dickens and Lang (1985) employ a switching regression model to show that the division of workers between sectors is better served by occupational-based classification schemes than by industrial ones. McNabb (1987), in his study using general household survey data and estimating earning's functions, concludes that 'the findings . . . support a form of labour market segmentation based on occupation rather than one associated with industry specific characteristics' (p. 271). As convincing as this evidence is, we believe that no segmentation theory necessarily precludes any other. Thus, there may be some industries which use higher percentages of occupations that exhibit secondary segmentation characteristics.

In the fourth level we move to the theory postulated by Doeringer and Piore (1970) in which they see the primary market as being distinguished by the type of 'mobility chain' that an employee may be on. The different mobility chains constitute the differences between the primary and secondary segments. The primary segment has mobility chains which are akin to career ladders, whereas the secondary market is described as having mobility chains that lead nowhere. They are unstable, dead-end jobs. Stewart *et al.* (1980) examine this with regard to the clerical labour market where 'they point out the difference between a permanent clerical job and a clerical job that is a trainee slot for management' (Burchell and Rubery, 1990). The mobility chain theory can also be used to disaggregate the primary sector into sub-segments by the employee's relative position on the mobility chain. Still, though, the two tiers on the primary sector mobility chain should be recognized as being in the primary sector.

The fifth level of segmentation theory is Atkinson's (1986) model of the 'flexible firm'. Here the division of core and periphery segments are divided within the firm according to their relative flexible attributes. In Atkinson's terms, this model of labour markets 'explores the extent to which more flexible working practices had been introduced, to ascertain under what circumstances particular kinds of change might be found, to consider how permanent they might be and to look at their implications for employers, workers and job seekers' (Atkinson (1986), p. 5). The agency, home working, sub-contracted employees are relegated to the outer periphery of this model. They are considered to be part of the secondary labour market, primarily because they lack the job security that the employees in the core of the firm have.

Because Atkinson's model categorizes job forms within one particular firm, it takes a particular demand-side view of job segmentation and stresses organizational reasons for various job forms. We have suggested reasons why experts may not desire to work long-term for any one firm. Atkinson's model also closes doors to analysis of other organizational forms such as agencies which may develop from a punctuated break. This is typical of labour market segmentation theory which views firms (or outside influences) as the principal component and responsible for barriers which result in segmentation in the labour market. It is the plight of some employees to go through life trapped in the periphery (or lower status job) because they have been segmented out of the core labour force via demand-sided influences. We suggest that this conclusion is misleading since it negates a discussion of the advantages of working outside a traditional firm setting and does not fully appreciate that skilled individuals might prefer to do so. Traditional labour segmentation theory takes aspects of traditional organizations, such as security, mobility, steady pay and uses these to describe primary labour market segments. *A priori*, therefore, any employment outside the traditional organization will be considered as secondary or inferior.

We contend that Atkinson's model, as well as other demand-side Labour Market Segmentation models, may be appropriate when discussing the structure of the traditional firm, and how different job forms are utilized within a firm, but they are less appropriate when discussing specific characteristics of job forms and how they might provide for the preferences of a specific group of individuals. Why is this the case? The reasons are straightforward. The traditional labour market approach views employment from an institutional point of view which tends to relegate employee preferences to a 'less than important' status. A temporary job harvesting sugar cane on a Southern Florida plantation may exhibit the same characteristics as a temporary clerking job in a law firm in London when comparing attitudes of the *firms* (numerical flexibility). But the two jobs, although both temporary, will not necessarily exhibit the same characteristics when comparing attitudes of the *employees*. (In traditional Labour Market Segmentation theory the former is emphasized; in our approach it is the latter.)

Where are the barriers now?

The expert employee brings complications to this system of barriers constructed by the labour market segmentationists. According to Reich (1991) these barriers exist. Reich sees a division in the United States between symbolic analysts (experts) and service workers (for example, waiters and people who repair cars). Symbolic analysts have the means to send their children to the best schools, provide them with the best materials and introduce them to the right people that provide the institutionalized system which allows them to become the symbolic analysts of the future. Recognizing this, says Reich, is a necessary prerequisite for the United States to build a structured system which allows the underprivileged service workers to acquire the skills of the symbolic analysts. This system, according to Reich, will break the barriers of segmented labour markets. Thus, while recognizing the importance of the expert, Reich also accepts the basic tenets of traditional labour market segmentation theory.

Reich's discussion has parallels with Ryan's (1981) conceptualization of 'in-market and pre-market segmentation'. The latter is segmentation of capabilities which restrict occupational choice. These are the inherent capabilities of an individual. Thus, if an individual does not have the skills to be a doctor then s/he will not become a doctor. Only a few have the capabilities to play basketball for the American National Basketball Association. These pre-market skills divide the population into occupational and career segments and are, in many ways, an advantage to a nation because of their resulting diversity of occupations. 'In-market' segmentation, on the other hand, is the system of institutionalized barriers that excludes those with capabilities from entering occupations which they might be best suited for. Among these institutionalized barriers are the disadvantages of not growing up in the household of expert employees. Reich hypothesizes that symbolic analyst households are more capable of providing the environment to develop future symbolic analysts.

We can argue that our segment of knowledge-based experts have similar advantages, but we emphasize that an expert's advantage lies in his/her tacit and explicit knowledge and an ability to disseminate this to a wide range of people and networks. This implies a different type of divide to the one considered by traditional Labour Market Segmentation theorists. We emphasize the availability of and demand for discretion over work and this is predicated upon enhanced information and networks. Not all experts (symbolic analysts) will utilize such networks and not all symbolic analysts will rely on formal education and social architectures, but rather on innovation and spontaneous networks. This attribute or paradigm suggests another form of segmentation: one which is less concerned about occupations and specific knowledge (we believe these to be as varied as individuals), but one concerned with a segment that develops from a punctuated break from traditional organizations.

The advantages of discretion and development of tacit knowledge may not be confined to the children and siblings of experts. Knowledge is becoming more affordable and more accessible and being delivered in less conventional ways. This suggests that the lessons of flexibility, adaptation and innovation may be acquired by a much wider range of individuals rather that those with symbolic analysts as parents. If innovation becomes the most valuable labour market asset, children from families that change and are able to adapt to various situations will best be able to cope with the knowledge-based industries and their environment for flexibility and innovation (not necessarily families which provide a secure consistent household). However, they still need the basic educational certificates to enter the knowledge-based industries and professions. Thus, rather than arguing forcefully against labour market segmentation, we assert that the barriers as they are now defined may be less relevant in a world that values change and innovation.

Labour market segmentation is a valid theory on many occasions, but its relevance to structured organizations seems to be tied to the manufacturing industries which appear to have been uppermost in the people's minds who developed them. Therefore, utilizing its barriers and systems to the knowledge-based firm may be a weakness of an otherwise insightful discussion.

CHAPTER TWELVE

Agents and intellectual capital

. . . the comparison of different . . . points of view has one purpose – changing the reader's point of view.

Sergie Eisenstein, *The Short Fiction Scenario*

As opportunities[1] and technologies change, it is reasonable to assume that consumption and preferences will also change (see Becker (1976) and Marshall (1946)). We have described how changing opportunities and technologies encouraged experts to abruptly leave traditional organizations in pursuit of greater control over their lives and careers. Conditions external to organizations influence this break as much as the internal dynamics of an organization. As long as organizations have in-built defence mechanisms that resist change, there will exist a motive for empowered experts to break from traditional organizations.

This break is not a *gradual* transformation of the labour market since: (i) the results of such breaks are incompatible with traditional organizations and (ii) for the first time in history technology permits information to be delivered on a one-to-one basis and thereby dispenses with the need for a centrally located information based workplace. It is because of these fundamental differences and characteristics that a break is said to *punctuate* relative stasis.

We do not, however, suggest that all organizational structures will become obsolete or that one form of organizational system is necessarily better than another. We simply emphasize that an examination of the supply-side preferences of expert employees can seriously affect arguments that surround organizational structures. What appears as a demand-sided change may, in fact, be significantly influenced by individuals.

Our theory suggests a lineage from changing opportunities and technologies to a break towards at-will contracts, agency-led, expert labour market. This is predicated upon an increase in value and utility for experts in making such breaks. It also hints at an increase in knowledge-based productivity. In light of this, we suggest that demand-sided theories which are frequently used to describe flexibility and the new work environment might benefit from a re-evaluation.

Our evidence consists of various case studies and indicators of the expert employee regarding increased discretion at work. Experts working through internal company employment agencies experience an increased lateral mobility (AT&T). A more explicit break is revealed through the professional temporary agency system which provides temporal discretion for its expert employees (London temporary accountancy firm). However, the industry which appears best to have engendered an agency led at-will contract labour market is that of Hollywood. Indeed, the qualities of the Hollywood industry are relevant to the emerged and emerging knowledge-based work. Hollywood's history reveals a distinct pattern of employment practices which characterize knowledge-dense products such as films. Hollywood is a key example, since it has always traded in intellectual capital.

Intellectual capital represents an individual's accumulated knowledge and know-how and is the source of innovation and regeneration.[2] It is the key ingredient to the expert's own value. Conventional wisdom suggests that economic performance is best understood in terms of ownership, control and influence of capital markets, but the importance of intellectual capital in fields ranging from law, biotechnology and entertainment is strategically important for those industries. Despite the strategic importance of intellectual capital, accountants, analysts, markets and, indeed, managers, do not adequately value and measure its worth. One would expect competitive pressures to have encouraged the evolution of effective accounting and managerial systems. One significant problem in this regard is that financial accounting dominates the assessment of performance. This has led to the human – intellectual – contribution to performance being understated or overlooked.

At first an industry of mavericks, Hollywood lapsed into a period of highly industrialized studios characterized by strangleholds on distribution. However, even during this period it was the talented star who held so much potential power. An appreciation of this power prompted individuals to break with the traditional large studios and thereby laid the foundations for the growth of a labour market, primarily based on agents and at-will contracts. As other industries and experts rely more and more on specific intellectual capital for competitive advantage, so there is a potential for experts to follow the route of their Hollywood counterparts and break with their organizations and create distinct labour markets.

Knowledge exchanges

Commodities such as steel, chemicals and oil are the key components of many industries. Over time their relative importance has led to a complex system of market exchanges, such as the New York Stock Exchange. These exchanges facilitate the consistency of supply (consistent with demand) of these key industrial inputs. If, as we argue, intellectual capital will provide a major source of wealth for Western nations in the future, then it seems reasonable to suggest that a similar market exchange of its basic inputs would aid in efficient distribution of resources within the economy: a knowledge exchange.

Throughout history, exchanges have grown up in several strategic geographic areas. They often have their roots in a localized group of buyers and sellers who have geographically located near each other, like the buyers and sellers of cattle who arranged themselves in a courtyard. The slaughter houses on one side and the curing and cooking on the other, with the livestock in the middle. Or, as in London, a localized area that became the coffee houses that lined 'Change Alley' before 1773. Here specialists would frequent one coffee house over another to broker and exchange shares in their particular industry. For example, the specialists in maritime insurance frequented Edward Lloyd's coffee-house and the fire insurance men Casey's. Of course, their final maturation brought stock exchanges like the exchanges of New York, London and Tokyo. Even today, in these large stock exchanges, there is a reduction in transaction costs because of the specialization of brokerage firms in transmitting information on market conditions for the decisions of potential buyers and sellers. These exchanges now communicate automatically with locations world-wide which creates a continuous global interchange of stocks, commodities and futures shares. It is at these exchanges that an exchange of intellectual capital might first be located.

The stock markets as a knowledge exchange

In the New York, London and Tokyo stock markets, shares are bought and sold in such corporations as Sony, and Dow Chemicals. Each of these companies and industries rely heavily on intellectual capital and therefore their purchase can be viewed as a means of exchanging the ownership of the intellectual capital these companies possess. However, these exchanges, with all their brokers and Wall Street pundits, have problems in accurately valuing companies based on intellectual capital (see Albert and Bradley (1995)). Perhaps this is because these exchanges grew and matured since the seventeenth century (the century in which the Amsterdam stock market first opened and sold shares) to exchange paper (shares) backed by physical goods like corn, wheat and automobiles. It is because of these long roots into the exchange of physical goods that these exchanges have developed a unique set of rules and customs which govern their means of transaction. In short, perhaps they cannot cope with intellectual capital since it is not a tangible commodity to be exchanged, but a debt. And yet it may be more fundamental than this. Traditional exchanges fail to be successful at valuing intellectual capital because they are designed to perform a different task. Still, one could make a case for the stock exchange acting as a place to exchange intellectual capital and knowledge (although there is a foreseeable limit as to the value of knowledge on this exchange, i.e. the total value of assets sold on the Exchange).

The labour market as a knowledge exchange

In another type of exchange market – the labour market – the value and amount of knowledge and information that is bought and sold may be significant. It is, in a sense, invoking one of the central themes of intellectual capital and of this book: that experts hold significant capital in the form of knowledge and skills, i.e. intellectual capital. In the current labour market, a person's skills are becoming increasingly specialized, at least specialized to a particular expertise or profession (see the rises of professionalism since 1950). And it is this expertise that usually can be defined as knowledge (or a component of intellectual capital) that determines a unique transaction between employee and employer. Here, the exchange takes place in no central area. The individual possessing knowledge exchanges the future application of his/her knowledge to a company for a specified period under specific conditions. This exchange on the labour market is direct. It is hard to see where the benefits of transaction cost reduction and liquidity that market exchanges provide to physical goods, could be developed in the labour market where, essentially, knowledge is exchanged.

However, if we again look at the development of market exchanges, we see a pubescent period where specialists traded from stalls along streets, where speculators were selling things they did not possess, and buying things they never would own ('blank buying'). It is this specialization that is the hallmark of an organized exchange. It is the specialist's ability to locate and bring buyers and sellers together that allows a profit to be made from the difference in the buying and selling price.

In the labour market – the market where human capital/know how/ intellectual capital is borrowed and lent – we see similar means of specialization. Employment agencies, company internal re-hiring policies, notice-boards, alumni associations and many other institutions act as brokerage houses for unique individual talents and knowledge in the form of jobs and careers. These institutions relay information from the person who owns the knowledge (i.e. the prospective employee) and information about the reliability of the borrower of the know-how of the person (the company). Institutionalized processes are arranged which screen individuals for different types of capacities, characteristics, traits, skills, talents, etc. As the exchange is made, the person's know-how is leased/given to the company.

The relative importance of these labour exchanges is enhanced because the basic labour exchange is no longer an exchange for a muscular-based product. Rather, the labour exchange is now a leasing of intellect, knowledge and know-how: a knowledge exchange. Just as large mechanical devices such as the bulldozer magnified muscle power, so the information superhighway magnifies intellectual capital. With the bulletin boards on the Internet, we are witnessing the birth-pains of such exchanges. These, like the coffee houses before them, stand to grow into significant places where knowledge is traded to create wealth.

Employment agencies as a knowledge exchange

Expert temporary employment agencies have developed which market unique professional skills and knowledge through the placement of professionals in various firms throughout an industry. Their know-how or intellectual capital is spread. And it is because agents act as specialists that they provide venues for buyers and sellers of knowledge. This question of specialized agents acting as the knowledge exchange should not be taken lightly. Employment services are becoming more sophisticated, more international, as the global information highways become more robust. Further, experts can work at a distance since their work is with knowledge which can be handled, more or less, from anywhere in the world.

This global interchange becomes more efficient by utilizing some form of agency system. It is the finding of the best exchange, or combination, that the agent provides an efficient market service to lubricate the knowledge economy. Shared knowledge, in the form of mobile employees, is more valuable knowledge. It is the employment agent that can cut transaction costs, both for the buyer and the seller (as in the stock markets) that aids the economy. And there is some evidence that these agents are becoming more sophisticated.

The agents of exchange have information about market prices for the employment of their skilled knowledge-based employees. They engage in buying and selling just as in the earlier stock market exchanges of the seventeenth century and their commission is in the difference between the two prices. It is convenient for many to point to employment uncertainties as the cause for the specialized agency expansion, but this seems premature. Rather, it may be the means by which knowledge, a highly valuable input, can be easily transferred from place to place. Again, though, this specialization within the labour market may not yet be fully developed. But it is certainly one market venue for the exchange of knowledge. An exchange that often takes place through an intermediary, such as an employment agent, who has no more connection to the skills bought and sold than does the commodities broker in the New York Stock Exchange about the bushels of corn they buy and sell.

Networking as a knowledge exchange

Maintaining the link between people and knowledge, as well as knowledge and intellectual capital, we look now at more informal settings where knowledge is exchanged via employment devices. Is it by chance that in the 1980s many companies and people entering the labour market found terms like 'networking' playing such a large role?

Perhaps not. There was a vast amount of literature on the appropriate way to network in order to find the appropriate situation for specific skills and knowledge; which parties to go to, who to meet, informational interviews, friends, relatives, etc. All of these were seen to form a web of contacts and information that provided a network for the labour market. This may have had less to do with a new attitude among aspiring young people than it did with the fact that they were now buying and selling a valuable product/service – their specific know-how and knowledge which are key components in the drive towards increasing a company's intellectual capital. These informal exchanges provided the venue for clearing the market of buyers and sellers.

Similar to the formation of earlier stock markets, groups of individuals concerned with similar problems and products gathered in a specific area, such as coffee houses, and exchanged information and availability of positions in companies and who was working where. These 'clubs' of knowledge can be equated, in a way, to the structures of a university, with its groups of specialists encouraged to teach and research in various fields. Indeed, a university system of knowledge exchange, with professors moving from one university to another, depending on the working conditions and contractual terms, is a market in knowledge. Where the professor goes also goes the potential future rewards of that person's know-how. And, as in the informal networking systems, the knowledge of the market place may be as critical and valuable as the knowledge that the professor holds. Most professors aware of their market worth will tend to end up in the most appropriate setting.

Again, one can imagine a labour market where some of these informal means of exchange, such as networking, could be formalized into a massive exchange of know-how and talent. For example, there has been a long tradition in Hollywood of using agents to bring people together to make films. These agents started by representing major stars. They now represent a gambit of talent, from stars to directors to lighting personnel. It is often said that some of the most powerful people in Hollywood are the agents, who have the ability to bring buyers and sellers together. They are critical in deciding which films get made. An agent who can bring a talented director together with a leading actor is a powerful person. But agents do more than bring people together. They act as brokers on a knowledge exchange. They call potential buyers, find out what is available in the market, report to their clients the going rates for deals, etc. They are clearing the market, finding the bid and ask prices for a client's know-how and skills. Most important to note is that it is an agent-enhanced market exchange for knowledge and human resources; both of which are key ingredients of intellectual capital. Not all industries rely so heavily on the skills of individuals, such as the Hollywood film industry, and thereby do not have such an extensive agency system. However, there are indications that such systems are beginning to appear more broadly. It is the ability of these exchanges to maintain the fluidity of the supply of skilled individuals that makes for an efficient distribution of scarce resources – experts. Agents also assist in minimizing the transaction costs of finding the appropriate person for a job or situation. Thus, through the exchange of experts and specialisation, agents have developed an infant knowledge exchange.

Conclusion

Exchanges taking place in the labour market are increasingly an exchange of knowledge. The increased relevance of intellectual capital to the Gross National Product of Western nations suggests that these labour market exchanges are increasingly important to the health of knowledge-based economies. A knowledge exchange that can accurately surmise the market conditions and efficiently allocate scarce resources will eventually produce higher levels of productivity. An economy predicated upon the distribution of knowledge might be referred to as intellectual capitalism.

Intellectual capitalism is the buying and selling of future options of returns to knowledge in the form of hiring and firing employees, experts and others that essentially represent future intellectual capital returns. This is then a major difference in economic systems, from those of the past. Traditional contracts based on companies producing physical products were the means of wealth creation through financing capital expenditures. Now investment in knowledge and intellectual capital is, at one level, the borrowing of know-how from skilled individuals. The exchange of which cannot, yet, be easily transferred to paper and negotiated in the same way as traditional market exchanges.

Intellectual capitalism relies more heavily on a vast array of specialist agents who can determine market conditions and produce an environment for an appropriate exchange. In this market setting, a contract is made with every stock holder (the employee) and the potential buyer of the employee or their intellectual capital. This suggests a different means in distributing scarce resources. Previously, transactions were based on commodities, companies, etc., that were so removed physically from the piece of paper being traded. The knowledge exchange, on the other hand, creates a transaction wherein the asset has a direct relationship with the purchaser. One can foresee a knowledge exchange based on systems such as the World Wide Web and the Internet, notwithstanding that agents will become essential as they develop a filter for the vast amounts of information which need to be distributed most efficiently to specific companies or groups. In the end, intellectual capitalism may be based on a confluence of people in a knowledge exchange that distributes scarce resources with those areas that most desire these, but doing so in an agency-led employment knowledge exchange.

This book is predicated upon the rise and importance of experts and their intellectual capital. It is this human and intangible asset, we suggest, that throws a spanner into the traditional organizational structures. The consequences of this is a break by expert employees to an at-will contract-driven labour market, motivated by an increase in utility for the individual and an increase in productivity.

Within each industry and each firm, and perhaps each individual, the move by expert employees to an agency system will occur differently. Some will not have the capacity to do so because of the investment they have already made in a large traditional organization. Some may still place a high value on firm internal job security, and still others may not be able to cope with the changing aspects that agency systems imply. But the advantages of this type of work to expert employees and to knowledge-based work are so great that some of these expert employees will take hold of such work environments and find that they can prosper. This does not imply the working conditions or work environment for all and all types of jobs is best under an agency contract, but that, as we have suggested, when knowledge-based work and the value of expertise coincide with changing opportunities for different work environments, the result will be a labour market niche that is filled by expert employees working through agency systems.

APPENDIX A

The formal exposition of Winston model

This appendix relies heavily on Winston (1982), as does chapter 8, and describes the important elements of Winston's model. Of prime consideration is the optimal switching rule (for utility-maximizing individuals) from activity to activity in a time-sensitive way. This appendix is also used to show how we have adapted Winston's model to labour market segmentation and the time-related aspects of job form. We also note those times when we depart from the perspectives of Winston's analysis.

Winston's model employs three activities: two consumption (or non-work) activities and one work activity. Although, within the mathematical notation, it may appear as if the sequencing of the activities is imposed exogenously, this is not the case. The sequencing itself will emerge from the model.

Accumulated household utility is:

$$U = \int_{t_o}^{t_1} u_1\Big(z_2\big(x_1(t);t\big)\Big)\delta t + \int_{t_1}^{t_b} u_2\Big(z_2\big(z_2(t);t\big)\Big)\delta t \qquad [1]$$

Where flows of utility from activity 1, u_1, is a function of the intensity of the activity z_1 and the amount of goods used x_1. The same holds for activity 2.

This utility is maximized subject to the constraint,

$$\int_{t_0}^{t_1} \bar{p}_1 x_1(t)\delta t + \int_{t_1}^{t_b} \bar{p}_2 x_2(t)\delta t = \int_{t_b}^{t_T} \bar{w}\delta t + Y_p \qquad [2]$$

where the price, p, is exogenous and goods x_i, are time-sensitive. They are constrained by the resources: w, flow of wages and Y_p wealth.

The similarities between Winston's model and regular household allocation models are abundant. Like the allocation of labour model, the optimal quantity of consumption and labour services is found.

However, since his terms are denoted as flows, he is also able to distinguish the optimal moments to switch from one activity to the next (t^*). He incorporates the timing (dates) of activities into the model. Thus, we have a model of household activities that occurs *within time*.

Most notably this is accomplished in the $z_i(x_i(t);t))$ term (speed of output). This term denotes the efficiency of production, and Winston suggests that this is time-sensitive since the production environment (Winston uses $E(t)$ to denote this) changes throughout the day (Winston relies heavily on cyclical variations like day to night altering the production environment). This changes the relative efficiency of production of the various goods throughout the day. Which means that 'the value of time spent in any one activity will change over the day' (p. 172). This is because the 'intensity' (or speed) of production, $z_i(t)$, changes via the external environment at different times in the day, ultimately changing satisfaction, $u_i(t)$ (The same effect on the value of time is felt through the time-sensitive cost of producing the input $x_i(t)$.). This means that labour services are time-sensitive.

The first order condition for optimal activity choice with respect to consumption activity timing is,

$$u_1\left(z_1\left(x_1(t_1^*)\right)\right) - u_2\left(z_2\left(x_2(t_1^*)\right)\right) - \lambda(\bar{p}_2x_2(t_1^*)) = 0 \qquad [3]$$

rearranging leaves,

$$\lambda = \frac{u_1(t_1^*) - u_2(t_1^*)}{\bar{p}_1x_1(t_1^*) - \bar{p}_2x_2(t_1^*)} \qquad [4]$$

and in a different form,

$$u_1\left(z_1\left(x_1^*(t_1^*)\right)\right) - \lambda\bar{p}_1x_1^*(t_1^*) = u_2\left(z_2\left(x_1^*(t_1^*)\right)\right) - \lambda\bar{p}_2x_2^*(t_1^*) \qquad [5]$$

we now more readily define for each activity i at each moment t of the day T its net utility flow:

$$\mu_1(t) = u_i(t) - \lambda\bar{p}_is_i(t), \quad i = 1, \ldots, m, t_0 \leq t \leq t_T \qquad [6]$$

$\mu_i(t)$ is the value of time spent in activity i at moment t. It is the value of the activity minus the cost. From this, Winston states the choice rule which generates the maximum utility flow: 'At any moment the optimal choice rule for the household is simply to do what will maximize the net flow of utility, $\mu_i(t)$ – in other words, to spend time, always, in the activity in which time has the most value. From the m

possible activities that can be done at any moment, only one is chosen' (p. 172).

At the optimal switching moment, t^*, time will have the same value in both activities,

$$\mu_1(t_1^*) = \mu_2(t_1^*) \qquad [7]$$

These equations are what lead to diagrams such as those in chapter 5.

In our discussions about the timing of activities and the decision to work, we are implicitly altering Winston's model by redefining the production environment, $E(t)$. Winston's production environment changes constantly via exogenous environmental rhythms, like the daily train schedule or the yearly weather conditions, etc. (p. 159). We accept this influence over the efficiency of production but find it too conservative. Therefore, we include in our production environment elements like one's father visiting, or an offer to play tennis, or an invitation to go to lunch. To us, these events which alter scheduling are all too common to be left out of the production environment. This has the effect of altering the perspective of the economic agent. Instead of solely planning all units of time from perfect rhythmic foresight, the agent plans different sets of units of time from both rhythmic foresight and production environment aberrations.

This means that we also leave Winston's analysis by implicitly redefining the function, $z_i(x_i(t);t)$, the intensity or speed of production. Since z_i, more explicitly denoted as

$$z(t) = f_i(x_i(t), l_i)E_i(t) = z_i(x_i(t), l_i; t), \text{ for } i = 1, \ldots, m, \qquad [8]$$

is a function partially explained by the production environment $E(t)$.

What does this model tell us? It simply says that the agent can maximize utility in time, given an exogenous production environment, by optimally timing his/her activities. Our discussion in chapter 5 uses the less formal diagrammatic methods of this model. The chapter shows how one set of individuals easily and readily accommodate to a production environment; the efficiency with which they produce/consume activities is not effected by the timing of doing those activities. Their consumption of activities other than work is time-insensitive. They can adjust the timing of activities (t_1^*, t_2^*, etc.) without altering utility because they are not severely effected by the production environment. Therefore rules about working-time set by institutions and organizations have little effect on their activities.

More importantly, we show how another set of individuals are very sensitive to the timing of their activities. The production environment, we implicitly assume, is most constraining to them (for example seeing one's daughter pirouette in a ballet, or taking French lessons). For them, the utility derived from their activities is closely tied to the timing of their activities. These are the time-sensitive employees. Therefore organizational restrictions may cause severe losses in utility; Winston (1987) implies this (see p. 581).

This means then that these two groups, when faced with two different production environments and the different working time flexibilities attached to them (one job form produces a very constraining or restrictive production environment, another job form produces another freer production environment), may possibly choose, if given the opportunity, different job forms.[1] Thus, we have a supply-side labour market punctuated organization and/or supply-side, firm-internal compensation package stratification, and a new application of Winston's 'Activity Choice' theory.

APPENDIX B

Agency employment and search costs

Whereas in the internal market an unstable equilibrium of sorts over working-time control can directly result between employer and employee, in the external labour market the problem of information costs develops. It has often been said that this is why the temporary agency will appear, because of the search costs that both sides of the temporary employment contract must incur in order to locate the complementary arrangement (see Magnum *et al.* (1985)). However, it has not been shown how instrumental the demand by the firm for flexibility *and the supply-side* issues of working-time control may together increase the search costs which facilitate a market mediated labour market – the temporary agency. Again, this is an important point of this book – to reassert the significant influences that supply-side preferences for elements like working-time control by expert employees may have in labour market arrangements, segments, organizations and in compensation packages. In this example, their effects are felt through search costs.

The role of search costs

In general, the analysis of external labour markets (the temporary agency) is stylized for clearer presentation. It will proceed in the following manner: assuming an instantaneous increase in the demand for labour services for a predetermined length, we will compare the difference in search costs incurred by the firm when searching in three different groups of labour service supply. The first group will generally be distinguished by an abundant labour supply with consistent, similar, time-insensitive preferences; the second group by a less abundant labour supply with consistent, similar, time-insensitive preferences; and the third group by a labour supply with inconsistent, dissimilar, time-sensitive preferences who desire greater control over their working-time.

Assume our profit maximising firm experiences a sudden need for labour (this could be due to an immediate increase in demand for their product, an ill employee, an employee on holiday, or a special project). Assume, for the time being, that the firm must employ a new employee for, we will say, a week. In a labour market where the labour supply is distinguished by a large group of employees who are willing to work for any length of time (assume, too, that they all have similar time-insensitive preferences – in other words, all the available workers' preferences are identical functions of time), the wage necessary to induce any one of them to work is identical at all times and they all are available. The firm need only make one phone call. That will be its search cost, since it is assured of obtaining the same type of worker for the same wage no matter who it contacts no matter when it needs them. The person comes to the job and fills in for the necessary week. This may be the case of a large group of unemployed workers who prefer work of any type at any time. (Indeed, they may be maximizing their income and disregarding entirely alternative non-work activities.)

If, however, there is scarce labour supply with varying time-sensitive preferences associated with varying opportunity costs of non-work activities over time (our expert employees) and, thus, varying availability at the offered wage, the search costs for the firm will rise considerably. One can imagine multiple phone calls to various employees before finding an available worker. It is obvious that the probability of finding an available employee is dependent upon the relative availability of employees; thus, the scarcity of the labour services. It is concluded that the more scarce the supply of workers, the higher will be the search costs.

Again, assume the firm has an increase in demand for labour services. However, the labour supply available is one person willing to work at all times. In this case, one phone call is all that is necessary in order to fill the position. Although the labour supply may be small, it is easily attainable. Therefore, the search costs are low. (Note the wage may not necessarily be low.) Now, compare this situation with a time-sensitive expert employee labour supply. This labour supply includes two workers. One is available for half the unit time, and the other for the other half. The firm does not know at any particular time which worker is available or willing to work. The probability of locating the appropriate person is 1:2. In the previous example, the probability was one. The supply of labour services in this case has not become any more scarce; there are the same amount of labour services available, but the search costs to the firm have increased. It has been shown more formally by Lippman and McCall (1976) that search costs increase when the probability of receiving a job offer decreases. This can be applied to the descriptions above. The probability of finding an available worker for the firm decreases from case one – an abundant supply of labour; to case two – one worker willing to work at any time; to case three – two workers willing to work only at specific times. (See also Mortensen, 1986, for a general discussion on search costs.)

Search costs in a Winstonian diagram

These examples are more concretely developed in a Winstonian diagram as in the four cases in figure B1: *a*, *b*, *c*, and *d*. In *d*, the firm's flow of demand for labour services is shown over the unit time T = 1 month. In *a*, the utility flows for the abundant group of consistent time-insensitive workers are shown; in *b*, the utility flow for the single person and in *c*, the utility flows for the two time-sensitive workers. In *a*, all workers derive less utility over time from activities other than work and are willing to work each week in the month. In *b*, the single worker is willing to work each week within the month. In *c*, two workers are shown with two different sets of time-sensitive preferences over time. Worker 1 is willing to work in weeks 1 and 2, and worker 2 is willing to work in weeks 3 and 4.

In figure B1 above, *a* shows many time-insensitive workers. For all of them the indirect utility derived from work U_w is greater than the utility derived from non-work activities U. During weeks three and four the employer should have no problem finding workers. In *b*, there is only one worker, but since that worker is time-insensitive, the employer need only ask that one to work during weeks three and four. In *c*, there are two time-sensitive workers and during weeks three and four the search cost to the firm to find an appropriate worker will increase since both of these workers may have to be contacted in order to find one willing to work. *d* shows the increase in demand for labour services during weeks three and four.

It is clear that if our firm, which is shown to have an increase in demand for labour services in weeks 3 and 4, were to face the labour

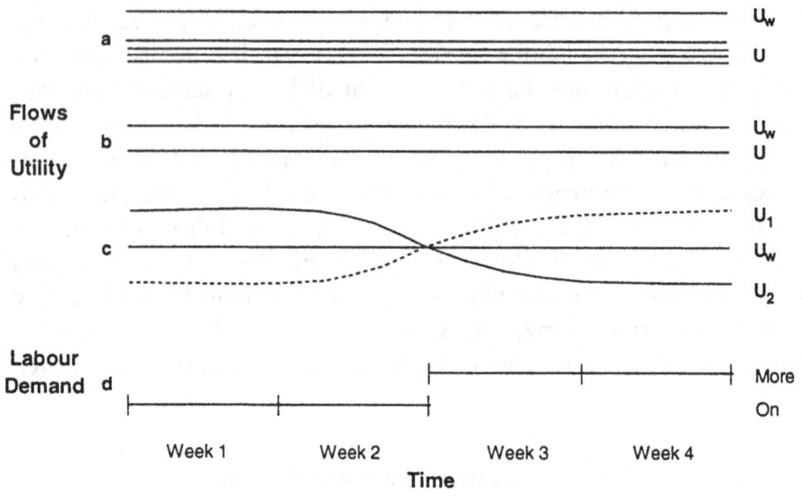

Figure B1 Comparison of different time-sensitive workers. In this figure *a* shows many time-insensitive workers. For all of them the indirect utility derived from work U_w is greater than the utility derived from non-work activities, *U*. During weeks three and four the employer should have no problem finding workers. In *b* there is only one worker but since that worker is time-insensitive the employer need only ask that one to work during weeks three and four. In *c* there are two time-sensitive workers and during weeks three and four the search cost to the firm to find an appropriate worker will increase since both of these workers may have to be contacted in order to find one willing to work. *d* shows the increase in demand for labour services during weeks three and four.

supply of numerous time-insensitive workers *a*, the search costs would be low compared to the two cases *b* or *c*. The more subtle difference in search costs is revealed when comparing *b* and *c*. In week four, if the firm faced the labour supply exemplified in *b*, one phone call would be sufficient (although the wage may be higher than in case *a*). But by facing the time-sensitive, not any more scarce, labour supply in *d*, the search costs will increase. It first must find the one worker where utility flow for non-work activities are low for week four. The firm will then be able to fill the vacancy with person 2, whose utility flow is shown by U_2.

If the firm contacted person 1, whose utility flow is shown by *U*1, they would receive a negative response at the wage offered w, since the utility from non-work activities during that week of the month (U_1), is greater than the indirect utility derived from the income from work.[1]

This causes a further complication for the firm. It can either attempt more searching, hoping to find person 1, or it can increase the wage offered until it reached the 'reservation wage' of person 2. This is the classic search cost theorist's stopping rule problem (for example, see Lippman and McCall (1976); Mortensen (1986); and Akerlof (1984)). One can generalize from this example over a large number of workers with various reasons for different time-shaped utility curves. The search costs to the firm, compared to other more stable labour supplies, could be higher.

When comparing the labour supply *b* and *c* with *a*, *the scarcity of labour* is low, the probability of locating a worker may be lower, and therefore the search costs are more likely to be high. When comparing *c* with *b*, the time-sensitivity of the labour supply, its need for *control over working-time*, is the basis for the differences in the probabilities of locating a worker. In *c*, the probability is lower than in *b*, therefore the search costs are higher.

The above analysis suggests then that *the search costs for the firm will increase with an increase in the scarcity of the labour supply and with an increase in the labour supply's time-sensitivity, their value of control over working-time*. Because the analysis was time-sensitive, an element of search costs previously hidden by traditional analytical approaches, namely the supply-side effects of a time-sensitive labour supply, was uncovered.

The expert employee's search costs

Assume now that the firm has a recurring seasonal need for an increase in labour services. This is shown in figure B2 as a seasonal increase in demand every March. If we assume our agents are rational and learn from the past, then we would expect this pattern to become known. A worker who prefers to work in March will know exactly where to go and accordingly the search costs will be low. This is often seen in agricultural labour markets, where the same group of pickers will show up at a farm when the fruit has become ripe. If we generalize this pattern of short-term demand over many firms throughout the year, we may have a systematic demand for temporary labour services. The demand could cover the entire year. Again, seasonal fruit pickers will often follow the harvests; for example, moving from apple picking one time in the year to hops picking at another time in the year. Informal discussions with apple farmers in Kent and Sussex have hinted that

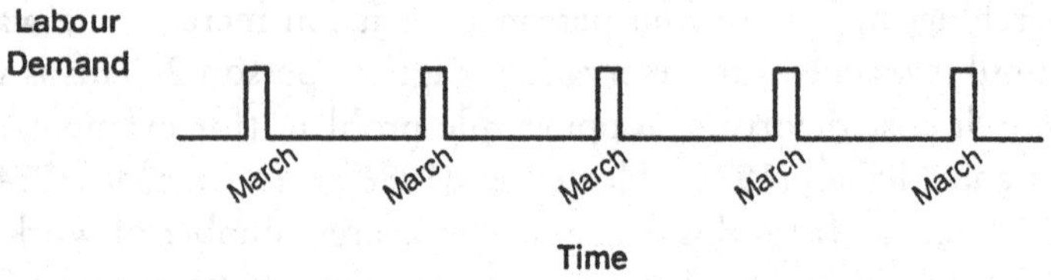

Figure B2 Repetitive increase in demand for labour services. The figure shows that March of each year is accompanied by an increased demand for labour services. This repetitive pattern implies that workers will know where to go to find work. The search costs for them will be low.

this is the case. They report that frequently the same apple pickers will show up at approximately the exact time that the apples are ripe. After picking apples they will then move on to pick hops from neighbouring farms, where at that exact time hops are ready to be picked.

If the firm has inconsistent increases in demand, the worker will not know when each firm demands temporary employees. The employee will then have trouble finding the appropriate place to work. On a given month, since there is no previous pattern, there will be no reason for the worker to search for a job at one location over another. It would become necessary for the worker at all times to search out all firms to find the firm which has need for labourers. The search costs for the worker will thereby have increased considerably.

If we add to this scenario two different types of groups of employees, the differences in search costs due to time-sensitivity will again become apparent. For a group of employees with very little time variation in their preferences, the job situation finally acquired can last a long time since the indirect utility derived from the wages earned will be sufficiently high for an extended period. The search costs therefore will be distributed over a longer period. A group of workers with a desire for more control over their working-time (time-sensitive workers) will, by changing jobs with more frequency, incur a relatively larger search cost. It is partly because their time-sensitive preferences will cause the wages earned to be insufficiently high for a sustained period that their job duration will be less. Thus, the search costs for the time-sensitive worker will be distributed over a much shorter period.

Of course, the duration of employment may be more directly linked to simply the duration of work available. But the consequences to the worker are the same. With a decrease in job duration, the search costs will be spread over a shorter period. The search costs per job will rise.

The above analysis suggests then that *the search costs for the potential worker will increase with an increase in a time inconsistent demand for labour services and with an increase in the labour supply's preference or need for control over their working-time.* Again, because the analysis was based on a time-sensitive labour market, a significant time element of search costs in temporary work previously hidden by traditional analytical approaches was uncovered. It is implicit in temporary work that the time erratic behaviour of the market implies significant search cost problems.

Search costs, agencies and networks

The search costs described above play a critical role in the development of a market-mediated labour market. For it is the ability of the agency to decrease the timing inconsistencies of supply and demand of temporary work that distinguishes it. It is its ability to provide a service that eliminates most of, if not all, the search costs described above that will make its service valuable and, of course, its ability to renegotiate contracts with various employers for a group of employees. This is what generates its ability to provide the at-will contract essential to the efficient use of expert employees.

The agency is able to eliminate search costs by providing all the information about all the employees and all the firms in the time-sensitive labour market. It attracts the temporary expert employee by providing information about jobs from *all* firms (thereby the agency obtains information on the individual's particular availability and reservation wage). It attracts the firm by providing information about *all* potential workers (thereby the agency obtains information about available jobs and offered wages). Because single firms and individual workers have only limited information, they cannot alone provide the necessary information to generate the frequency of at-will contracts that is necessary to provide the expert employee with the type of compensation package that they prefer.

The only information a single firm can provide about jobs to potential workers is its own. Since its demand for services is either time constraining or time erratic, this is insufficient. Workers must search at many different firms before they find an appropriate match for their desire to work at any one particular time. This increases the potential workers' search costs. The only information an individual worker can provide about potential employees for the firm is their own. Since their supply of services is time erratic, this is insufficient. The firm must search for many different workers before it finds a match. This increases the search cost for the firm. It is not possible for the single firm or the individual temporary employee to provide the information a temporary agency can provide. It is the timing inconsistency of labour supply and labour demand and the dispersion of various preferences both of the employer and the employee that make this mediator necessary. It is the time-sensitivity of the temporary employee that is critical in forming this labour market segment. It is their preference for control over working-time that drives the labour market segment or causes the punctuated break from exclusive employment in the traditional firm.

Because the expert temporary employee labour market is distinguished by time inconsistencies (or preferences for control over working-time) and scarce labour, the search costs for both the firm and the individual will be higher than in other markets. This high search cost will induce alternative organizations to appear that can provide information at a lower cost. So that, whereas before the search costs may have been prohibitively high for either the firm or the individual to trade, because of the temporary agency the trade will occur.

An example of search costs in a temporary agency

A firm will pay for a temporary worker so long as the wage offered is lower than alternative forms of filling the need for increased demands of labour services; for example, overtime.[2] It will also pay as long as there is a marginal benefit of the extra labour services. These are the two necessary conditions. More formally, a firm will pay a wage W(temporary) = W^*(wage offered to the temporary worker) + search costs, as long as W(temporary) < W (overtime). This implies that an increase in search costs then will decrease the wage offered to a temporary worker, W^*.

The time-sensitive employee will work as a temporary employee as long as the indirect utility derived from work is greater than the utility derived at that point in time from performing non-work activities.

More formally, the temporary employee will work for a firm at any moment in time as long as the U(W^{**} – search cost of finding job) > U(non-work activities) at that moment (this is the Winstonian model). An increase in search costs then will increase the necessary wage to induce the worker to work, and therefore decrease the likelihood of taking a job.

These two statements above imply that the temporary arrangement will occur if and only if W^* (Wage offered to the worker) $\geqq W^{**}$ (Wage necessary to induce worker to work) at the given moment in time (see Gronau (1986)). This condition in turn is dependent on the search costs for both the firm and the temporary worker, and the search costs, as shown above, increase as working-time inconsistencies increase in supply and demand. If search costs are so high for either the firm or the temporary employee so that $W^* < W^{**}$ then there will be no employment.

If $W^* < W^{**}$ and this condition is primarily due to the high search costs an agency which can lower these search costs may be able to capture the gains. For example, a firm may be willing to pay a total cost of £56/hr to hire a temporary worker. Of this £56/hr, say, £10/hr is search costs. This means that the firm will only offer the temporary employee £46/hr (total wage = paid wage + search cost). A temporary worker would be willing to work for £45/hr but one must add on the search cost of finding the job. We'll say this is £6/hr. This means it will be necessary to offer the temporary worker £51/hr (total wage = wage + search cost).

In this example W^* (£46/hr) < W^{**} (£51/hr) and the transaction will not occur. It is the search costs which drives the firm and the temporary worker apart. If there were no search costs the firm would offer £56/hr and the temporary worker would demand £45/hr. A negotiated equilibrium would then occur: at, say, £50/hr.

The temporary agency on the other hand could get £56/hr from the firm and offer the temporary worker £45/hr so long as it made the search costs for both firm and the worker = £0/hr. The difference between the £56 and £45:£11, is the income to the agency. It is because the search costs were prohibitively high that the agency was able to make revenues from this difference. The £11 in revenues minus the costs of the agency are the profits for the agency. The trick for the temporary agency is to (a) offer a worker to the firm that costs just less than W^* + search cost (of firm) in finding an employee and to (b) offer a wage W to the temporary employee that is just greater than W^*

– search cost of finding job. This gives them the widest margin between the wage they get from the firm and the wage they pay to the employee.

In some sense it might be argued that these profits are exploitive of the labour market. They do not merely capture the search costs of the agency, but they capture the inability of the individual to search efficiently. It could be argued that if the profits of the agency are very high this will induce other agencies to form, which could drive down the profits. Competition then might be relied upon to drive profits down to the search costs of the agency.

Still, because we are talking about human beings performing work, profits like these are very controversial. They must be sensitively addressed as opposed to profits from a train load of coal. This has lead to intense debates within the International Labour Organization (ILO) about the acceptability of temporary agencies. Although they recognize the agencies' ability to provide work arrangements where it may not have been provided before hand, the ILO feels it is necessary to regulate these agencies.[3] A neoclassical economist might argue that if the profits are high enough this will attract other entrepreneurs to engage in business. Ultimately the profits are driven down to a point where they just cover the temporary agencies own costs. The final wage for the employee is determined by either a bidding war between agencies for the employee or a bidding war between agencies for the job. More generally, Bakels in Albeda *et al.* (1978) notes that the 'ethical objection to profit making on labour is, strictly speaking, not directed at the agencies, as such, but applies to practically every employee in our society' (p. 295).

Notes

Introduction

1 Whether profits are generated from (i) appeasing changing consumer tastes (demand-fed), or (ii) the firm *a priori* making available a wide range of products convincing consumers they need to purchase them (supply-led), is inconsequential. The result for the firm is the same: the firm demands the know-how to produce a variety of new and changing product lines.

2 However, they were unable to determine the type of work performed by sub-contracting. This may be significant to theories we put forth in this book.

3 Wood (1992) explains the progress of such demand-driven debate in clarifying the origins of flexible specialization, numerical flexibility, neo- and post-Fordism, etc.

4 Atkinson's work (1986) is most often cited regarding the theoretical divisions within a firm.

5 Thompson (1989) argues that such breaks in work organizations are inconsistent with what has been learned from the labour process debate. To this end we address the 'break' problem head-on by carefully defining what we mean by a break and justifying the use of the terms throughout the book.

6 The financing for the study came from fifteen companies and Foundations: Salt River Project, a Phoenix, Arizona utility company; Sears, Roebuch and Co's Allstate Insurance Unit; American Express Co; American Telephone and Telegraph Co; Commonwealth Fund; Dupont Co; General Mills Foundation; International Business Machines Corp; Johnson and Johnson; Levi Strauss & Co; Merck & Co; Mobil Corp; Motorola Inc.; the Rockefeller Foundation; and Xerox Corp. It was conducted using representative statistical procedures, contacting 2,958 wage and salaried workers via in-depth telephone surveys of approximately an hour long. Brief analysis of the survey is given in Shellenbarger (1993).

7 Working as a temporary employee has its life-style advantages as well. As Sooz Edwards, a temporary senior benefits analyst for Chalres Schwabb, San Francisco, says, it gives her time to volunteer for several non-profit

groups, she finds it a relief not getting bogged down by strategy sessions, and the tensions are lower. For Laura Masurovsky, a graduate from Harvard Law School, working as a temporary lawyer means that she does not 'have to look over my shoulder when I have three paediatrician appointments in a row. And I don't have to answer if I only have three billable hours.' This is a far cry from the preferences of Dave Harrison, one of the subjects of William H. Whyte Jr's seminal work, *The Organization Man* (1956) as well as Leinberg and Tucers' book, *The New Individualists* (1991), who provides one well-researched case study of this US middle-class ideal of the 1950s. Dave Harrison had worked for Chevrolet most of his life. In so doing, he successfully obtained ever greater sums of wealth. He was able to buy ever bigger cars and to buy ever larger houses. He could support a family as well as send kids through college. These were his rewards for his hard work. 'I'd leave home at six on Monday and be out there until Friday night, working my way home calling on dealers. I was home only on weekends . . . . Things were opening up, and that's when my financial situation began to improve.' His concern for the quality of family life was negligible. The Harrisons' concern for job security is best summed up by Dave's wife Helen's concern for her own daughter's career. 'I'm real proud of her . . . but I do worry about her future, what will happen when she's in her sixties. It's just that we are used to having a big corporation behind us.' (Leinberg and Tucker (1991) The Harrisons demanded life-long job security and an ever-increasing income.

8 Wood (1992) distinguishes between Fordism and Taylorism, where the former 'is a more wide-ranging strategy of organizing production' and the latter is 'principally concerned with shop-floor labour management through the techniques of work-study' (p. 10). Both imply a disciplined work environment.

1 Trends in the labour market

1 The data used to compile these figures are from the US Department of Labor Statistics' *Employment and Earnings* various issues and from the US Department of Education Statistics, *Earned Degrees Conferred*. Data were also obtained from publications by the Federal Security Agency, Office of Education's various circulars of Earned Degrees Conferred by Higher Education Institutes as reported in US Department of Commerce *Statistical Abstracts*. These education data are complete from 1949 to the present. However, in the period 1940–1944, only total enrolment by gender is available rather than degrees conferred. Since 1940, the number of degrees conferred is known, as well as the numbers enrolled. Thus, it is possible to make a calculation of the likely percentage of degrees conferred per number enrolled. This facilitates estimations of the numbers of degrees conferred in the period 1941–1944. For the gap between 1945 and 1948, we estimate using an average of 1944 and 1949.

2 See e.g. Spurr (1990) who argues that within the legal profession, women are less likely to be promoted. Cox *et al.* (1991), Hagan (1990), Adam and Baer (1984) and Kanter (1977) all report that a wage gap is produced not by occupational choice alone but also by gender discrimination in these professions.

3 These estimates are made without allowing for any growth in the number of women obtaining professional degrees. This is conservative, we feel, because trends suggest that there will be an increased percentage of women obtaining these degrees. Some sociologists, however, have argued that the feminization of specific professions have coincided with their demise (for example, see Hill, 1981).

4 The working hours of Members of Parliament in the UK will be reviewed 'because of the growing pressures of women and those with young families' (London *Times*, 28 June 91). Further, an *Employment Gazette* article (2.92) on firms that have changed their employment policies revealed the importance to women of flexible hours in order to return to work.

5 These numbers were calculated by the authors from Table 637 of the *Statistical Abstract of the United States 1994*, US Department of Commerce.

6 These statistics for Great Britain were calculated by the authors from January 1987, October 1989, April 1991 and May 1992 issues of the *Employment Gazette*.

7 These numbers were calculated using average earnings reported in *Employment and Earnings*, January 1993. Weekly earnings for lawyers, physicians, engineers, computer programmers and business executives were multiplied by fifty-two weeks in a year and then multiplied by totals of each occupation. These earnings were then compared to the national average earnings for all occupations multiplied by the total employed in all occupations.

8 Shelley (1992) looks closely at occupations and jobs that require college degrees. Using data from the Bureau of Labor Statistics, she shows that jobs requiring a college degree will grow from 23.2 million to 32.3 million between 1990 and 2005. But this demand, she believes, may be more than compensated for by an increasing number of college graduates entering the labour force and concludes that 'the job market will be less favourable to college graduates from 1990–2005 than during the 1984–90 period'. Using other estimations, she shows that these differences in supply and demand could be better than shown or worse, depending on estimated variables of occupational growth, supply of graduates and immigration. None of these estimations takes into account an increase in new occupational job growth like that derived from new technologies such as 'virtual reality', for example, but can be used as the best estimates available. Hadlock *et al.* (1991), using novel definitions of high technology, believes that 'Level I' technology industry employment is estimated to grow at about average rates when compared with total employment. However, their statistics are derived primarily from commodity-based production enterprises which exclude the knowledge-dense industries we are discussing here.

9 Noll (1992) describes well the development of the picturephone system by AT&T as early as 1933–34, when such a system was displayed at the Chicago World's Fair. By 1964 a 'See as You Talk' service was offered between Chicago, New York City and Washington DC. Throughout the 1970s trials were held and experiments within companies were launched, but its apparent uselessness as a business tool undermined its success. It appeared that management valued a transmission system that could transport hard copies of text, etc. This demand by consumers was met by the fax machine and its success as a business tool is proven.

10 Jussawalla (1992) gives an overall survey of the conditions of the telecommunications infrastructure of the Pacific Rim countries such as South Pacific Islands, China and Singapore (which has the best developed telecommunications infrastructure), India, Latin America, the Arab world, and Africa. The conclusion is that Asia has made great leaps in improving and investing in its infrastructure. Latin America and Africa are much worse off, with Africa causing the greatest concern because of political instability within parts of that continent.

11 Of course, the effects of technology may be a consequence of how they have been implemented by an organization. Few technologies have properties in them which cannot be altered by the way in which they are implemented; see e.g. Austrin (1991), Burnes (1989), Buchannan (1984) and Dy (1990). But in this book the stress is on the 'expert' professional employee. The power that this type of worker can have in determining how technology is used is assumed to be strong.

12 Sequencing a knowledge-based product with the advent of computers with their large memory systems, may be unnecessary. Data or knowledge collection, considered to be a first step in many knowledge-based products, now, with computers, is a continually updated phenomena. It is no longer necessarily a sequenced precursor to a knowledge-based product. Concurrent production between processes in a knowledge-based industry may take place miles away from each component and even at different times. A knowledge-based discussion (production) can take place concurrently through the transportation of information from one user to another through the computer. This can happen not only at different places, but also at different times. The information is stored and can be withdrawn to be used concurrently at any time. Timed production (externally imposed deadlines) is most constraining on products that are non-storable (the product, if non-storable, must be produced, in time, close to deadlines). Knowledge can now be stored, updated and retrieved quite easily so that deadlines do not as severely constrain production backwards in time. Production duration (the time necessary to complete a task) is less constraining in that stopping and start-up costs continue to shrink as knowledge becomes more readily accessible through increased powers of technology. The important consequence of this freeing up of production processes in time is not that they necessarily dismember the employee

from the employer and the firm, or that they entirely relieve work of all its time constraints, but that the production process itself of an expert employee (now more likely to be knowledge-based) may be radically altered. In light of these changes, though, one must be aware that knowledge as a marketable product is intertwined with the timing of production. Having knowledge first is an important competitive advantage and therefore this aspect of knowledge-based work may develop increases in time constraints. Still, the time constraints that were most severe in manufacturing production have become less severe in knowledge-based industries, because of the technology-driven changes in the production process of knowledge-based products. This is a fertile environment from which the expert employee and their new ideas about a work environment can flourish, either within the firm or in the external labour market.

13 Another development in attitudes includes the description of the development ethic, described as a goal to develop oneself in totality and can be linked to the holistic management style (Hampden-Turner and Trampenaar (1993)). This includes the development of the physical, intellectual, emotional, spiritual and also includes the earning of a basic salary. Hampden-Turner and Trampenaar argue that no longer does more necessarily mean an increase in utility. Two cars may not be better than one. The most expensive suit may no longer bring the admiration of one's peers. Basic economic logic is being called into question. Does increased material affluence necessarily bring psychological well-being? This leads authors like Karesek and Theorell (1990) to develop new models with labels like 'New Value'. They define this as a value that is 'process oriented not product oriented' (p. 192). It adds value to a person or an organization, as opposed to adding a physical input into the making of a final physical product. Recall that the Families and Work Institute study showed that 60 per cent of those surveyed considered the effect of their work on their family or personal life a very important reason in deciding to take their current job. In relation to this, 46 per cent regarded their employer's family supportive policies as an important reason for taking their current job. Furthermore, 55 per cent believed that control over their work content was an important reason for taking their job, as well as 38 per cent citing control of their work schedules. As before, these numbers then give some evidence that a broader definition of compensation for the employee is needed rather than just income. These attitudes are already being reflected in some of the top management courses in the United States. The Wharton School of the University of Pennsylvania has brought together eighteen work–family experts to search for ways to include in courses a way to balance work and family life. They will teach their students 'how to work things out' between work and the family; the managerial skills necessary to become a successful manager of a family-friendly organization. 'Managers need for example to be flexible and allow employees to start work at different times.' (*New York Times*, 27

February 94, p. 41.) This business school is feeling the pressures of the demands of employees for greater discretion over their work. They are teaching subjects that would seem an impossible addition to the curriculum just five years ago.

14 Malecki and Bradbury (1991) have shown that research and development laboratories locate in areas that attract professional and technical workers. The firms are following the locational preferences of their employees.

2 Adaptations in the labour market and the expert employee

1 See Beniger (1989) for more on this. He describes the evolution of control and gives a clear explanation of many terms used to describe transformation in a useful table.

2 Organizational learning literature is disparate, ranging from routines in an organization (Levitt and March, 1988) to individual processes (Daft and Weick (1984) and Argyris and Schön (1978)). For Huber (1991) organizational learning is used to describe impending organizational adaptation.

3 Work describing transformation has been criticized by Thompson (1989) because of its 'idealised view of craft work; unproblematic readings of skill; over-rationalistic conceptions of management strategy (towards flexibility); and the presentation of changes in work organisation as if they were complete historic breaks' and that 'no qualitative break has been made in the organisation of the capital to labour process'; furthermore, 'the nature and significance of flexibility vary according to the context in time, sector, nation and choices of actors in the labour process' (pp. 228–29). In this chapter we discuss exactly what we mean by a 'break' and we thoroughly contextualize our discussion.

4 One example of the work of natural scientists is insights made into the peppered moths chameleon adaptation to environmental situations, as described in the quotation at the start of this chapter. This demonstrates the Darwinian (and Gilbert White) theory of natural selection with its premises of variation and environmental pressures which combine to affect the probability of survival. It should be noted now that the well-known evolutionist's phrase that the fittest survive means that some survive because they better fit their environment. This does not mean that they are 'better' than any other. Indeed, it is the misfits and oddities that sometimes ensure the survival of a species. For when environments change, those who have prospered previously because of their superior adaptation, may find it impossible to survive, like the pallid peppered moth of the mid-nineteenth century, and it is those that were once considered misfit that will survive.

5 One answer has always been associated with the emergence of Christianity. However, according to George Duby (1974) 'Christianity did not condemn slavery; it dealt it barely a glancing blow.'

6 In general, slaves were sold like livestock, as shown by the law of the Bavarians: 'A sale once completed should not be altered, unless a defect is found which the vendor has concealed, in slave or the horse or any other livestock sold . . . for animals have defects which a vendor can sometimes conceal' (quoted from Lex Baiwariorum, XVI,9. in Bonnassie (1991)). Serfs were free, but under the iron rule of strong lords.

7 Note we use the term 'punctuated break' to emphasise the abrupt change (break) and to recall the naturalists' description of equilibriums marked by such breaks (punctuated). Perhaps we could have used 'punctuating break', but deferred to 'punctuated break' to emphasise the link with the natural sciences 'punctuated equilibrium'.

8 Examples of this are *Patriot Games* filmed in London and or *Apocalypse Now* filmed in the jungles of the Philippines.

9 The literature on demand-driven flexibility is well documented for its stance on the cost-saving aspects of transforming to a 'flexible organisation'. Our contention is that the flexibility debate can be made more robust by including supply-side elements into the equation which was discussed in the introduction.

10 Huyssein (1986) is referring to the debate in post-modern art history. The relevance to our own discussion lies in the battle between two understandings of post-modernity. 1. For many of these writers the development of art beyond modern art can be seen as a continuous route stemming from modern art. These are post-modern responses to modern culture that tend to criticize modern life. One is reminded of Andy Warhol's silk screen images of Marilyn Monroe and Jackie Onassis. In these paintings, Warhol calls into question and boldly examines the consequences and effects of the mechanically reproduced image: a process that is modern. In a way, he commodifies these stars. Similarly, Warhol's sculptures of Brillo boxes and his silkscreened images of the Coca Cola bottle or the Campbell's soup can show his obvious references to the increasing preoccupation of commodities for the actors in capitalist society. Thus, Warhol's work can be considered post-modern, because of his commentary and critique of the product of a fordist hierarchical organization. The connection between post-modern and modern is strong, as between the Fordist organization and either the flexible specialization or the global firm of the US film industry. 2. Dramatic explanations of another definition of post-modernity include Charles Jencks' (1977) claim that the symbolic end of the modern era of architecture was 15 July 1972 at 3.32pm; where in St Louis the destruction of the Pruitt Igoe Housing Estate began. Several of the buildings were dynamited and they collapsed in a dramatic manner which was shown on the evening news. This exemplifies the desire for some artists and architects to make a break from all that is modern or Fordist. To destroy it and build anew. This we consider a punctuated break with a new equilibrium

3 From the firm to the agency

1 Rapoport (1995) reports that business writer Handy (1994) also reflects on the development of partnerships in knowledge-based firms. Handy believes that 'organizations today have to be based on trust. How many people can you know well enough to trust? Probably 50 at most. So, increasingly organizations will be made up of groups of 50 that will bond together for different projects or needs.'

4 Expert agency employment as a facilitator of intellectual capital

1 For an annotated bibliography, see Flamholtz (1985), pp. 356–74.
2 Recall the 1960s and 1970s was the time when the de-skilling thesis dominated much of social science and significantly influenced the way the workplace was perceived (for example, see Braverman (1974) and Hill (1981)). The de-skilling thesis suggested that the development of technology and production line manufacturing processes made skills redundant and reduced people to perform simple, repeatable tasks. This took away any discretion people had over their work. Although influential, the thesis concentrated on manufacturing and neglected to consider other economic sectors which were changing and requiring different, more cognitive skills.
3 At this point in time, business schools and Universities began to offer courses in Human Resource management (see Beer *et al.* (1984)).
4 Eccles (1991) uses the term 'grammar' to refer to a basic model for performance measurement.
5 Over time, there have been developments of these two basic models: see the annotated bibliography in Flamholtz (1985), pp. 356–74.
6 See, for instance, Jauch and Skigen (1974).

5 The temporal advantages of agency work for the expert employee

1 Deserpa (1971) also develops a theory of time, distinguishing between activities that are a necessity and activities which can be chosen. He utilizes a non-linear programming model.
2 Bosworth and Dawkins (1980) examine how the variations in utility over the day may affect wage premiums at unsociable hours. Hicks was also sensitive to the fact that commodities may be differentiated, not only according to their attributes, but also to their date (Currie and Steadman (1990), p. 109). In this thesis, though, the physical attributes are endogenous to the date.
3 Winston emphasizes the cyclical nature of time in his book. We emphasize the heterogeneous nature of time. Hassard (1990) suggests that studies utilizing either approach are scarce (p. 13).
4 This time constraint differs from Becker's in that it allows for the timing of

activities to be generated from the model, not just the amounts of time devoted to different activities.

5 This differs from Becker in that t^* is a moment in time, not a level of time allocated.

6 This is akin to Groneau's (1986) discussion of the 'shadow price of time'.

7 Owen (1979) suggests that flexitime will not increase leisure time. We suggest that it might change the quality of leisure time. Owen's analysis suffers because time is treated as a commodity: *the number* of leisure hours takes precedence. We suggest that *the timing* of leisure hours is most relevant.

8 Allen's (1981) empirical investigation of work attendance suggests that the flexibility of the work schedule directly relates to attendance. See also Schappi (1988). He also states that 'there was no empirical support that certain classes of individuals are absence prone regardless of scheduling flexibility provided by their employers or the opportunity costs of taking a day off'. This gives some evidence that preferences over working time are true exogenous preferences, not traits (see chapter 3). Hepple (1990) suggests that full-time permanent employees need to be paid more than others, to decrease their incentive to be absent.

9 See also Staten (1982) for more on incentives to shirk.

6 Taking stock

1 'Economic theory is a game which makes you think in simple examples and then gets you to extrapolate without thinking too much about problematic settings' (Kreps (1990)). Preferences and choices are the very determinants of basic micro-economic theory. It describes the consumer's behaviour by analyzing the theoretical consequences of his choices, on the bases that his preferences are revealed by his choices and of course these preferences must behave according to the strict rules of preferences governed by economists. These are summarized in the consumer's utility function which harbours all the preferences of the individual and measures all the subject's choice on a numerical scale, thus changing a choice problem into a numerical maximization problem. Given a set of preferences, we can think of a utility function that includes preferences and then use optimization theory to solve the choice problems. Therefore, an economist can prescribe what choices will optimize utility.'

7 AT&T's special employment policies for expert employees

1 The authors are indebted to Doug Merchant, resource officer at AT&T who was good enough to discuss aspects of this chapter. Some of the material for this chapter was also taken from 'Attempting to Reduce Employment Risk and Increase Stability at AT&T: A Creative Approach',

an unpublished paper authored by Thomas D. Sugalski, Louis Manzo and Jim Meadows. The views expressed, however, are those of the authors and not of AT&T or any of its personnel.

2 It is interesting to note that within Resource Link's promotional material it includes a core-periphery diagram similar to that of Atkinson (1986).

8 An external temporary agency and expert employees

1 Data were retrieved by way of questionnaire survey and in-depth interviews with key personnel. The final design of the questionnaire followed an initial pilot study of 10 contemporary accountants. Their responses were considered and follow-up telephone interviews were performed to inform alterations and adjustments to the questionnaire. Several large firm employees were also administered the questionnaire and the refinement process repeated. Furthermore, several managers were sent a questionnaire to make detailed design comments and suggestions in order to increase its readability and reduce confusion in its format. The questionnaire was also organized with care to enhance its internal validity, taking into account possible spurious relationships. Overall, the questionnaire had approximately 200 data points, which included a range of questions about different aspects of working conditions and personal work histories. This facilitates the testing of numerous relationships, not just control over working time. Two firms were surveyed using an identical questionnaire in Autumn 1991. The large London accountancy firm was divided into six divisions: three of these were randomly chosen as perspective respondents. This amounted to 265 questionnaires distributed to employees. The questionnaires were delivered by firm internal mail under the authors' supervision, with a cover letter with London School of Economics (LSE) letterhead, stating that responses would be used for academic purposes and that all responses were confidential and that no individual would be traceable to a particular questionnaire. The participants were also given a stamped addressed envelope so that questionnaires were returned directly to the authors at the London School of Economics. The firm itself never handled the completed questionnaires. This survey yielded 175 responses, a response rate of 66 per cent. A similar process was used for the temporary accountancy agency. All the agency accountants (75) were sent a questionnaire through the post to their homes. Also included was a cover letter which explained the project without referring to it specifically as a project about temporary employment, rather about working conditions. Completed questionnaires were returned by post directly to the authors at the LSE. Confidentiality of the responses was expressed. Of the 75 mailed, we received 50 responses, thus yielding a 67 per cent response rate.

2 There is some evidence to suggest that, in general and for all occupations, as unemployment increases, temporary agency employment decreases (for

example, see Albert and Garcia (1995)). When unemployment decreases, temporary agency employment increases. Perhaps as employment conditions become increasingly favourable to the expert employee, individuals are more likely to work from a temporary agency; perhaps to gain some type of advantage. These general statistics suggest that employers do not off-load employees from their organizations and then use the temporary agency system as a pool from which to employ someone for the same job. If this were the case, there would be an increased number of temporary agency employees during periods of unemployment. This is not so.

3 In the 1980s, the London accountancy profession grew almost 33 per cent (the number of students in the profession grew more than that – for example, see Harvey (1991)). However, the summer of 1991 (the time-frame in which data was collected for this study) was, by all accounts, a period of recession for most industries in London and the accountancy market was no exception. As reported in several trade journals as well as newspapers, the London accountancy market was, for the first time in over a decade, contracting. Staff across the board were being made redundant: '225 redundancies at KPMG, Peat Marwick McLintock, United Kingdom's second largest firm . . . 120 staff cut from London office, 60 from the London region and the remainder from the Northeast . . . Redundancy terms at 3–4 months salary' (*The Accountant*, May 1991). This is also reflected by the responses to telephone interviews we conducted with over twenty agencies. Of the respondents, 75 per cent reported that, 'there had been fewer jobs available for their staff over the past 18 months'. Several even noted that the drop had been severe. Two of the respondents felt that there had been not 'too much drop', and one other reported that there was actually a slight increase. They explained this by the use of temporary accountants when companies are going out of business 'to clear up and clean up their accounts'. The table below justifies this response to some degree. It shows that insolvency work for some of the larger accountancy firms had increased as well.

Percentage Increases in Insolvency Work by the Big Six Firms 1990–1991

Company	*% Increase*
Coopers & Lybrand	56
Deloitte	100
KPMG Peat Marwick	100
Price Waterhouse	30
Ernst & Young	54
Touche Ross	64

Source: The Accountant, June 1991

This recessionary moment in the London accountancy labour market is in some ways an ideal setting for investigating a supply-side break with traditional organizations towards agency work. Indeed, if traditional and demand-driven theories are correct, it is at the point of contraction that job security would be weakest for agency employees and income would be significantly lower because of the renegotiation of the at-will contract agency employment implies. If there are no differences in these key elements of the demand-driven ideas about agency employment and the flexible firm, then one can assume that the agency employee is not being forced to work through a secondary job by demand-driven forces like organizations that want to increase numerical flexibility; rather, it implies that other elements of the compensation package that agency work provides are drawing specific employees to the agency.

4 The variable 'Job Security' conflates the questions: (i) 'My amount of job security is an important advantage of my job'; (ii) 'In the next two years I will expect to be made redundant'; and (iii) 'An increase in my job security would improve my situation'. Similarly, the 'Mobility' variable is constructed from two questions: (i) 'My chances for promotion are an important advantage of my job'; and (ii) 'An increase in my responsibilities would improve my situation'. The 'Income' variable from: (i) 'The amount of income I receive for my work is an important advantage of my job'; and (ii) 'My income, including all assets, gives me more than enough to feed and house my family comfortably'. The variable of 'Control Over Working Time' is derived from four questions: (i) 'I have control over the time of the day that I work'; (ii) 'I have control over the total number of hours that I work'; (iii) 'I have control over which days of the week that I work'; and (iv) 'I have control over which weeks of the year that I work'. The variable of 'Control Over Other Items' is a conflation of: (i) 'I have control over the location that I work from'; (ii) I have control over the types of tasks that I perform'; (iii) 'I have control over the amount of work that I must complete'; (iv) 'I have control over the setting of deadlines'; and (v) 'I can choose who I work with'.

5 We also measured respondents preferences over other items of working conditions. For example, we asked respondents to choose two items from a list of six which might improve their work situation. The items they could choose from were: (i) an increase in pay (ii) an increase in job security (iii) a change of job location (iv) an increase in their responsibilities (v) an increase in control over the types of tasks they perform and (vi) a change in the people they work with. With these elements there was no reported difference between the agency employees and the large firm employees.

6 It may be the case that preferences are being reported for only those items that are present in a job form. The possibilities for a research instrument (the questionnaire) being biased in this way can be tested. For example, although there is no significant difference in preference for control over the types of tasks performed between the temporary agency employee and the large firm employee, this element is still highly valued by the temporary agency employees; 56 per cent of the temporary employees reported a preference for this. However, only 12 per cent reported that they have

control over the types of tasks performed. Similar percentages were reported by the large firm employees; 52 per cent preferred control over tasks performed and 20 per cent had control over tasks performed, so that for this item, although it is not present, preferences are still being reported.

9 The Hollywood agency system

1 See Bordwell, Staiger and Thomson (1985) *The Classical Hollywood Cinema*; Dyer (1991) *Stars as Social Phenomenon*; Gomery (1991) *Movie History; A Survey*; Balio (1985) *The American Film Industry*; and Shipman (1979a and 1979b) *The Great Movie Stars; The International years* and *The Great Movie Stars; The Golden Years* for more on the history of Hollywood and stars.

2 This break registered here should also include earlier attempts by Hollywood stars to form their own companies and break from the restrictions of the studio system. We believe there was a constant pressure for control that would reveal itself at various moments throughout film history, for example, Charlie Chaplin and Mary Pickford forming United Artists, James Cagney producing his own movies, and Burt Lancaster forming Hecht-Lancaster productions. What we are asserting here is that the break in the late 60s was wide-sweeping and crucial in describing a new Hollywood production process (see e.g. Albert (1996)).

10 The Internet as agent

1 The brief history of the Internet in this section is largely drawn from *The Economist* article 'A Changling's Tale', 'The Internet Survey', p. 9.

12 Agents and intellectual capital

1 Although we use the phrase 'change in opportunities', this also implies a change in opportunity costs. For example, a family where both husband and wife work means that there is less opportunity cost if the husband were to cut back on hours at work in order to pursue another interest. The lost earnings (and/or lost career gain) are a smaller fraction of the family income. The changing opportunities for women also implied a change in opportunity costs for their spouses. Another example, an increase in pollution implies a scarcity of pristine eco-systems. Fewer opportunities are available to view natural grandeur. These fewer opportunities also implies a greater opportunity cost when polluting the environment through production for increased economic activity. The changing opportunities for the eco-system means a rise in the opportunity cost of manufacturing another car.

2 Although in this book we emphasize the importance of the capacity for innovation and growth residing in individuals, the exploitation of know-

how requires structural assets – such as information systems, knowledge of markets, customers and management focus. Discussions of these aspects have been rejected, as it is our intent to emphasize and highlight the consequences of knowledge in the shaping of labour markets and organizations.

Appendix A

1 Winston (1982, 1987) mentions the possibility of night shift work being selected by a group of individuals who find night work most appealing.

Appendix B

1 The fluctuations in availability of temporary workers may also be due to their being at another job. It can be argued, though, that this type of search cost is not necessarily any greater for temporary labour hiring or permanent labour hiring. It just determines the relative amount of labour supply available in the market.

2 Another reason noted by Abraham (1990) is taking 'advantage of outsiders' special expertise' which may be an 'important factor in many contracting decisions, particularly those involving highly paid workers' (p. 10).

3 ILO Convention 69 addresses the problems of temporary agencies for workers (see Albeda, *et al.* (1976), p. 412, for more on this).

References

Abraham, K. G. (1988) 'Flexible Staffing Arrangements and Employers Short-term Adjustment Strategies', in R. Hart (ed.), *Employment, Unemployment and Labour Utilization*, Boston: Unwin Hyman, pp. 288–313.

Adam, B. and Baer, D. (1984) 'The Social Mobility of Women and Men in the Ontario Legal Profession', *Canadian Review of Sociology and Anthropology*, 21: 22–46.

Akerlof, G. (1984) 'Gift Exchange and Efficiency Wage Theory: Four Views', *The American Economic Review*, 72, May: 79–83.

Albeda, W., Blanpain, R. and Veldkamp, G. M. J. (1978) *Temporary Work in Modern Society – A Comparative Study of the International Institute for Temporary Work*, Zurich: The Foundation Internationale pour la Promotion de l'étude du Travail Temporaire.

Albert, S. (1996) *Considerations on the Economics of Stardom and the Impact on the Hollywood Film Industry.* Open University Business School Working Paper Series 96/12.

Albert, S. and Bradley, K. (1995) *The Management of Intellectual Capital*, Business Performance Group, London School of Economics.

Albert, S. and Garcia, P. (1995) 'Temporalidad y Segmentacion En El Mercado De trabajo', *Actualidad Financiera*, no. 7, February: 9–38.

Alchian, A. A. and Demsetz, H. (1972) 'Production Information Costs, and Economic Organization', *American Economic Review*, 62, no. 2, December: 777–95.

Allen, S. (1981) 'An Empirical Model of Work Attendance', *The Review of Economics and Statistics*, 63, no. 1, February: 77–87.

Allison, G. (1971) *Essence of Decision: explaining the Cuban Missle Crisis*, Boston: Little, Brown.

Appelbaum, E. (1989) 'The Growth in the US Contingent Labor Force', in R. Drago and R. Perlman (eds.), *Microeconmic Issues in Labour Economics: New Approaches*, Hemel Hempstead: Harvester.

Argyris, C. (1993) *Actionable Knowledge: Changing the Status Quo*, San Francisco: Jossey-Bass.

(1991) 'Teaching Smart People How to Learn', *Harvard Business Review*, 69, no. 3, May–June: 99–109.

(1990) *Overcoming Organizational Defences: Facilitating Organizational Learning*, Bostona: Allyn and Bacon.
Argyris, C. and Schön, D. (1974) *Theory in Practice*, San Fransisico: Jossey-Bass.
Askoy, A. and Robins, K. (1992) 'Hollywood for the 21st Century: Global Competition for Critical masss in Image Markets', *Cambridge Journal of Economics*, 16, 1–22.
Atkinson, J. (1986), *Changing Working Patterns – How Companies Achieve Flexibility to Meet New Ends*, NEDO London: National Economic Development Association.
Austrin, T. (1991) 'Flexibility, Surveillance and Hype in New Zealand Financial Retailing', *Employment Work and Society*, 5, June: 201–21.
Balio, T. (ed.) (1985) *The American Film Industry*: Madison: University of Wisconsin Press.
Bardach, E. and Kagen, R. A. (1982) *Going to the Book*, Philadelphia: Temple University Press.
Baudrillard, J. (1986) *Simulations*, trans. Foss P. and Patton, P. and Beitchman, P. New York: Semiotext inc.
Becker, G. S. (1965) 'A Theory of the Allocation of Time', *Economic Journal*, 75: 493–517.
(1976) *The Economic Approach to Human Behaviour*, Chicago: University of Chicago Press.
Beer, M., Spector, B., Lawrence, P., Mills, D. Q., and Walters, R. (1984) *Managing Human Assets*, New York: Free Press.
Beer, S. and Barringer, R. (eds.) (1970) *The State and the Poor*, Cambridge, MA: Winthrop.
Belous, R. (1989a) *The Contingent Economy: The Growth of Temporary, Part-time and Subcontracted Workforce*, U.S. Bureau of Labour Statistics National Planning Association Report, No. 239.
(1989b) 'How Firms Adjust to the Shift Toward Contingent Workers', *Monthly Labor Review*, 11, no. 3, March:. 7–12.
(1991) 'The Two Tiered Work Force in US Corporations – Box 7.2 and 7.3' in Doeringer *et al.*, *Turbulance in the American Workplace*, New York: Oxford University Press.
Beniger, J. R. (1989), 'The Evolution of Control' in T. Forester (ed.), *Computers in the Human Context*, Oxford: Basil Blackwell.
Block, F. (1990) *Postindustrial Possibilities: A Critique of Economic Discourse*, Berkeley CA: University of California Press.
Blyton, P., Hassard, J., Hill, S. and Starkey K. (1989) *Time, Work and Organization*, London: Routledge.
Bonnassie, P. (1991) *From Slavery to Feudalism in South Western Europe*, trans. by J. Birrell, Cambridge: Cambridge University Press.
Bordwell, D., Staiger, J. and Thompson, K. (1985) *The Classical Hollywood Cinema*, London: Routledge & Kegan Paul
Bosworth, D. L. and Dawkins, P. J. (1980) 'Compensation for Workers' Disutility: Time of Day, Length of Shift and other Features of Work Patterns', *Scottish Journal of Political Economy*, 27, no. 1: 80–96.

Boudling, K. E. (1953) *The Organizational Revolution: A Study in the Ethics of Economic Organization*, New York: Harper.
Braverman, H. (1974) *Labor and Monopoly Capital: the Degradation of Work on 20th Century*, New York, London: Monthly Review Press.
Bridges, W. (1995) *How to Prosper in a Workplace without Jobs*, London: Nicholas Brealy.
Brunsson, N. (1989) *The Organization Hypocricy*, NewYork: Wiley.
Buchanan, D. (1984), *The Impact of Technical Implications and Managerial Aspirations on the Organization and Control of the Labour Process*, paper presented to the Second Annual Conference on the Control and Organization of the Labour Process, UMIST/ASton, 28–30 March.
Buchanan, R. A. (1994) *The Power of the Machine*, London: Penguin Books.
Burchell, B. (1989) 'The Impact of Precariousness in the UK Labour Market,' in Rodgers and Rodgers (1989), pp. 225–48.
Burchell, B. and Rubery, J. (1990) 'An Empirical Investigation into the Segmentation of the Labour Supply', *Employment Work and Society*, 4, no. 4, December: 551–75.
Burnes, B. (1989) *New Technology in Context*, Aldershot: Avebury.
Burnett, J. (1994) *Useful Toil*, London: Routledge.
Cagnon Thompson, S. and Barton, M. (1994) 'Ecocentric and Anthropocentric Attitudes Toward the Environment', *Journal of Environmental Psychology*, 14: 149–57.
Cain, G. (1976) 'The Challenge of Segmented Labour Market Theories to Orthodox Theory: A Survey', *The Journal of Economic Literature*, 14, no. 4: 1215–57.
Calabrese, A. and Jung, D. (1992) 'Broadband Telecommunications in Rural America', *Telecommunications Policy*, 6, no. 3, April: 225–36.
Carey, M. and Hazelbaker, K. L. (1986) 'Employment Growth in the Temporary Help Industry', *Monthly Labor Review*, 109, no. 4, April: 37–44.
Casey, B. (1988), *Temporary Employment – Practice and Policy in Great Britain*, London: Policy Studies Institute.
Christensen, K. (1991) 'The Two Tiered Workforce in US Corporations' in Doeringer *et al.* (1991).
Christensen, K. (ed.) (1988) *The New Era of Home Based work: Directions and Policies*, Boulder: Westview Press.
Clark, D. G. (1992) 'The Effectiveness of Incentive Payment Systems: An Empirical Test of Individualism as a Boundry Condition', unpublished PhD dissertation, London School of Economics.
Clegg, S. R. (1990) *Modern Organizations: Organization Studies in the Postmodern World*, Sage Publications: London
Coase, R. H. (1937) 'The Nature of the Firm' *Economica*, 4 November: 386–405.
Cohen, W. and Leventhal, D. (1990) 'Absorptive Capacity: A New Perspective On Learning And Innovation', *Administrative Science Quarterly*, 35: 125–52.

Colclough, G. and Tolbert, C. (1992) *Work in the Fast Lane: Flexibility, Divisions of Labour, and Inequality in High Tech Industries*, Albany: SUNY Press.

Cox, T. H. and Nkomom, S. M. (1991) 'A Race and Gender-Group Analysis of the Early Career Experience of MBA's', *Work and Occupations*, 18, no. 4: 431–46.

Currie, M. and Steadman, I. (1990) *Wrestling with Time*, Manchester: Manchester University Press.

Daft, R. L. and Weick, K. E. (1984) 'Toward a Model of Organizations as Interpretation Systems', *Academy of Management Review*, 9: 284–95.

Dale, A. and Bramford, C. (1988) 'Temporary Workers: Cause for Concern or Complacency?' *Work, Employment and Society*, 2, no. 2: 191–209.

Davis-Blake, A. and Uzzi, B. (1993) 'Determinants of Employment Externalization: A Study of Temporary Workers and Independent Contractors', *Administrative Science Quarterly*, 38: 195–223.

Deserpa, A. (1971), 'A Theory of the Economics of Time', *The Economic Journal*, 81: 828–46.

Dickens, C. (1978) *Nicholas Nickleby*, London: Penguin Books.

Dickens, W. T. and Lang, K. (1985) 'A Test of the Dual Labour Market Theory', *American Economic Review*, 75, no. 4: 792–805.

Dockès, P. (1981) *La Libération Médiéval*, trans. A. Goldhammer as *Medieval Slavery and Liberation*, Chicago: University of Chicago Press.

Doeringer, P., Christensen, K., Flynn, P., Hall, D., Katz, H., Keefe, J., Ruhm, C., Sum, A., and Useem, M. (1991) *Turbulence in the American Workplace*, New York: Oxford University Press.

Doeringer, P. and Piore, M. J. (eds.) (1985) *Internal Labor Markets and Manpower Analysis – with a new Introduction*, London: M. E. Sharpe.

Dosi, G., Freeman, C., Nelson, R., Silverbrg, G., and Soet, L. (eds.) (1988) *Technical Change and Economic Theory*, London: Pinter.

Drucker, P. F. (1992) 'The New Society of Organizations', *Harvard Business Review*, 70, no. 5, September–October.

Duby, G. (1974) *The Early Growth of the European Economy, Warriors and Peasants from the Seventh to the Twelfth Centuries*, trans. Clarke, H., London: Weidenfeld and Nicholson.

Dy, F. (1990) *Advanced Technology in Commerce*, A study prepared for International Labour Office. Aldershot: Avebury.

Dyer, R. (1979) 'Part One: Stars as a Social Phenomenon' in *Stars*, London: British Film Institute.

Eccles, R. (1991) 'The Performance Measurement Manifesto', *Harvard Business Review*: 69, no. 1, Jan–Feb: 131–7.

Economist, The (1994) 'Schools Brief, The War Between The Sexes', March: 96–7.

(1995) 'A Survey of the Internet', 336 supp. 3, July.

Eisenstein, S. M. (1985) *The Short Fiction Scenario*, Calcutta: Seagull Books.

Eldridge N. and Gould, S. J. (1972) 'Puncuated Equilibria: An Alternative to Phyletic Gradualism', in Thomas J. (ed.) *Schopf Models in Paleobiology*, San Fransisco: Freeman, Cooper, pp. 82–115.

Epstein, R. A. (1985) 'Agency Costs, Employment Contracts, and Labor Unions', in Pratt, J. W. and Zechauser, R. J. (eds.), *Principles and Agents: The structure of Business*, pp. 127–48. Boston Mass: Harvard Business School Press.

Fernandez, J. (1986) *Child Care and Corporate Productivity: Resolving Family/Work Conflicts*, Lexington, MA: Lexington Books.

Fernie, S. and Metcalf, D. (1995) 'Participation, Contingent Pay Representation and Workplace Performance: Evidence from Great Britain', Discussion Paper 232, Centre for Economic Performance, London School of Economics.

Ferris, T. (1989) *Coming of Age in the Milky Way*, New York: Anchor Books.

Fierman, J. (1994) 'The Contingency Work Force', *Fortune*, no. 2 24 January: 20–5.

Flamholtz, E. G. (1969) 'The Theory and Measurement of an Individual's Value to an Organisation', unpublished PhD dissertation.

Freeman, C. and Perez, C. (1988) 'Structural Crises of Adjustment: Business Cysles and Investment Behavviour', in Dosi *et al.* (1988), pp. 38–66.

Frieden, R. (1995) 'Universal Personal Communications in the New Telecommunications World Order', *Telecommunications Policy*, no. 1, 19: 43–9.

Galensen, W. (1991) *New Trends in Employment Practices – An International Survey*, Contributions in Labour Studies, No. 34, New York: Greenwood Press.

Gannon, M. (1984), 'Preferences of Temporary Workers: Time Variety and Flexibility', *Monthly Labour Review*, 107, no. 8, August: 26–8.

Gates, B. (1995) *The Road Ahead*, London: Viking, Penguin.

Gerson, J. and Kraut, E. (1988) 'Clerical Work at Home or in the Office: The Difference it Makes', in Christensen (ed.) (1988).

Gomery, D. (1991), *Movie History: A Survey*, Belmont CA: Wadsworth.

Gould, S. J. (1994) 'Hooking Leviathan by Its Past', *Natural History*, 103, no. 5: 8–15.

(1995) 'Spin Doctoring Darwin', *Natural History*, 104, no. 7: 6–9 and 70–1.

Groneau, R. (1986) 'Home Production – A Survey', in O. Ashenfelter and R. Layard, *Hand book of Labor Economics*, New York: Elsevier Science Pub. (1986) I, pp. 273–304.

Guest, D. (1992) 'Right Enough to be Dangerously Wrong: An Analysis of the In Search of Excellence Phenomenon', in G. Salaman (ed.), *Human Resource Strategies*, London: Sage Publications, pp. 5–19.

Hadlock, P., Hecker, D. and Gannon, J. (1991) 'High Technology Employment: Another View', *Monthly Labor Review*, 114, no. 7, July: 26–30.

Hagan, J. (1990) 'The Gender Stratification of Income Innequality Among Lawyers', *Social Forces*, 68, no. 3: 835–55.

Hakim, C. (1984a) 'Homework and Outwork – National Estimates From Two Surveys', *Employment Gazette*, 92, no. 1, January: 7–12.

(1984b) 'Employer's Use of Homework, Outwork and Freelance', *Employment Gazette*, 92, no. 4, April: 144–50.

(1990) 'Core and Periphery in Employers' Workforce Strategies: Evidence

from the 1987 ELUS Survey', *Work Employment and Society*, 4, no. 2, June: 157–88.
Hall, J. and Hall, P. (1979) *The Two Career Couple*, Redding MA: Addison Wesley.
Hammond, J. L. and Hammond, B. (1920) *The Skilled Labourer 1760–1832*, London: Longmans, Green and Co.
Hampden-Turner, C. (1990) *Corporate Culture*, London: Hutchinson.
Hampden-Turner, C. and F. Trampenaars, D. (1993) *The Seven Cultures of Capitalism*, NewYork: Doubleday.
Handy, C. (1984) *The Future of Work – A Guide to a Changing Society*, Oxford: Basil Blackwell.
(1994) *The Empty Raincoat*, London: Hutchinson.
Hart, J. Reed, R. and Bar, F. (1992) 'The Building of the Internet', *Telecommunications Policy*, 16, no. 8, November: 666–89.
Harvey, M. (1991) 'An Accounting Odyssey', *Certified Accountant*, November: 27–9.
Hassard, J. (1989a) 'Time and Industrial Society', in Blyton and Hill (1989), pp. 13–34.
(1989b) 'Time and Organization' in Blyton and Hill (1989), pp. 79–104.
Hassard, J. (ed.) (1990) *The Sociology of Time*, Basingstoke: Macmillan.
Hayek, F. A. (1975) 'The Pretence of Knowledge', *Les Prix Nobel en 1974*, Stockholm: P. A. Norstadt and Somry.
Hayes, R. H., Wheelwright, S. C. and Clark, K. B. (1988) *Dynamic Manufacturing: Creating the Learning Organization*, London: The Free Press.
Hayghe, H. V. (1990) 'Family Members in the Work Force', *Monthly Labor Review*, 113, no. 3, March: 14–19.
Hayghe, H. V. and Bianchi, S. M. (1994) 'Married Mothers' Work Patterns: The Job-Family Compromise', *Monthly Labor Review*, 117, no. 6, June: 24–30.
Heckscher, C. (1988) *The New Unionism*, New York: Basic Books.
Helvey, T. C. (1971) *The Age of Information: An Interdisciplinary Survey of Cybernetics*, Englewood Cliffs, NJ: Educational Technology Publications.
Hepple, B. A. (1978) 'The Temporary Worker', in Albeda *et al.* (1978), pp. 493–512.
(1990) *Working Time a New Legal Framework?* Institute for Public Policy Research Employment Paper No. 3. London: Instutute for Public Policy.
Heydebrand, W. (1989) 'New Organizational Forms', *Work and Occupations*, 16, no. 3: 323–57.
Hicks, J. R. (1946) *Value and Capital: An Inquiry into Some Fundamental Principles of Economic Theory*, Oxford: Oxford University Press.
Hill, S. (1981) *Competition and Control at Work: The New Industrial Sociology*, London: Heinemann Educational.
(1984) *Worksharing: Some Costs and Other Implications*, London: Unemployment Unit.
(1989) 'Time at Work: An Economic Analysis' in P. Blyton and S. Hill *et al.* (1989), pp. 57–78.

(1991) 'How Do You Manage a Flexible Firm?' *Work, Employment and Society*, 5, no. 3:. 397–416.
Hirst, P. and Zeitlin, J. (1991) 'Flexible Specialization versus post-Fordism: Theory, Evidence and Policy Implications', *Economy and Society*, 20, no. 1: 1–55.
Hong, S., Adams, R. and Love, H. (1993) 'An Economic Analysis of Household Recycling of Solid Wastes: The Case of Portland, Oregan', *Journal of Environmental Economics and Management*, 25: 136–46.
Housekneckt, S. K. and Macke, A. S. (1981) 'Combining Marriage and Career: The Marital Adjustment of Professional Women', *Journal of Marriage and Family*, 43: 651–61.
Huber, G. P. (1991) 'Organizational Learning: The Contributing Process and the Literature', *Organizational Science*, 2, no. 1: 88–115.
Hunter, L., McGregor, A., MacInnes, J. and Sproull, A. (1993) 'The "Flexible Firm": Strategy and Segmentation', *British Journal of Industrial Relations*, 31, no. 3: 383–407.
Huws, U. (1989) *The New Home Workers: New Technologies and the Changing Location of White Collar Work*, London: Low Pay Unit.
Huws, U., Kork, W. B., Robinson, S. (1990) *Telework: Towards the Elusive Office*, Chichester: Wiley
Huxley, J. (1942) *Evolution: The Modern Synthesis*, 3rd edn, London: George Allen & Urwin Ltd.
Huyssein, A. (1986) *After the Great Divide: Modernism, Mass Culture, Postmodernism*, Bloomington: Indiana University Press.
Irish, V. (ed.) (1991) *Intellectual Property: A Manager's Guide*, London McGraw Hill.
Jameson, F. (1984) 'Post-Modernism or the Cultural Logic of Late Capitalism', *New Left Review*, 146: pp. 53–92
Jaques, E. (1955) 'Social Systems as a Defence against Persecutory and Depressive Anxiety', in M. Klein, P. Heimann and R. E. Money Kyrle (eds.), *New Directions in Psycho Analysis*, London: Tavistock Publications, New York Basic Books.
Jauch, R. and Skigen, M. (1974) 'Human Resource Accounting: A Critical Evaluation', *Management Accounting*, 55, no. 11, May: 33–6.
Jencks, C. (1977), *The Language of Post-Modern Architecture*, New York: Rizzoli.
Johnson, H. T. (1992), *Relevance Regained*, New York: The Free Press.
Johnson, H. T. and Kaplan, R. S. (1987) *Relevance Lost: The Rise and Fall of Management Accounting*, Boston: Harvard Business School Press.
Jussawalla, M. (1992) 'Is the Communications Link Still Missing?' *Telecommunications Policy*, 16, no. 6, August: 485–503.
Kanter, R. M. (1977) *Men and Women of the Corporation*, New York: Basic Books.
Karesek, R. and Theorell, T. (1990) *Healthy Work: Stress Productivity and the Reconstruction of Working Life*, New York: Basic Books.
Keggunder, M. N., Jorgensen, J. J. and Hafsi, T. (1983) 'Administrative and

Practice in Developing Countries: A Synthesis', *Administrative Science Quarterly*, 25: 66–86.

Kinsman, F. (1987) *The Telecommuters*, Chichester: Wiley

(1990) *Millennium: Towards Tomorrow's Society*, London: W. H. Allen.

Kiser, J. W. (1993) 'Eastern Europe's Intellectual Capital: Possibilities for the West', in *Management of Human Assets*. Mimeo, Business Performance Group: London School of Economics.

Krepps, D. (1990) *A Course in Micro-Economic Theory*, Princeton, NJ: Princeton University Press.

Kroll, E. (1994) *The Whole Internet*, 2nd Edition, Sebastapol: C. G. O'Reilly and Associates.

Krueger, A. (1993) 'How Computers Have Changed The Wage Structure: Evidence From Microdata, 1984–1989', *The Quarterly Journal of Economics*, 58, February: 33–60.

Larson, J. R. Jr. and Christiansen, C. (1993) 'Groups as Problem-solving Units: Toward a New Meaning of Social Cognition', *British Journal of Social Psychology*, 32: 5–30.

Lash, S. and Urry, J. (1987) *The End of Organized Capitalism*, Cambridge: Polity Press.

Leinberg, P. and Tucker, B. (1991) *The New Individualists*, New York: Harper Collins.

Levitt, B. and March, J. (1988) 'Organizational Learning', *Annual Review of Sociology*, 14: 319–40.

Likert, R. and Bowers, D. G. (1973) 'Improving the Accuracy of P/L Reports by Estimating the Change in Dollar Value of the Human Organisation', *Michigan Business Review*, 25: 15–24.

Lippman, S. A.. and McCall, J. J.. (eds.) (1976) *Studies in the Economics of Search*, Amsterdam, New York: North Holland Publishers.

Lyotard, J. (1984) *The Postmodern Condition: A Report on Knowledge*, trans. by Geoff Bennington and Brian Massumi, Manchester: Manchester University Press.

Lyth, I. M. (1990) 'Social Sytems as a Defense Against Anxiety' in Trist and Murray (eds.) *The Social Engagement of Social Science*, Philadelphia: The University of Pennsylvania Press.

Machlup, F. (1962) *The Productaion and Distribution of Knowledge in the United States*, Princeton, NJ: Princeton University Press.

Magnum, G., Mayell, D. and Nelson, K. (1985) 'The Temporary Help Industry: A Response to the Dual Internal Labour Market', *Industrial and Labour Relations Review*, 38, no. 4: 599–613.

Malecki, E. and Bradbury, S. (1991) 'R&D Facilities and Professional Labour: Labour Force Dynamics in High Technology', *Regional Studies*, 26, no. 2: 123–36.

Marshall, A. (1946) *Principles of Economics – An Introductory Volume*, London: Macmillian.

(1989) 'The Sequal of Unemployment: The Changing Role of Part-time Workers in Europe', in Rodgers and Rodgers (1989), pp. 17–48.

Martin, J. K. and Shehan, C. L. (1989) 'Education and Job Satisfaction: The

Influences of Gender, Wage Earnings Status and Job values', *Work and Occupations*, 16, no. 2: 184–99.
McNabb, R. (1987) 'Testing for Labour Market Segmentation in Britain', *The Manchester School of Economics and Social Studies Journal*, no. 3, September: 257–73.
Meadows, D. H. , Delaunay, Jaque and Delaunay Janine (1972) *The Limits to Growth: A Report for the Club of Rome's Project on the Predicament of Mankind*, New York: Universe Books.
Meadows, D. H., Meadows, D. L. and Randers, J. (1992) *Beyond the Limits – Global Collapse or Sustainable Future*, London: Earthscan Publications.
Mill, J. S. (1911) *Principles of Political Economy*, London.
Mitchell, A. N. (1994) 'Telework: The Business Opportunities' in Mecklermedia (1994) *Internet World and Document Delivery World International 94: Precedings of the Second Annual Conference*, London: Mecklermedia, pp. 37–46.
Mortensen, D. (1986) 'Job Search and Labour Market Analysis', in Ashenfelter, O. and Layard, R. (eds.), *Handbook of Labour Economics*, Amsterdam: North Holland, II, pp. 849–920.
Natale, R. (1989) 'The Price Club', *American Film*, 14, June: 42–4 and 65.
Nelson, R. and Winter, S. (1982) *An Evolutionary Theory of Economic Change*, Cambridge: Harvard University Press.
Nonaka, I. (1991) 'The Knowledge-Creating Company', *Harvard Business Review*, 69, no. 3, November–December: 96–104.
Noll, M. A. (1992) 'Anatomy of a Failure: Picturephone Revisted', *Telecommunications Policy*, 16, no. 4, May/June: 307–16.
Norwood, J. and Klein, D. (1989) 'Developing Statistics to Meet Society's Needs', *Monthly Labour Review*, 112, no. 10, October: 14–19.
O'Connell, M. (1993) 'Where's Papa? Fathers' Role in Child Care', *Population Trends and Public Policy*, Washington DC: Population Reference Bureau, September.
Orpen, C. (1981) 'Effect of Flexible Working Hours on Employee Satisfaction and Performance: A Field Experiment', *Journal of Applied Psychology*, 66, no. 1: 113–15.
Oster, G. (1979) 'A Factor Analytic Test of the Theory of the Dual Economy', *The Review of Economics and Statistics*, 61: 33–9.
Osterman, P. (1988) *Employment Futures – Reorganization, Dislocation, and Public Policy*, New York: Oxford University Press.
Owen, J. D. (1971) 'The Demand for Leisure', *Journal of Political Economy*, 79, no. 1, Jan–Feb: 56–71.
(1979) *Working Hours*, Lexington, Mass: D. C. Heath and Co.
(1988) 'Work Time Reduction in the US and Western Europe', *Monthly Labor Review*, 111, no. 12, December: 41–5.
Parain, C. (1979) *Outils, Ethnies et Developpement Historique*, Paris.
Peters, T. and Waterman, B. (1982) *In Search of Excellence: Lessons from America's Best Run Companies*, New York, London: Harper and Row.
Pfeffer, J. and Baron, J. (1988) 'Taking the Workers Back Out: Recent Trends

in the Structuring of Employment', *Research in Organizational Behaviour*, 10: 257–303.
Piore, M. and Sable, C. (1984) *The Second Industrial Divide: Possibilities for Prosperity*. New York: Basic Books.
Piore, M. J. (1970) 'Jobs and Training', in S. Beer *et al.* (1970).
Prahalad, C. K. and Hamel, G. (1990) 'The Core Competence of the Corporation', *Harvard Business Review*, 68, no. 3, May–June: pp. 79–91.
Pym, D. (1978) 'Employment as Bad Ritual', *London Business School Journal*, 3.
(1981) 'The Other Economy: The Possibilities of Work Beyond Employment', in Richards (ed.) (1991), pp. 137–48.
Quine, W. V. (1990) *Quiddities: An Intermittently Philosophical Dictionary*, Harmondsworth: Penguin.
Rapoport, C. (1995) 'Charles Handy Sees the Future', *Time*, 13 February: 'Fortune' section.
Reich, R. (1991) *The Work of Nations*, London: Simon and Schuster.
Rheingold, H. (1995), *The Virtual Community*, London: Minerva.
Richards, V. (ed.) (1990) *Why Work? – Arguments for the Leisure Society*, London: Freedom Press.
Ritzer, G. (1989) 'The Permanently New Economy: The Case for Reviving Economic Sociology', *Work and Occupations*, 16, no. 3: 243–72.
Robinson, J. P. (1988) 'Who's Doing the Housework?' *American Demographics*, 10 December: 24–8.
Robinson, J. P. and Gershuny, J. (1988) 'Historical Changes in the Household Division of Labor', *Demographics*, 25 November: 537–52.
Rodgers, G. and Rodgers, J. (1989) *Precarious Jobs in Labour Market Regulation – The Growth of Atypical Employment in Western Europe*, Geneva: International Institute for Labour Studies.
Rosenberg, S. (1989) 'From Segmentation to Flexibility' *Labour and Society*, 14, no. 4, October: 363–407.
Rosener, J. B. (1990) 'Ways Women Lead', *Harvard Business Review*, 68, 119–25.
Royal Society of Arts (1995), *Tomorrow's Company Inquiry*, London: Royal Society of Arts.
Ryan, P. (1981) 'Segmentation, Duality and the Internal Labour Market', in Wilkinson, F. (ed.) (1981) *The Dynamics of Labour Market Segmentation*, London: Academic Press, pp. 3–20.
Sampson, A. (1995) *Company Man – The Rise and Fall of Corporate Life*, London: Harper Collins.
Schappi, J. V. (1988) *Improving Job Attendence*, Washington DC: The Burea of National Affairs Inc.
Schein, E. H. (1993) *Organizational Culture and Leadership*, rev. edn, chapter 14, 'Deciphering Organizational Culture', San Francisco: Jossey-Bass.
Senge, P. (1990) *The Fifth Discipline: The Art and Practice of the Learning Organization*, New York: Doubleday.
Shellenbarger, S. (1993) 'Work-Force Study Finds Loyalty is Weak, Divisions of Race and Gender are Deep', *Wall Street Journal*, 3, September: B1 and B5.

Shelley, K. (1992) 'The Furture of Jobs for College Graduates', *Monthly Labor Review*, 115, no. 7, July: 13–21.

Shipman, D. (1979a), *The Great Movie Stars; The International Years*. New York: St Martin's Press.

(1979b), *The Great Movie Stars; The Golden Years*. New York: St Martin's Press.

Silvestri, G. and Lukasiewicz, J. (1991) 'Outlook: 1990–2005. Occupational Employment Projections', *Monthly Labor Review*, 115, no. 11, November: 64–102.

Smith, A. (1976) *The Wealth of Nations*, ed. Edwin Canan. Chicago: University of Chicago Press.

Smith, V. (1994) 'Institutionalizing Flexibility in a Service Firm', *Work and Occupations*, no. 3. August: 284–307

Sorrentino, C. (1990) 'The Changing Family in International Perspective', *Monthly Labor Review*, 113, no. 3, March: 41–58.

Spence, A. (1991) 'Employment Changes in Central London in the 1980s – The Record of the 1980s', *The Geographical Journal*, 157: Part 1, March: 1–12.

Spurr, S. J. (1990) 'Sex Discrimination in the Legal Profession: A Study of Promotion', *Industrial and Labour Relations Review*, 43, no. 4: 406–17.

Staiger, J. (1979) 'Dividing Labor for Production Control: Thomas Ince and the Rise of the Studio System', *Cinema Journal* 19, no. 2: 16–25.

Staten, M. (1982), 'Information Costs and Incentives to Shirk: Disability Compensation of Air Traffic Controllers', *American Economic Review*. 72, no. 2: 1023–37.

Stewart, A., Prandy, K. and Blackburn., R. (1980) *Social Stratification and Occupations*, London: Macmillan.

Stewart, T. A. (1994), 'Measuring Company I.Q', *Fortune*, 129, no. 2: 24.

Stockman, D. H. (1986) *The Triumph of Politics: How the Reagan Revolution Failed*. NewYork: Harper Colins.

Storper, M. (1989) 'The Transition to Flexible Specialization in the US Film Industry: The Division of Labour, External Economies and the Crossing of the Industrial Divides', *Cambridge Journal of Economics*, 13, no. 2: 273–305.

Storper, M. and Christopherson, S. (1987) 'Flexible Specialization and Regional Industrial Agglomerations: The case of the US Motion Picture Industry', *Annals of the Association of American Geographers*, 77, no. 1: 104–17.

Tahvonen, O. and Kuuluvainen, J. (1993) 'Economic Growth, Pollution, and Renewable Resources', *Journal of Environmental Economics and Management*, 24: 101–18.

Taylor, F. W. (1947) *Scientific Management*, New York: Harper and Brothers.

Thompson, E. P. (1967) 'Time, Work-Discipline, and Industrial Capitalism', *Past and Present*, no. 38, pp. 56–97.

Thompson, P. (1989) *The Nature of Work*, New York: Humanities Press.

Towers, B. (1978) 'The British Temporary Work Labour Market' in Albeda *et al.* (1978), pp. 91–136.

Toynbee, A. (1920) *Lectures on the Industrial Revolution of the Eighteenth Century in England* (1884), London: Longmans, Green.
Turgenev, I. (1859) *A Month in the Country*, trans. I. Berlin, Harmondsworth: Penguin.
Wells, H. G. (1926) *The World of William Clissold Vol. II*, London: Ernest Benn Ltd.
Whyte, W. (1956) *The Organization Man*, New York: Simon and Schuster.
Wilkinson, F. (ed.) (1981) *The Dynamics of Labour Market Segmentation*, London: Academic Press.
Williamson, O. E. (1971) 'The Vertical Integration of Production: Market Failure Considerations', *American Economic Review*, 61, no. 2, pp. 112–23.
Winston, G. C. (1982), *The Timing of Economic Activities – Firms, Households, and Markets in Time-Specific Analysis*, Cambridge: Cambridge University Press.
(1987) 'Activity Choice. A New Approach to Economic Behaviour', *Journal of Economic Behavior and Organization*, 8: 567–85.
Winston, G. C. and McCoy, T. O. (1974) 'Investment and the Optimal Idleness of Capital' *Review of Economic Studies*, 127: 419–28.
Wood, S. (ed.) (1992) *The Transformation of Work?* Second edition, London: Routledge.
Yu, L. C., Wang, M. Q., Kaltreider, L. and Chien, Y. (1993) 'The Impact of Family Migration and Family Life Cycle on the Employment Status of Married, College Educated Women', *Work and Occupations*, 20, no. 2: 233–46.
Zeytinoglu, I. U. (1992) 'Reasons for Hiring Part-Time Workers', *Industrial Relations*, 31: 489–99.
Zick, C. D. and McCullough, J. L. (1991), 'Trends in Married Couples Time Use; Evidence from 1977–78 and 1987–88', *Sex Roles*, 28: 459–88.

Index

Printed in the United States
By Bookmasters